THE
TANGO WAR

THE
TANGO WAR

THE STRUGGLE FOR THE HEARTS, MINDS, AND RICHES
OF LATIN AMERICA DURING WORLD WAR II

MARY JO
McCONAHAY

ST. MARTIN'S PRESS ❧ NEW YORK

www.stmartins.com

Designed by Omar Chapa

Library of Congress Cataloging-in-Publication Data is available upon request.

ISBN 978-1-250-09123-9 (hardcover)
ISBN 978-1-250-09124-6 (ebook)

Our books may be purchased in bulk for promotional, educational, or business use. Please contact your local bookseller or the Macmillan Corporate and Premium Sales Department at 1-800-221-7945, extension 5442, or by email at MacmillanSpecialMarkets@macmillan.com.

First Edition: September 2018

10 9 8 7 6 5 4 3 2 1

To the memory of my parents, James Cornelius McConahay, U.S. Navy, and Mary Thérèse Rakowski McConahay, U.S. Navy. They made the world a better place.

CONTENTS

PART IV. THE WARRIORS

PART V. THE END WITHOUT AN END

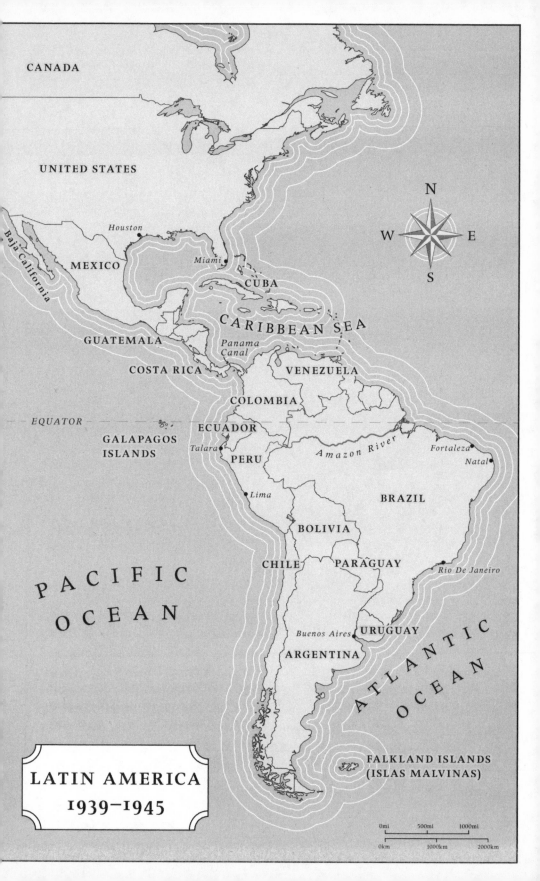

CANADA

UNITED STATES

Baja California

MEXICO

Houston

Miami

CUBA

CARIBBEAN SEA

GUATEMALA

Panama Canal

COSTA RICA

VENEZUELA

COLOMBIA

EQUATOR

ECUADOR

GALAPAGOS ISLANDS

Talara

PERU

Amazon River

Fortaleza

Natal

Lima

BRAZIL

BOLIVIA

PACIFIC OCEAN

CHILE

PARAGUAY

Rio De Janeiro

Buenos Aires

URUGUAY

ARGENTINA

ATLANTIC OCEAN

FALKLAND ISLANDS
(ISLAS MALVINAS)

LATIN AMERICA
1939–1945

N
W   E
S

0mi   500mi   1000mi
0km   1000km   2000km

INTRODUCTION

STORMFRONT

At a café on the Tiergartenstrasse, women meet over Black Forest cake and Apfelstrudel, planning a film night for their chapter of the NS-Frauenschaft— the National Socialist (Nazi) Women's League. Outside the café, girls in pinafores, blonde braids bouncing, and boys wearing lederhosen pass the wide windows, returning from the Neue Deutsche Schule. Some of the young- sters look up to the sky in hopes of catching sight of "the Zepp," the silver dirigible Graf Zeppelin, *passing overhead. Newspaper vendors hawk* Der Urwaldsbole *and the* Deutsches Volksblatt, *and in an empty lot very young boys wearing swastikas on armbands practice marching under the tutelage of teens from the Nazi Youth Club and the Gymnastics Society. Hitler's birth- day is just around the corner. There will be parades! The party men will march in their uniform shirts, arms raised straight out before them, salut- ing like the Fuehrer . . .*

These moments on a "Tiergartenstrasse" might be unfolding in 1930s Ger- many, but instead the afternoon scene is typical of a host of towns in southern Brazil, where a million ethnic Germans lived on the eve of World War II. Ethnic Italians and Japanese, too, resided in countries from Mexico to Argentina. As World War II loomed in Europe, President Franklin Delano Roosevelt's greatest fear was that fascist—especially Nazi—subversion in Latin America would threaten the security of the United States. Of one hundred meetings of the Joint Planning Committee of the U.S. State, Navy, and War Departments in 1939 and 1940, all but six had Latin America at the top of the agenda.

While covering the region for more than thirty years as a reporter, I sometimes heard tales with roots in the Second World War years. But under the pressure of writing about the civil wars in Central America and other issues of the day, I did not pursue them. My father, a U.S. naval officer who served in the Pacific, the Mediterranean, and South America during the war, had let drop over time intriguing bits of stories about Brazil, Uruguay, and Argentina. He mentioned that the U.S. base at Fortaleza was opened on Sundays to the entire local community, a day "For All," as it was called, when Brazilians and Americans played their music for each other. He told of the time his crew was ordered to appear in as many different places as possible on shore leave at night in Buenos Aires to convey the impression that there were more Americans around than there really were—Argentina then was considered pro-Nazi. But when I finally found the time to pursue more details about his stories my father was gone, my questions about the war among many I never asked. I would have to satisfy my curiosity on my own.

What I discovered was that a shadow war for the Western Hemisphere reverberated in every country and that Latin America influenced the global war. Powerful and glamorous figures known better in other scenarios played major and highly imaginative roles: Roosevelt; Nelson Rockefeller; Walt Disney; Orson Welles; the legendary Reich spymaster Admiral Wilhelm Canaris and his opposite, FBI chief J. Edgar Hoover; and "Wild Bill" Donovan, founder of the precursor to the CIA. The Axis and the Allies competed for the hearts and minds of the continent's people, for their sea lanes and natural resources—from oil and rubber to wolfram and industrial diamonds—to feed their war machines. Their spies operated out of embassies, corporate offices, dockside bars. Each side closely shadowed the steps of the other, like dancers in a tango.

This book tells the story of the people behind the events that unfolded on the Latin continent during the global conflict. Not all the names are famous: they include families kidnapped in Latin countries and brought to concentration camps in the United States to be used as pawns in a little-known prisoner exchange program; Jewish families who tried to reach the continent to escape the Holocaust; Latin American–born businessmen and immigrant community leaders who had the misfortune to have German, Japanese, or Italian roots, making them vulnerable to Allied blacklists that froze their assets, and worse. They include princes of the Roman Catholic Church who laid down the clandestine escape routes that brought fascist war criminals like Joseph Mengele and Klaus Barbie to safety in South America. And the book tells the story of a scrappy, unsung force of twenty-five thousand Brazilians—the only Latin American unit to bear arms in Europe—who fought for the Allies in Italy, and how the Battle of the Atlantic, the longest continuous military campaign of the war, was joined by ships great and small in southern seas.

Just as the tango can be danced fast or very slowly, even with one partner holding still while the other moves, the rhythm of the competition between the Allies and the Axis varied in each country. And the territory covered was vast—a distance of 6,640 miles from the Rio Grande river border in Texas south to the Argentine Antarctic. To do justice to the subtle intricacy of the interlinked maneuvers of this deadly contest, I chose to present the elaborate story of World War II in Latin America in connected narratives, like tiles in a mosaic that, seen together, give a picture of the whole.

At this distance in time, since we know the outcome of the war, it is difficult to imagine how strong the Reich was before 1943, how grievous a threat to the Allies, how unsure anyone was about which way the conflict would go. In the run-up to the war and during the hostilities in Europe and the Pacific, the Latin American region was up for grabs.

In writing this book I came to admire the intelligence and energy of those who fought the war in many different ways, without receiving medals, often without recognition. I also came to realize that the era was not simply history but the taproot of issues we face today, such as the practice of extraordinary rendition in Washington's "war on terror"—the kind of forcible capture and relocation that families like the Naganumas, the Sappers, and others suffered more than seventy years ago. It was the beginning of U.S. intelligence gathering and CIA operations of the kind that have saved lives but also meddled to disable governments inconvenient to U.S. policy. And the war years mirror painful discussions we have now on whom we invite into the country to be Americans and whom we shut out and why.

People of Latin American heritage are by far the largest driver of demographic growth in the United States. In 2004 Latinos with roots in countries covered by this book surpassed the number of non-Hispanic whites in my home state of California, the nation's most populous. Yet the lands from the Rio Grande to Tierra del Fuego are seldom in our headlines and histories. The long-standing assumption that nothing much happens in that vast region, despite its population of 650 million, continues. In the United States, lands south of the border are still viewed as, somehow, our "backyard."

It is time that the engrossing story of how World War II developed in Latin America is more widely known.

PART I

The Prizes

1.

THE FIGHT FOR SOUTHERN SKIES

Images of South American cities burst forth on movie screens across the United States in the 1930s, sun-kissed and glittering as in *Flying Down to Rio* or swank with hippodromes and landscaped parks as in *Down Argentine Way*—the kinds of places an American girl like Betty Grable might go on vacation. The far-off cities, alive with the music of samba and tango or the blithesome voice of Carmen Miranda, materialized before audiences as exciting and inviting. The picture was romantic, and in many ways true.

In Buenos Aires and Rio de Janeiro, cash did flow. Cars, buses, and trucks shuttled people and goods from the ports and around the streets in effervescent movement. The Uruguayan capital, Montevideo, the continent's third-largest metropolis with European-looking buildings set among shady streets, prospered too, commanding commerce on the Rio de la Plata—the Plate River, named for silver, *plata*—upstream from Paraguay all the way down to where the wide river feeds the Antarctic seas.

Drive an hour or two outside these waterfront centers, however, and the isolation of most South American towns hit home with the first flat tire on a rutted dirt road or the first experience of a highway that had become an impassable river of mud. Rail travel was uncomfortable, with schedules undependable. Everyone wanted to fly. In the grand finale of the immensely popular *Flying Down to Rio* film, dancers perform on the wings of aircraft swooping high over city and shore while enthusiastic crowds watch from below. What the Hollywood movies did not show was how thoroughly German planes were masters of the air above South America. It was easier for passengers from the southern continent to travel to the heart of the Reich than to the heartland of the United States. Most routes were flown by German- or Italian-owned companies, or local companies using German pilots, or pilots who were naturalized German-born citizens. In 1934, when Brazilian generals wanted to map the country's remote interior, they contracted the new aerial photography unit of a German-controlled airline to record its every square mile. Whether the initiative for the mapping came from the Brazilians or in some way from the Germans is not clear.

Germans, and thousands of Japanese immigrants in agricultural settlements, lived in six countries on the Amazonian littoral: Ecuador, Peru, Brazil, Venezuela, Colombia, and Bolivia. Few North Americans inhabited the resource-rich region, however, especially after Fordlandia, an Amazonian rubber-growing enterprise of Henry Ford, largely collapsed. An Associated Press editor sent his correspondent from New York on assignment to "tell us whether the South Americans are really our friends." The reporter, John Lear, survived a 1942 plane crash in the Peruvian desert to report that at regular distances, "over an area larger than the United States, the Amazon was lined with airports cut from the wilderness by German technicians."

The United States was well into the war by the time Lear wrote that "at least several times a week, sometimes each day, German planes piloted by German flyers came down on these airports on a fixed schedule." He noted that U.S. intelligence officers called the ubiquitous German pilots a threat to defense of the Panama Canal, only a short flying distance away. "Taking these planes from German hands would not deprive the Germans of their maps or flying knowledge of this almost unknown terrain," Lear wrote.

How did Germans come to be the virtual owners of South American skies? The answer lies partly in an unforeseen consequence of the Treaty of Versailles, which ended World War I after Germany's military defeat. Signed in June 1919, Versailles, among its punishing terms, forbade Germany to have an air force. That ended the careers of many military pilots and eliminated an otherwise natural career path for German youth attracted to aviation. From their devastated homeland, German aviators joined thousands of entrepreneurs of all stripes in turning their eyes across the Atlantic to South America, with its reputation as a frontier region that offered fresh starts, especially where German colonies already existed.

A GOSPEL OF FLIGHT

Airlines, German-owned or not, grew in South America within a global atmosphere of enthusiasm for the potential of human conquest of the skies. The dreams began in 1903 with the Wright brothers' first short flight at Kitty Hawk, North Carolina. Poignantly, it seems now, some early designers and pilots saw aircraft as a technology that would knit the world together and make war obsolete. The Pomeranian Otto Lilienthal, considered the founder of the science of wing aerodynamics and an inspiration to the Wright brothers, represented this "gospel of aviation." In January 1884, Lilienthal wrote a letter to the Prussian naval officer Moritz von Egidy, a current of excitement rippling through his words.

> Numerous technicians in every nation are doing their utmost to achieve the dream of free, unlimited flight and it is precisely here where changes can be made that would have a radical effect on our whole way of life. The borders between countries would lose their significance . . . national defence would cease to devour the best resources of nations . . . the necessity of resolving disagreements in some other way than by bloody battles would, in its turn, lead us to eternal peace.

In the United States men and women took to the air with what author Gore Vidal called a "quasi-religious" fervor. Vidal's father Gene, an intimate of Amelia Earhart and President Roosevelt's director of the Bureau of Air Commerce, served as an executive of three commercial airlines. Just as Henry Ford envisioned putting every family on the road with his Model T, Gene Vidal saw a day when the simple "Everyman's Plane" would put everyone on the skyways. "Flight would make men near-angels," wrote Gore Vidal, "and a peaceful world one."

Brazil's own air pioneer, Alberto Santos-Dumont, spent many evenings gazing at the starry skies above the coffee plantation where he grew up. Born in 1873, he read voraciously as a boy, especially Jules Verne. "With Phileas Fogg I went round the world in eighty days." Santos-Dumont moved to France, where he joined the enthusiasts called aeronauts, who were exploring the new technology of aviation. In 1901, the young Brazilian became one of the most celebrated personalities of the day by circling the Eiffel Tower at record speed in a dirigible. (He made history another way, too: he asked his friend Louis Cartier to come up with a timepiece that he would not need to pull out of his pocket in flight, resulting in what would come to be called the "wristwatch.") In those days before air traffic controls, Santos-Dumont could be spotted by morning drifting in his personal hydrogen gas–powered flying machine over Parisian boulevards, then lunching smartly dressed at his favorite café, Maxim's.

But Santos-Dumont was no rudderless dandy. He made the first controlled fixed-wing flight in France and developed a series of improvements for heavier-than-air craft, including a precursor to ailerons. He was showered with honors until his career stopped at age thirty-six, when he was stricken by multiple sclerosis. Tragically, perhaps affected by the depression that sometimes accompanies the condition, he burned his papers and drawings and hanged himself in 1932. Like the emblematic early Argentine flier Jorge Newbery, who died in 1914 and is interred in Buenos Aires, Santos-Dumont too lies buried under a massive statue of Icarus, in Rio.

If you come to Rio, you may land at Santos-Dumont Airport—the aeronaut remains lionized in Brazil as the father of aviation. But it took German presence and know-how to establish the industry on Santos-Dumont's native continent.

In 1919, a full five years before Delta, the oldest operating U.S. airline, began sending crop dusters over the Georgia cotton fields, Germans had already established the first carrier in South America. Called SCADTA (Sociedad Colombo-Alemana de Transportes Aéreos), the Colombian line flew German-made Junkers seaplanes from a base alongside an island in the Magdalena River near Cartagena. The money behind SCADTA, its pilots, and management all came from Germany after World War I. Some SCADTA pilots who had learned to fly in the war maintained their commissions in the Luftwaffe reserve.

As adequate airfields were built on the mainland, SCADTA soon was flying passengers and cargo throughout the Andes, to the enormous satisfaction of Colombians. Their country was divided by three high mountain ridges that made land travel a long, slogging nightmare. Anyone who could afford it now took a plane.

Six years after SCADTA began, the prosperous German community in Cochabamba, Bolivia, took up a collection to buy a modern, four-passenger Junkers F.13, the world's first all-metal transport aircraft. With no more than the single plane, they grandly founded Lloyd Aéreo Boliviano (LAB), purposely choosing the name to echo "Lloyd's of London," the British enterprise with a sterling reputation for security. Soon a fleet of LAB aircraft linked Bolivian cities to points in Argentina, Uruguay, Chile, and southern Brazil.

Given the size and wealth of the Brazilian German colonies, it was no surprise when an airline appeared in 1927 with the specific aim of serving *teuto-brasileiros*, the Germans of Brazil. Germans had been establishing agricultural settlements in South America since the 1850s; German businesses followed and thrived, with entire cities growing up around *teuto-brasileiro* industries such as cloth manufacture and meat processing. Sindicato Condor, a subsidiary of the German company Luft Hansa, provided overnight flights from Rio to other Brazilian cities, cutting days from overland journeys, and soon flew to Uruguay and Argentina. Luft Hansa also took a controlling share in the SEDTA (Sociedad Ecuatoriana Alemana de Transportes Aéreos) line of Ecuador, operated it exclusively with German pilots, and fought off U.S. airline penetration into the country.

When the Bolivian LAB and the Brazilian Condor airlines joined forces in 1936, German hegemony in southern skies took another leap forward. The companies brought their respective passengers to a central hub, the Brazilian city of Corumbá on the mineral-rich Pantanal, the world's largest wetland, where passengers spent the night. The next morning, passengers and cargo brought in by one company flew out on the equipment of the other, effectively giving each airline international connections neither possessed alone.

In the 1930s, German lines often used airplanes that were simply better than the competition in Latin America, including U.S.-owned airlines. Panair do Brasil, a subsidiary of Pan American, vied for the Brazilian trade but often lost out because it used only traditional seaplanes until 1937, limiting its routes to seacoast, lake, and river cities. Meanwhile, the Condor line was flying the most up-to-date product of the German aviation industry, the Focke-Wulf Fw 200 Condor, a four-engine monoplane suited for hard-surface runways. (In a sign of pride in the model, German foreign minister Joachim von Ribbentrop flew a Condor to Moscow in 1939 to sign the Non-Aggression Pact with the Soviet Union.) Designed as a long-distance, high-altitude passenger carrier, which saved fuel by cruising at more than ten thousand feet while other planes flew at a maximum of five thousand, the Condor was later modified by the Luftwaffe for use as a warplane.

When the Italian LATI (Linee Aeree Transcontinentali Italiane) began to fly out of Rio in 1939, U.S. and British diplomats raised a warning flag. LATI flew regularly between South America and Rome, with connections to Nazi Europe.

Not every airline in South America was run by Germany and Italy. An airplane mechanic from the United States founded a line in Peru. The French Aeropostale, whose pilots included Antoine de Saint-Exupéry, the author of *The Little Prince* and *Wind, Sand and Stars*, ran mail. Argentines established a spin-off of the Aeropostale amid national enthusiasm for flying balloons, and then airplanes, over the River Plate. The heroics of native aviators like Jorge Newbery, who began his love of flying when he met Alberto Santos-Dumont, inspired hundreds of tangos with titles such as "Night Flight" and "Chile by Night." A tango called "El Gato" was named for a flier renowned for surviving accidents the way a cat survives a fall.

The German and Italian airlines, however, worried the Allies the most. Reporting on Axis espionage in 1941, U.S. journalist Curt Reiss wrote, "In the case of South America, no intelligence apparatus had to be organized. It was already there in the many airlines which spanned the entire continent."

On the surface, the struggle for the southern skies looked like a fight between big international companies, but in reality it was a high-stakes duel among governments: the United States and Great Britain on one side, with Germany and Italy on the other. The grandfather of Latin airlines, SCADTA, flew routes within two hundred miles of the Panama Canal, constituting "an immediate and extremely serious threat to U.S. security" according to the Joint Planning Committee of the U.S. State, Navy, and War Departments. SCADTA and LATI had to be neutralized.

The effort began in Colombia, where a deep historical grudge existed against the United States. In 1903, Washington orchestrated the secession of Colombia's northernmost province, arming "rebels" and recognizing the region as a new country named Panama, making a deal with its government to build the canal. In the 1930s, feelings in Colombia still ran strong against the United States for the loss of national territory. President Eduardo Santos pledged that no attack on the Panama Canal would be launched from Colombian soil, but he could not be persuaded to eject the Germans. SCADTA had become vital to Colombia's economic growth, and it kept families and friends connected who lived far apart. Many of the company's Germans had taken Colombian citizenship; they participated in civic affairs and otherwise contributed to the life of the country. Why should Santos kick them out?

What the Colombian president wanted was beside the point to Spruille Braden, a blustering newcomer to the U.S. Embassy. A Montana businessman with stakes in companies active in Latin America—United Fruit, Standard Oil, and his own Braden Copper—the ambassador was not a diplomat at heart, but comfortable with political intervention. After the war, as assistant secretary of state for Western Hemisphere affairs, he made the cover of *Time* magazine with a story about him inside under the headline "DEMOCRACY'S BULL." Corpulent, with dark eyes that stared out from under thick brows, Braden led the charge against SCADTA. He liked the nickname "Buffalo."

For months after presenting his credentials in Bogotá in February 1939, Braden treated unsuccessfully with President Santos about removing Germans from SCADTA. Meanwhile, Juan Trippe, the shrewd, legendary founder of Pan American Airways, held information close to his chest that neither Santos, important Pan Am executives, nor key U.S. officials knew about who really owned the "German" airline in Colombia: he did. In 1931, Trippe had surreptitiously bought 85 percent interest in the company by way of a secret compact with its Austrian owner, who eventually also obtained Colombian citizenship. Making the transaction known would have stoked the anti-gringo ire of Colombians, reckoned Trippe, who had also failed to inform U.S. authorities at the time.

In March 1939 Trippe was summoned to Washington by military officials who knew he controlled SCADTA. The War Department generals told him to eliminate its "Germans," Colombian citizens or not, in the interest of U.S. national security. Pan Am, with its extensive air routes and responsibility for carrying U.S. mail, was considered by the State Department and the military as an arm of national defense.

Ambassador Braden had discovered the truth about SCADTA's ownership only on the eve of his departure for Colombia. In February 1940, he called a secret meeting with Pan Am representatives at the U.S. Embassy in Bogotá. It was the middle of the day, but the men arrived to find Braden's office dark, all the drapes drawn. The only light came from candles sputtering in their holders on a grand piano. Solemnly, as if he were delivering a death sentence, Braden announced that SCADTA must be "deloused." The Germans, like insects, were to be picked off and the airline purified.

Even with war coming, however, Trippe dragged his feet about "delousing" the airline, concerned that the state might take it over and he would lose money. Finally in June 1940, more than nine months after war had begun in Europe, and only after being assured his expenses would be covered, Juan Trippe bent to pressure from Washington and the "Buffalo's" diplomatic charge.

In an operation worthy of a spy film, Pan Am smuggled 150 U.S. pilots and dozens of maintenance technicians into Colombia, keeping them hidden and communicating with them in code. Early one morning, Trippe's local operations manager surprised all of SCADTA's German personnel with simultaneous dismissal notices and replaced them with the Americans. SCADTA did not miss a day of flying. President Santos could do nothing. The U.S. Treasury cushioned the costs of firing the Germans for the resourceful Juan Trippe "in the interest of the national defense of the United States." After Pearl Harbor, German pilots and other SCADTA employees were interned in camps in Colombia or in the United States.

While SCADTA's Germans were being eliminated, LATI's Italians were smuggling spies, intelligence, and contraband between South America and the Reich. LATI's fast, three-engine Savoia-Marchetti SM.79 airplanes, nicknamed "Sparrowhawks," carried fascist secret agents, diplomatic pouches, and propaganda books and films. At a time when even small amounts of rare materials were in demand for war industries, LATI secretly carried them out of South America: industrial-use diamonds, tungsten for aircraft manufacture, mica for insulation and heat transfer in electronics.

LATI secretly delivered to the Nazis one of the earth's rarest elements: platinum, a metal so strategic that the United States banned its use during the war for any purpose other than military. Essential for catalytic converters and for electronic and oil-refining processes, platinum is found in few places in the world, among them Colombia. Thanks to LATI and roundabout airline routing, Colombia became for Germany and Japan the only wartime source for platinum. In 1940, a mine operator named Theodor Barth smuggled out small amounts at a time to the chief *Vertrauensmann*—V-man, or confidential agent—of the German secret service, the *Abwehr*, in Chile. The agent contacted a collaborator, the German manager of the Condor-LATI office in Santiago. Together the V-man and the airline office manager repackaged the platinum into one-pound packets, sending them clandestinely on a series of separate Condor flights to Brazil, where they were transferred to LATI planes. In this way a significant lode—twenty-five pounds altogether—of the metal reached the Reich between August 1940 and February 1941. In like manner, other precious commodities mined from South American earth evaded the British naval watch of European coasts, literally flying over His Majesty's ships to supply the German war machine.

If the Allies were going to take LATI down, they must do it in Rio, its Latin American headquarters and continental hub. But the Italians were ahead in the game. From its first days in Brazil, LATI had hired President Getúlio Vargas's son-in-law Pedro Cavalieri, a lawyer, as one of its top directors in South America. Members of Brazil's social elite held key administrative positions, and wealthy Brazilian investors stood to lose if the airline were closed down. President Vargas was unsympathetic to pleas from Washington and London that, for their benefit, he should upset an arrangement that was serving his country well. He saw little value in uprooting a key player in Brazil's growing economic sector, not to mention cutting a lifeline to the European continent, especially with no substitute in sight to provide a direct bridge across the Atlantic.

Washington's efforts to eliminate LATI looked feeble. The Brazilian branch of the Rockefeller family's Standard Oil of New Jersey provided fuel to the Sparrowhawks, despite State Department protests. The U.S. ambassador in Rio, Jefferson Caffery, a career diplomat from Louisiana, complained to Washington for months about the airline without results.

At last, in August 1941, a cable from Secretary of State Cordell Hull informed Caffery that the federal Reconstruction Finance Corporation would create a branch specifically to eliminate Axis control of airlines in South America. In its first action, the new office negotiated with Pan American, promising loans, and Pan Am agreed to establish a route from New York to Lisbon by way of cities on the Brazilian hump, an alternative passage to compete with the Italians. In huffy-sounding language, Secretary Hull cabled Ambassador Caffery that the idea had better work, given that "the sole reason for the establishment of this new service is, of course, the elimination of LATI." Even with the prospect of a Pan Am route to Europe, however, President Vargas hesitated to act against the airline.

As war ravaged England in the summer of 1941, British leaders decided they could not wait for the Americans to manage developments. They suspected LATI's pilots of spotting for German submarines that sank British ships. "L.A.T.I. constituted the biggest gap in the British economic blockade," wrote British Security Co-ordination (BSC) agent H. Montgomery Hyde. Something drastic needed to be done.

An order came to the BSC office in New York, the British secret intelligence outpost that covered the Americas: eliminate LATI operations in South America. Details of the order were left to the agent in charge. The scheme that unfolded, led by a Canadian code-named "Intrepid," would erase the Sparrowhawks from the southern skies and go down as one of the most successful single blows to the Axis in the history of wartime spycraft in Latin America.

High above New York City, in "his highly mechanized eyrie in Rockefeller Center" as author Ian Fleming described it, William Stephenson presided over the BSC offices. On Churchill's orders, Stephenson had installed the office in May 1940 with the support of President Roosevelt and knowledge of FBI director J. Edgar Hoover. The task of confronting the Nazis in Latin America in July 1941 was on the desk of an extraordinary man.

As a young boy in his native western Canada, William Stephenson had become fascinated with radio technology and taught himself Morse code. During World War I, he flew fighter planes and fought in the trenches, escaped German captivity, and earned medals for valor from Canada, Great Britain, and France. Slender, with clear blue eyes, young Bill's nickname was "Captain Machine Gun," not for combat proclivities but for his boxing style. Stephenson won the interservice lightweight world boxing championship at the same time the heavyweight title was won for the U.S. Marines by the legendary Gene Tunney, who would become Stephenson's good friend and business partner. Stephenson invented a kind of early wireless technology, traveled around Europe to grow his business, and was a millionaire by age thirty.

Stephenson became Winston Churchill's intelligence point man. Churchill charged him with establishing a global network of information gathering and sabotage to help besieged England survive the onslaught from Germany. No armchair administrator, the man called "Intrepid"—Churchill gave him the code name—took on certain dangerous missions himself.

"He is the man who became one of the great secret agents of the last war," Ian Fleming wrote of Stephenson. Fleming, creator of James Bond, one of the best-known fictional spies of all time, was an intelligence agent for the British Navy on a plainclothes mission when he first met "Intrepid," describing him as "a man of few words" who possessed "a magnetic personality and the quality of making anyone ready to follow him." Added Fleming, "He also used to make the most powerful martinis in America and serve them in quart glasses."

The British secret operations executive office in London entrusted Stephenson with the mission of destroying LATI in South America "by any means necessary." With full discretion, Stephenson considered his options. A coup changing the Brazilian government was a possibility, but the potential consequences of an attempt, successful or not, were considered too grave to risk: if traced to the British undercover office in New York, the operation could jeopardize the BSC's still-covert cooperation with officially neutral Washington. President Roosevelt supported the British intelligence team only in secret because isolationists, such as those in the America First Committee, were a strong political force, constantly challenging the president, who was up for reelection. Stephenson would do nothing to threaten the position of the American president upon whom so much depended in England's darkest days, from circuitously supplying warships and armaments to sharing intelligence.

Another option was to blow up a LATI commercial flight as an unmistakable warning to the Nazi network in Latin America. There were occasions when civilian lives had to be sacrificed, went the thinking of the time. Stephenson decided the need to crush LATI, however, was not such an occasion; besides, as a pilot he could not condone the deaths of fellow pilots if an alternative could be found.

Instead, the intelligence chief sought out the skills of operatives at Camp X, a clutch of fields and buildings forty miles from Toronto, a school for assassins and a factory of dirty tricks carved out of Canadian farmland. Describing the place in his memoirs, Stephenson used the language of his boxing life: Camp X was "the clenched fist," he said, "preparing for the knockout." Forty miles of Lake Ontario, rough and icy cold much of the year, lay along one side like a forbidding moat. A perimeter of dense scrub and woods around the rest discouraged accidental discovery. A corps of security agents trained in silent killing patrolled constantly against the possibility of deliberate intrusion.

Stephenson knew Camp X well, because he had helped to create it earlier in 1941. By September the camp already housed classrooms, stage sets, and a massive radio transmission station where men and women from more than a dozen countries trained as spies, saboteurs, and recruiters of resistance forces. Before radio operators were flown out and dropped behind enemy lines, they learned Morse code at Camp X, practiced new identities, and underwent realistic training to prepare them for harsh interrogation should they be captured, which most of them were. Five future directors of the Central Intelligence Agency and its predecessor, the Office of Strategic Services (OSS), trained at Camp X.

Alongside the professional spies labored forgers, chemists, tailors, Oxford tutors, and filmmakers such as the Korda brothers, Alexander and Zoltán, famous for Hollywood successes such as *The Thief of Bagdad* and *The Private Life of Henry VIII*. Artists created locales to mimic corners of Nazi-occupied territories in Europe where operatives would carry out their missions, such as the spectacular murder of SS general Reinhard Heydrich, an architect of the Final Solution, outside a Czech village in 1942.

A spy's spy, "Intrepid" believed that the best method to complete a mission—the smartest way—used violence only as a last resort. From his New York office, Stephenson contacted a Camp X unit called Station M (for "magic"). Headed by a master illusionist famous among British schoolboys before the war, Station M invented ways to fool the enemy, even creating the semblance of air bases, troops, or seagoing fleets at various points of the world. Once, on a clandestine visit to Camp X, FBI director Hoover was amazed to look out from a hut to see what appeared to be several German warships on the Great Lake, an illusion produced by the Station M master with mirrors and toy boats. Station M also manufactured special inks and forged documents that could be sneaked into diplomatic pouches or caused to materialize on desks where they might do the most harm. Stephenson had an idea: could Station M produce a letter that would pass all tests to look like a missive sent from the president of LATI airlines in Rome?

The creation of a believable letter entailed a series of steps that went far beyond finding an agent with language skills in colloquial Italian. Stephenson requested the BSC chief in Rome to pilfer a sheet of paper from LATI headquarters that carried the personal letterhead of company president General Aurelio Liotta.

Before forgers in Canada could create a convincing forgery, however, authentic primary materials had to be made from scratch. This was not beyond the reach of the experts at Station M: in order to outfit spies who would infiltrate Nazi strongholds, operatives in Europe regularly collected items such as baggage decals, belt buckles, and a host of wardrobe elements for duplication at the Canadian site, lest a secret agent be betrayed in the field by some fault in appearance. Likewise, a letter putatively written in Rome must appear on what seemed like local paper. That meant finding straw pulp, because in much of Europe, where trees were scarcer than in the Americas, paper was manufactured by pulping annual plants—mostly wheat, but also rye and oat.

While agents of the magic group went about producing the required paper, others at Camp X created a typewriter whose every imprinted letter, comma, and space would mimic those that came from the typewriter of General Liotta's secretary because, as Sherlock Holmes once said, "A typewriter has really quite as much individuality as a man's handwriting." Stephenson's experts examined the purloined letter and determined the secretary used an ancient Olivetti with quirks they incorporated into the duplicate machine. General Liotta's letterhead was reproduced and embossed onto the newly fabricated paper so accurately that the experts reckoned it could withstand microscopic inspection; the fateful missive was composed, typed, and photographed. A copy of the letter was sent as a microfilm to Stephenson's chief agent in Rio, a trick within the trick that would help persuade those about to read the letter of its authenticity.

On the morning of November 14, 1941, a small item appeared on inside pages of Rio de Janeiro newspapers reporting a burglary at the home of Comandante Giovanni Coppola, the local director of LATI. A bedside clock and other small items had gone missing, according to the police report. The next day a Brazilian operative of the British intelligence service, posing as one of the thieves, approached the Rio office of the Associated Press with a microfilm photograph he claimed to have found among the comandante's things. Was it of interest? The AP reporter recognized the letter's explosive content and surmised it had been sent as microfilm to avoid interception. He carried the tiny photo to the U.S. Embassy to gauge its authenticity.

When Ambassador Caffery examined enlargements and determined the letter was genuine, he might have been excused for thinking the long-sought way to eliminate LATI had fallen into his lap. Caffery delivered the microfilm and enlargement to President Vargas, who broke into a rage.

Not only did the letter call the president a bloated buffoon, it suggested a fascist conspiracy was afoot. The letter said the Italians were planning to deal with Vargas's domestic enemy, the Integralist Party, a far-right political movement commonly called "Greens" for their uniform; Vargas had already beaten down one coup attempt by the Greens. The president forbade publication of the letter, but it soon made its way into diplomatic circles and beyond.

"There can be no doubt that the fat little man is falling into the pocket of the Americans and that only violent action on the part of our green friends can save the country," the phony letter said. "Our Berlin collaborators . . . have decided to intervene as soon as possible."

Intervention from Germany meant Luft Hansa might compete in Brazil, said the letter. The local LATI director was encouraged to befriend "the green gentlemen" to assure that LATI's privileges would continue under a new regime, and to discover whom "the green gentlemen" might name the next air minister, all plausible exhortations in the face of a supposed coup. To ice the cake, Stephenson ended the letter with an insult that could not be ignored. "The Brazilians may be, as you have said, a nation of monkeys, but they are monkeys who will dance for anyone who will pull the string."

Furious, President Vargas canceled LATI's landing rights. Events happened so fast that protest from Italy was useless. Brazilian soldiers took over the line's aircraft, landing fields, and maintenance equipment, and they interned flight crews. Comandante Coppola, the local director, withdrew a million dollars from a bank and tried to flee to Argentina, but authorities captured him just short of the border and threw him in jail.

U.S. ambassador Caffery took full credit for the culminating affair. He had a copy of the letter shown quietly to a member of British intelligence working at the British Embassy, saying U.S. intelligence had "pinched" the damning evidence that tore LATI from the landscape. Later, FBI chief J. Edgar Hoover would also take credit for bringing down LATI. The British agent, secretly cognizant of the letter's true backstory, made sure to compliment the U.S. ambassador's work effusively.

With LATI's demise in 1941, the domination of South American airways by German and Italian lines, a presence so strong in the 1930s, came to an end.

SOARING AZTECS, FORGOTTEN FLIERS

In pre-Columbian times, Mexico City's Chapultepec Park was a verdant space reserved for the rest and recreation of Aztec rulers. Today it is a fifteen-hundred-acre oasis in the middle of the largest Spanish-speaking city in the world. In the park stands a castle where six "Boy Heroes" fell, military cadets defending a hill against U.S. troops in 1847 during the Mexican-American War.

Ironically, another monument stands nearby, this one commemorating a Mexican air unit that flew under U.S. command in World War II. The Mexican Air Force Squadron 201, nicknamed the "Aztec Eagles" by its members, consisted of three hundred pilots and crew trained in the United States who made bombing runs over Luzon and Formosa in 1945 and ferried aircraft from Papua New Guinea to Pacific theater airfields for Allies fighting Japan. Eight of the Aztec Eagles were killed in the line of duty.

But don't expect to find the monument to the World War II fliers by asking directions from Mexicans enjoying the park.

"There is a Metro station named for them, I know that," said one person I asked, the first to show a spark of recognition about the squad.

I approached two indigenous-looking men before a giant *ahuehuete*, a Montezuma cypress. They said they had been praying at the tree, a species sacred to native people. We stood no more than a hundred feet from the flying Aztecs' monument, a massive stepped semicircle standing at least a story high, but they said they had not heard of the squadron. "We do not concern ourselves with war," said one, Tenoch, who identified himself as a Nahuatl priest.

The big monument to the Aztec Eagles and the little excitement their name arouses is a contrast that symbolizes Mexico's split attitude toward participation in the war. Both Washington and Mexico City knew some military participation was necessary to ensure that Mexico would have a seat at the table in the new postwar world order. But for historical reasons, supporting Washington was not a popular cause among the Mexican people. The United States was the Big Brother to the north who had taken away a large chunk of Mexican territory and threw a long shadow over the country.

Toward the war's end, however, Mexican president Manuel Ávila Camacho found a way to support the Allies militarily with a pretext that played upon Mexican pride. In May 1942, two Mexican tankers supplying oil to the United States had been sunk by U-boats, one on the way to New York, the other returning from Pennsylvania. Mexico declared war on the Axis. In 1944, President Ávila Camacho sent the aerial fighter squadron to fight with the Allies and "to clean the national honor" for Mexico's sunken ships.

As they trained in Texas and Idaho, the Aztec Eagles sometimes faced discrimination.

"The Americans looked down on us at least a little bit," Captain Reynaldo Gallardo recalled in 2003 in an interview for a San Diego, California, newspaper. "They didn't say so, but I noticed it. We made up our minds that we wouldn't say anything, but instead would show these people what we had."

On a combined U.S.-Mexican sortie in the Philippines, Gallardo, attached to the 58th U.S. Fighter Group, completed his mission of strafing a line of Japanese troops and vehicles. As he pulled up, he "got a little crazy" and maneuvered his plane into a celebratory roll, a move that earned him a scolding over the intercom as a "crazy Mexican." Gallardo found this offensive and blindly challenged the offender. On the ground, he saw that the American was "three times as big and four times as heavy," wearing a big grin on his face. They fought anyway, fortunately for Gallardo a mere tussle, but the Mexican's spunk earned him respect among the pilots. The gladiators became fast friends, breaking the ice between the Mexican and American airmen.

After the war, the Aztec Eagles were welcomed back home with a grand parade in Mexico City before being promptly shuttled into the background of the national landscape. The Mexicans received new fighter aircraft and other war matériel through the U.S. Lend-Lease program that aided U.S. allies. But the image of a fighting partnership with Washington did not fit the Mexican profile of independence from the United States. Ávila Camacho's successor, Miguel Alemán Valdés, turned his back on much of what his predecessor had done—and besides, no one in the ruling party wanted to entertain the prospect of war heroes competing with its handpicked, old-boy network candidates for political offices. The flying veterans faded into history, despite some ceremonial appearances over the years.

Mexico City's American Legion post in a charming old house in the leafy Condessa district is one of the few places the fliers are remembered. The post is a comfortable relic of another time, with a bar that opens at 2:00 p.m., a used bookstore, and memorabilia adorning the walls, including a photo of poet Alan Seeger—uncle of American folk singer Pete Seeger—who died at the Battle of the Somme in World War I. A secretary named Margarita dug out photos of the handsome young men of the Aztec Eagles for me. In some they posed with the propeller aircraft they flew, Thunderbolt single-seat fighters. In the past, Margarita said, the post hosted celebrations on Veterans Day—11/11 at 11:00 a.m.—"for those who came back alive." On Memorial Day, the Aztec Eagles joined American Legionnaires and U.S. Marines from the embassy at a cemetery to honor the dead. Mostly, however, the fliers were forgotten warriors in a country where the man on the street had little interest in the Second World War—even though Mexico had played an important part in supplying manpower to replace U.S. agricultural workers gone to fight, and providing oil and other natural resources.

"We fought in defense of sovereignty and independence of the nation," said former sergeant Héctor Tello Pineda of Xalapa, Veracruz, in a televised interview before his death in 2017. Tello, who entered the Mexican forces at age twenty, said the experience "shaped" him for the rest of his life.

"We did our duty as soldiers, and we did it with valor and discipline for the liberty of Mexico," he said. "For the whole world. Because in reality, it was a world war. That's what it was called."

2.

BLACK GOLD, OIL TO FUEL THE WAR

For centuries before the Europeans arrived, warriors in northeast Brazil covered their arrows with oil pitch and resin and sent them flaming through the air to destroy the huts of their enemies. In 1500 when the Portuguese came, the Indians launched the arrows against the houses of the first European settlers.

Almost five thousand miles to the north, on the rainy Gulf Coast of Mexico, natives were burning *chapopote*—petroleum tar—to honor their gods. They gathered small quantities of seeping oil for dye and glue, or smeared it over their skin as medicine. When the Spanish landed in 1519, the conquistadores used the pitch to caulk their boats.

Otherwise, Latin oil remained undisturbed until the turn of the twentieth century, when explorers from Europe and the United States began drilling wells in Brazil, Peru, Venezuela, Bolivia, Colombia, and Mexico. Petroleum had become a new kind of gold: all over the world oil powered electricity, asphalt made from it covered roads, and crude was refined into gasoline to fuel automobiles, buses, and, increasingly, trains. Early in World War I, Great Britain's First Lord of the Admiralty Winston Churchill turned oil into an indispensable wartime resource by overseeing the British fleet's conversion from coal power. By the 1930s, countries preparing for the next war coveted petroleum wherever they could find it.

Of thirty-three countries in Latin America, Mexico possessed the largest known reserves. The struggle for its prize involved international bankers, spies, manipulation in high places, and, sometimes, mayhem, with grave consequences for the beginning of the war. Mexican oil sold to Germany, Italy, and Japan gave the fascists a head start. Oil shook Mexico's relationship with other countries, especially the United States. European and U.S. companies produced oil in Venezuela, Colombia, Brazil, Bolivia, Peru, and Argentina, but in the lead-up to the war, when industrialized nations the world over were stockpiling arms and resources, Mexico stood at the center of the drama in Latin America.

Poor Mexico, so far from God, so close to the United States.

—ATTRIBUTED TO PRESIDENT PORFIRIO DÍAZ, 1830–1915

Unfortunately for the Allies, Washington's history of relations with its neighbor was ugly. Since Mexico declared independence from Spain in 1821, the U.S. military had attacked and occupied its territory or made cross-border raids at least a dozen times. Mexicans believed that many of their woes, and lack of true independence, derived from their location next door to the giant of the north. During the nineteenth century, the United States absorbed more than half of Mexican national territory, annexing present-day Texas in 1845 and, after the Mexican-American War ended in 1848, almost all of present-day California, Utah, Nevada, Arizona, and New Mexico.

A new wave of tension crested in 1914. Mexico jailed nine U.S. sailors who went off-limits into a fuel-loading facility at the port of Tampico, a major oil-exporting site. In retaliation, President Wilson ordered the U.S. Navy to seize the port of Veracruz, about three hundred miles south. The sailors were immediately released, but the U.S. commander demanded an apology and a twenty-one-gun salute for what has come to be known as the Tampico Incident. Mexico refused to humble itself by complying. When word reached Washington that a German boat was preparing to offload weapons for one of the contenders in a violent fight for the Mexican presidency—the side Wilson didn't like—Wilson ordered the city of Veracruz taken too. A characteristic Big Stick operation, the U.S. occupation lasted for seven months. The Mexican government was so outraged that it refused to support the United States in the First World War, remaining neutral and continuing to trade with Germany for the duration.

In the early 1920s Mexico ranked second in world oil output, outdone only by the United States. The producers generally came from abroad with capital or experience or both. Skilled local employees were paid a fraction of what the foreign managers and workmen made. Every attempt by Mexican authorities to increase taxes on production or otherwise gain some profit from the country's major natural resource was thwarted by the companies and the governments who backed them. Not only did Mexico lose significant territory to the United States in the nineteenth century, it also saw portions of its most valuable land in Big Oil's international grip as the twentieth century began.

Formula for success: rise early, work hard, strike oil.

—J. PAUL GETTY

The unequal relationship between foreign companies and their Mexican hosts began in 1901, when the California oil tycoon Edward L. Doheny sank his first Mexican well at El Ebano, a lonely spot on the railroad line about thirty-five miles southwest of Tampico. Doheny already had productive wells around Los Angeles; he cobbled together investments from the California operation, and from railroad entrepreneurs interested in replacing coal fuel with oil, and headed south. He announced that he would pay five pesos to anyone who could lead him to tar pits, those bubbling brown nuisances where cattle might wander and become stuck. But for the prospector in Doheny, the pits were a sign of oil. He wrote:

> We found a small conical-shaped hill—where bubbled a spring
> of oil, the sight of which caused us to forget all about the dreaded

climate—its hot, humid atmosphere, its apparently incessant rains . . . the dense forest jungle which seems to grow up as fast as cut down.

Doheny struck gushers, and the word spread. Others seeking a windfall arrived by boat and rail, men from companies with plans and maps but individual wildcatters too, often leaving behind the strikes they had been working in Ohio, Illinois, Kansas, and East Texas. From the United Kingdom came another moneyed entrepreneur, Weetman Dickinson Pearson, a Scottish contractor already well known for feats of construction: the first Aswan dam, a tunnel under the Thames, and two subway tunnels under the Hudson River.

Pearson's engineers in Mexico, who were building a railroad across the Isthmus of Tehuantepec, told him about the oil finds. His friend Porfirio Díaz, the Mexican president, gave the Scotsman concessions in five states, partly to prevent Standard Oil and the Americans from cornering production. In 1908 Pearson set up El Aguila, which would soon be Mexico's largest oil company, becoming part of Royal Dutch Shell.

By the end of the decade, more than 155 separate enterprises, including Doheny's and Pearson's, the Southern Pacific Railroad, Gulf Oil from Texas, and the Rockefeller Standard Oil companies, and 345 individuals and partnerships were operating in fields from El Ebano south to the Isthmus of Tehuantepec.

In 1910 came the Mexican Revolution, the first great social upheaval of the twentieth century. Since he took office in 1876, Porfirio Díaz had built railroads and improved the economy, but he did so by taking land from those who were working it, especially the indigenous, and dividing it up for private enterprises. The wealth they produced went to a tiny few. There was also deep resentment of seemingly unbridled foreign investment, such as in oil, whose profits failed to improve lives.

The revolution did not stop oil production, which generally took place on the Gulf Coast away from most of the fighting. Besides, the foreign companies had their own militias, strong and well equipped, so belligerents were unlikely to venture into the fields.

Americans, Brits, and Dutch as well as some Frenchmen lived in comfortable enclaves while Mexican employees ate separately and inhabited inferior, sometimes squalid housing. The outsiders seemed to care not a whit for local peasants who lived around the petroleum installations, a condition noted by a young cavalry officer who commanded troops in the Tampico region for three years in the 1920s, the future Mexican president Lázaro Cárdenas del Río. One oil company refused to install a spigot on its waterline that crossed a village, forcing residents to continue trekking to a river for water; the same company offered Cárdenas a sleek new Packard in a typical gesture of currying favor with the military. Cárdenas turned it down and continued to drive his Hudson clunker.

But Lázaro Cárdenas never forgot what he saw. Brutal company militias, the infamous *guardias blancas* (white guards), kept order. "In how many of the villages bordering on the oil fields is there a hospital, or school or social center, or a sanitary water supply, or an athletic field, or even an electric plant fed by the millions of cubic meters of natural gas allowed to go to waste?" he asked the nation years later, with the authority of one who had seen with his own eyes.

Out of the turmoil of the revolution—as many as 3.5 million persons died between 1910 and 1921—came a remarkable constitution that incorporated social rights, mandated land reform, and established the right to collective bargaining for workers. The document's famous Article 27 carried tectonic implications for the oil industry: the government might grant limited concessions, but from now on, rights to substances found underground, such as oil, gold, copper, and silver, belonged to the nation.

The international oil companies reacted with umbrage—possessing a concession, they said, meant that what was under the earth belonged to them, period. The executives seemed to agree with American oilman J. Paul Getty's famous words: "The meek shall inherit the Earth, but not its mineral rights."

The oil companies and their governments did not want to give in to the new law for reasons that went beyond Mexico: a snowball effect might reach holdings in Peru, Colombia, Venezuela, and Bolivia. Mexico had to be stopped.

• • •

When General Plutarco Calles, a veteran of the revolution, became president in 1924 and tried to implement Article 27, the U.S. ambassador called him a "communist." (He wasn't; indeed, Calles was an admirer of Mussolini, but it did not help appearances that Mexico had been the first country in the Americas to host a Soviet embassy.) The oil companies urged Washington to repeal an embargo on arms sales so that Calles's enemies could topple him. To cool tensions and find a compromise, President Coolidge named a class-mate of his from Amherst College as ambassador to Mexico City, a banker named Dwight Morrow. The appointment turned out to be enlightened.

Dwight Morrow was a patrician-looking J.P. Morgan Company executive who had served as the chief civilian aide to General John J. Pershing in France during World War I. As soon as he arrived in the Mexican capital, Morrow changed the name of the diplomatic headquarters from "American Embassy" to "United States Embassy," defusing long-standing ire from Mexicans who said the word "American" belonged to Latin countries as well.

At J.P. Morgan, Morrow had been the financial advisor to Charles Lindbergh, the first aviator to fly alone across the Atlantic, and he invited the pilot to Mexico on a goodwill tour. Adoring crowds received the world's most famous man. One hundred thousand workers paraded in his honor. The visit had romantic consequences, too. Lindbergh met the ambassador's daughter, Anne, and married her in 1929.

In nearby Cuernavaca, where Morrow and his wife built a weekend home, the ambassador expressed respect for the national culture by commissioning the muralist Diego Rivera to paint a massive narrative fresco in a palace off the central square, once the home of Hernán Cortés. The resulting panorama is one of the artist's most magnificent works, an image of the Conquest by a revolutionary: metal-clad Spanish invaders mounted on fine horses fight indigenous warriors who struggle in combat on the ground without shoes.

Years before President Roosevelt introduced the Good Neighbor policy in 1933, Dwight Morrow seemed to sense the end of the Big Stick. Since 1823, U.S. relations with countries south of the border had been ruled by what would come to be called the Monroe Doctrine, a declaration to

Europe and the rest of the world that Latin America fell within the U.S. sphere of influence. For a hundred years thereafter, Washington imposed its will on Latin countries, often by force, frequently on behalf of U.S. businesses. Morrow instead represented dialogue, partnership.

He also anticipated Nelson Rockefeller's program of Goodwill Ambassadors that would bring Hollywood stars and notable intellectuals to South America during the war, a propaganda offensive aimed both north and south. Morrow invited the wildly popular humorist Will Rogers to travel around the country with him and President Calles and send favorable dispatches about Mexico and its president back to the United States.

In 1928, the Calles-Morrow Agreement alleviated strains by introducing a kind of grandfather clause into the oil crisis, reaffirming the rights of foreign companies in the tracts they worked prior to the 1917 Constitution. The agreement said future disputes would be resolved by Mexican courts.

Even Dwight Morrow's diplomatic presence, however, could not put a lid on the roiling activism of oil industry workers. And members of the nationalistic middle class, who had supported the revolution as a way of subordinating foreign capital, knew foreign companies lost little in the 1927 pact, even though Shell and Standard continued complaining about even minor changes to the status quo.

Meanwhile, Germany, Italy, and Japan were beginning to explore ways to stockpile oil as they prepared for war. This was the situation faced by Lázaro Cárdenas, Mexico's greatest twentieth-century president.

Tall, part Tarascan Indian, with thoughtful dark eyes, Cárdenas was elected in 1934 on the pledge to carry out the reforms—finally—that had been promised by the long and bloody revolution. The son of a shopkeeper from Michoacan, he fought with such skill and ambition during the revolution that he rose to the rank of brigadier general by the time he turned twenty-five. Cárdenas's national project—expanded federal government, liberal social programs, and a policy of controlling natural resources to serve the public interest—had much in common with that of his colleague in the north, Franklin Roosevelt. Indeed, Lázaro Cárdenas had his own kind of New Deal.

The new president was bent on fundamental change. His reputation for personal incorruptibility gave him moral authority. But the reforms also placed Mexico on a collision course with the world's most powerful nations, the United States and Great Britain, over oil.

Workers sparked the dispute. Before the 1930s, the oil industry's organized labor sector was relatively weak. When faced with strikes, companies typically threatened to cut production and jobs, and the government reluctantly went along with the companies, fearing a domino effect from work stoppages that could upset the entire national economy. Refinery employees, engineers, and workers in the field were among the best-paid laborers in Mexico, but the disparity between their compensation and that of foreign employees, often for the same jobs, was an affront to dignity and respect.

In a way, the pay and benefits gap was a symbol of what rankled Mexicans overall about foreign control of their oil: the nonrenewable national resource was dwindling toward depletion even as the wealth it produced flew into pockets abroad. "The government or individual that delivers natural resources to foreign enterprises betrays the fatherland," Cárdenas would write at the end of his life.

On August 15, 1935, ten thousand oil workers united their nineteen disparate unions. They joined the fast-growing Confederation of Mexican Workers, effectively the ruling party's labor sector, demanding wage increases and benefits. They drafted the industry's first collective bargaining contract and submitted it to companies in 1936. The die was cast.

Some companies had amicable relations with their workers and accepted the contract, but seventeen American and European firms that produced most of the oil did not, saying they could not afford to comply. They included the giants—Royal Dutch Shell and the Rockefellers' Standard Oil. The Mexican Board of Conciliation and Arbitration, set up in the Constitution to resolve intractable labor-management disputes, wrote a twenty-seven-hundred-page report deciding in favor of the unions. Companies appealed to the Mexican Supreme Court, which sustained the board's decision.

In March 1938, Cárdenas's control of the country was under threat from two sides: from the fascist-supported political right that opposed his

wide reforms and from Mexican labor and the public who demanded he
confront Big Oil. Events in Europe were reaching a boiling point. Hitler
triumphantly entered Vienna with tens of thousands of troops. Out of
more than sixty countries in the League of Nations, only Mexico protested the *Anschluss*, Hitler's invasion of Austria. French commanders
ordered troops on the Maginot Line to stand by; the British home secretary called for a million air raid volunteers; Spanish troops loyal to the
elected Republican government were fleeing before Generalissimo Francisco Franco's legions, supported by Nazi arms and planes.

Cárdenas had to make the most momentous decision in the nation's history since independence—whether to nationalize the country's
petroleum—while keeping in mind Mexico's geographical reality, "so
close to the United States." He had two cards in his favor: oil would be
the lifeblood of the coming world conflict, required by all sides; and Roosevelt had pledged, at inter-American conferences in 1933 and 1936, that
the U.S. military would never again invade Latin countries. Cárdenas
reckoned that the American president could not go back on his word for
the purpose of securing Mexican oil, even if he wanted to. War was on
the way, and Roosevelt would be risking the allegiance of all Latin American nations with such rash action.

Cárdenas held face-to-face talks with the dissenting firms, offering
compromises they did not accept. "Even in today's terms, the arrogance
of the oil negotiators toward President Cárdenas himself and the symbolic
power of his office is surprising," wrote historian Friedrich Schuler.

At 10:00 p.m. on March 18, 1938, Mexicans gathered around their
radios to hear the president, whose voice sounded husky and firm. "It
is the sovereignty of the nation which is thwarted through the maneuvers
of foreign capitalists who, forgetting that they have formed themselves
into Mexican companies, now attempt to elude the mandates and avoid
the obligations placed upon them by the authorities of this country."

The morning newspaper *El Nacional* ran the headline "OIL COMPA-
NIES REFUSE TO ABIDE BY SUPREME COURT DECISION, THE GOVERNMENT WILL
FOLLOW THE PATH OF THE LAW."

Cárdenas offered compensation, but the companies turned it down.
They launched a crippling international boycott of the new Mexican state

oil company, PETROMEX, later called Pemex. They deprived Pemex of tankers to carry its oil and cut off its supply of tetraethyl lead, a compound necessary to turn crude into sellable high-octane gasoline. Working together, the State Department and the companies dissuaded Latin American customers from buying Mexican oil. The companies organized secondary boycotts to prevent sales of machinery that Pemex needed, sometimes resorting to threatening to withhold their business from suppliers. A press campaign orchestrated by the companies pictured Mexicans in racist caricatures.

Big Oil argued to Washington that the Mexican expropriation was a dangerous precedent, that losing control over the Southern Hemisphere's petroleum was a threat to the vital interests of the United States. Secretary of State Cordell Hull agreed. Labor costs had been kept low in the Latin oil fields. What would happen if other nations followed and companies lost their ability to procure cheap oil all over Latin America? In 1932 it cost US$1.90 to produce a barrel of oil in the United States, but only US$1.60 in Colombia, Ecuador, and Peru; US$1.41 in Mexico; and just US$0.87 in Venezuela.

Maintaining the position of the oil business into the future was conflated with maintaining the U.S. sphere of control in Latin America. In June 1938, an advisor warned Hull and Roosevelt, "Should the government of Venezuela follow the government of Mexico and expropriate the foreign owned oil properties . . . without adequate payment therefor, the proper interpretation of the Monroe Doctrine will become the gravest problem the State Department will have to face."

The peso fell and Mexicans suffered a 20 percent rise in prices, but the public supported the nationalization across class lines. Cárdenas believed oil had a social function, and Mexicans agreed that its value for the nation transcended money: expropriation was an economic Declaration of Independence. Cárdenas pledged that despite the circumstances, "Mexico will honor her foreign debt," and a call went out for public donations. "State governors, high Church officials, patriotic grand dames, peasants, students—all the numberless and picturesque types of Mexicans—pitched in what they had, including money, jewels, even homely domestic objects, chickens, turkeys and pigs," wrote a historian.

But donations of jewelry and pigs would neither meet the Mexican budget nor pay off the national debt, nor would they cover social programs to modernize the nation. With Mexico's traditional markets blocked, Cárdenas had to look elsewhere to sell oil. Germany, Italy, and Japan were at the door.

Cárdenas was by conviction a democrat; his political opponents were supported by Mexican fascist organizations and Franco's Spanish Falange. But he would make his decisions about where to send oil based on what was best for Mexico.

ENTER THE MYSTERY MAN

William Rhodes Davis, a larger-than-life international trader who made and lost entire fortunes by the time he was in his forties, could not have chosen a better moment to appear on the scene. In 1941, the *New York Times* referred to Davis as "the mystery man" of international wartime politics. A natural salesman with a magnetic personality and contacts that ranged from Roosevelt to Hitler, Davis gave Cárdenas what he needed to make nationalization work: a secure market for Mexico's oil. At the same time, the American entrepreneur also assured Nazi Germany of the fuel it needed to start the war.

Born in Montgomery, Alabama, William Rhodes Davis always said he traced his ancestry to the British empire-builder Cecil Rhodes and to Jefferson Davis, president of the Confederate States of America—forbears possibly more aspirational than factual. He learned the oil business from the bottom up in Oklahoma, beginning by doing dirty work on oil rigs, starting his first wildcat company at age twenty-four. Over the years he made the transition to dressing in elegant suits, smoking a cigarette European-style, held between thumb and forefinger, cultivating the air of a worldly entrepreneur. Inveterately optimistic, Davis was also a hard-fisted businessman who possessed a chameleonlike capacity to switch his persona as the occasion demanded, from that of a poorly spoken hick to a smooth, cultured gentleman. Not physically imposing, with a slight limp from an injury suffered during service in World War I, Davis was always the man with the biggest plans in the room.

In 1933, attracted by the possibility of selling oil to Germany as the

National Socialists came into power, Davis dispatched a company officer to Berlin. After a few weeks, his envoy reported there was no chance for their small, independent company to succeed against Standard and Shell, which had a stranglehold on the market. That iron wall of Big Oil had stood in the way of Davis's plans more than once—he deeply resented the giant companies and called them "the international combine."

Undeterred, Davis got financing from his perennial stand-by partner, the Bank of Boston, and went to Germany himself. He acquired an oil storage company in Hamburg, drew up a plan for a massive refinery, and, with his trademark confidence, peddled his proposal to German banks. When a banker introduced him to aristocratic twin brothers Karl and Werner von Clemm, Davis befriended them, and his star began to rise in Berlin.

The von Clemms, through a web of wives, mistresses, and blood kin, were related to influential Germans and Americans whom Davis might not have met on his own: Rudolf Diels, head of the Gestapo; top diplomat Joachim von Ribbentrop, Hitler's foreign minister after 1938; and Harry T. S. Green, a vice president of National City Bank of New York (today, Citibank). Werner von Clemm arranged a reception for Davis to meet corporate leaders, including the chairman of IG Farben, the powerful cartel of chemical and pharmaceutical companies that had poured more money than any other donor into Hitler's election campaign and would be among the war's biggest profiteers. Davis made a calculated but terrific first impression: he entered the banquet room giving the Nazi salute. The businessmen eased his introductions to government officials.

But Davis knew his project would never proceed without the approval of the Fuehrer himself. He sent a copy of the plan for the huge refinery operation, to be called Eurotank, directly to Hitler. A few days later, Davis was presenting his plan to a table of skeptical directors at the Reichsbank, feeling their resistance, when Hitler walked through the door. The men shot to their feet.

"Gentlemen, I have reviewed Mr. Davis' proposition and it sounds feasible, and I want the bank to finance it," Hitler said.

The Fuehrer raised his arm in the Nazi salute, turned on his heel, and was gone. Eurotank got its financing without a single dissenting vote.

Davis hired Winkler-Koch Engineering, a construction and design firm from Wichita, Kansas, to repurpose the Hamburg oil storage facility. For Davis, it was a wise choice. Fred Koch, the firm's owner, traveled to Germany often in the 1930s on oil business and knew how to get things done in the Reich. Father of the Koch brothers Charles and David, who would become billionaire forces in radical-right politics in the United States, Fred Koch had turned Davis's facility into one of the largest oil refineries in the world by 1935.

Eurotank refined a thousand tons of crude per day, and was one of the few refineries in Germany that could produce the high-octane gasoline demanded by fighter planes. Eurotank fueled the Luftwaffe. The business owned by Davis and built by Koch became "a key unit of the Nazi rearmament campaign."

Whether Hitler favored Davis because of his impressive Berlin connections or whether he gave the Reich's business to the independent American because he thought he could control him more effectively than he could manage Shell or Standard, Davis became a principal conduit for Germany's oil. Clearly Berlin saw his U.S. citizenship as an advantage in North and South America. Hermann Goering, one of the most powerful members of the Nazi party, said later in reference to Davis that "at the time of the American depression I was desperately looking for someone who would [be] useful to me in America in exploiting the economic situation."

William Davis needed a steady supply of oil to feed Eurotank. From 1934 to 1938 he bought small Mexican concessions, set up his company in Tampico, and developed a sales and political network that threw him into the kind of competition with Big Oil he had always dreamed about. He met with Mussolini and sold fuel to Italy for its war in Ethiopia (1935–40), helping to boost Il Duce to his apex of popularity at home. He met with Hitler six times after the Fuehrer's surprise appearance at the Reichsbank. In Washington, through labor leader John L. Lewis, he met with President Roosevelt to propose a complicated three-way barter deal: the Bank of Boston would buy U.S. surplus cotton and send it to Germany in exchange for railroad equipment, which the bank would then trade to the Mexican government for oil, which the bank would resell to Davis, who would refine it at Eurotank and sell it on the world market.

Roosevelt was enthusiastic about the idea: an important New Deal commodity law was in trouble because U.S. cotton farmers would not voluntarily limit production, and the administration desperately wanted to offload the crop. It was a time—the mid-1930s—when U.S. banks, businesses, and Washington traded with Nazi Germany as they did with any government, dictatorship or not. After his White House meeting, Davis made donations that added up to the single largest contribution to the Democratic Party in the 1936 elections. Roosevelt sent Davis a photo signed "To Major W.R. Davis, from his friend," which Davis prominently displayed on a mantel in his New York office. The president took the oilman's calls.

In the end the cotton deal didn't go through because U.S. ambassador to Mexico Josephus Daniels argued effectively against it, on the grounds that it would not benefit U.S. companies enough. Daniels had been secretary of the navy during World War I when Roosevelt served as assistant secretary, and the president valued the older man's judgment and friendship.

But Roosevelt did not put a stop to Davis's oil business in Mexico, or anyone else's, often heeding counsel from Ambassador Daniels. Once a South Carolina newspaper editor—and at age seventy-five, an even-tempered elder statesman—Daniels advised flexibility and a hands-off attitude toward the oil crisis when it came to respecting the Mexican president. Daniels believed that if Cárdenas fell, Mexican fascists would take over. State Department hard-liners disparagingly called Daniels "more Mexican than the Mexicans," which was an irony given that it was Daniels, in his former role as navy secretary, who had issued the orders to U.S. Navy ships to fire on Veracruz in the wake of the Tampico Incident, carrying out President Wilson's policy of "moral diplomacy."

OILING THE FASCIST WAR MACHINES

Secretary of State Hull, Ambassador Daniels's superior, referred to the Mexicans as "those Communists." He took the side of the oil companies in the dispute with Cárdenas, just as he took the side of American property owners fighting the terms of Cárdenas's land reforms. Americans possessed vast tracts in Mexico, and for some, the deeds came with an astonishing sense of entitlement, mirroring the attitude of some oil firms. Newspaper tycoon William Randolph Hearst owned a twenty-five-hundred-square-mile "ranch" in the northern state of Coahuila, inherited from his father, as well as timber and mining interests; visiting the spread as a young man, Hearst wrote to his mother, "I really don't see what is to prevent us from owning all of Mexico and running it to suit ourselves."

Roosevelt believed that Hull's legalistic hard line in defense of Americans' Mexican property was outmoded in the middle of the twentieth century, and he thought the terms of indemnification that Mexico offered the oil companies were not unreasonable. The companies erred when they insisted their compensation should include the value of oil still in the ground, he told reporters in April 1938, using the example of the "Little White House," his residence in Georgia. "If I have a piece of land at Warm Springs that is worth $5000, and the Government, or the State of Georgia wants to take it over, I ought to get $5000 out of it," he said. "I ought not to be able to say, 'In a few years this is going to be worth $20,000, so you have got to pay me $20,000.'"

Nevertheless, even though Roosevelt did not intervene directly for the companies, he stood by and allowed them to hold their uncompromising stand on claims, enabling their private proprietary concerns in Mexico to override concern for strengthening America's enemies in the coming war. Mexican oil was shut out of the United States, even as it flowed to the Axis.

That was not the way Cárdenas might have wished it. In his radio speech announcing the expropriations, he said that Mexico would not "depart a single inch from the moral solidarity maintained by Mexico with the democratic nations." He sent the head of the Bank of Mexico to sell oil to democratic France and the Spanish republic, but the effort did not succeed.

Meanwhile, almost all independent companies besides that of Davis shied away from Mexican oil out of fear of angering the international corporations. Independents relied on shipping extra loads for the big companies for a significant part of their business, and knew that part of their trade would dry up if they marketed Mexican petroleum. Also, the independents had to count on speedy loading and offloading at ports where

most traffic came from the major companies; they did not have the money
or legal infrastructure to fight Standard and Shell, which threatened con-
fiscation of Mexican oil as "illegal" cargo. At the same time, besides sending oil to mainland Spain, the Rockefellers' Standard Oil Company was
shipping to the Reich through the Canary Islands, using German crews
on some of its tankers.

Five months after he nationalized the production of Mexican oil,
Cárdenas was still looking for a way to sell it to democracies and align
himself with the enemies of fascism. He entrusted the United Mine Workers president John L. Lewis, who was visiting Mexico City for a mass
meeting of the International Congress Against War and Fascism, with a
coded message for Roosevelt. Hitler had just annexed the Sudetenland of
Czechoslovakia; Cárdenas proposed a Pan-American economic boycott
against aggressor nations to deprive them of raw materials for their international arms buildup. He suggested the move even though he knew it
would destroy Mexico's German market, now in place thanks to Davis.
But Roosevelt, Ambassador Daniels later wrote, was under too much pressure from the oil companies to pursue the proposal.

Meanwhile, William Davis was exporting half of Mexico's monthly
production; in 1938 and 1939, Germany and Italy were the biggest customers. A company called La Laguna, owned by a naturalized Mexican citizen
of Japanese descent, Kiso Tsuru, sent smaller quantities to Japan. Isoroku
Yamamoto, who would one day lead the attack on Pearl Harbor as admiral
of the Japanese fleet, was Tokyo's naval attaché in Washington in the late
1920s, and he visited the Mexican oil fields with Tsuru. Yamamoto, who
studied the petroleum industry as a student at Harvard, saw oil's potential
for fueling a modern navy. Eventually Tokyo found that importing oil
from California directly across the Pacific was more cost-effective than
shipping Tsuru's crude from Tampico through the Panama Canal.

When war broke out in Europe in September 1939, Great Britain established a naval blockade of Germany, halting the flow of Mexican oil
across the Atlantic. So Davis rerouted his tankers across the Pacific to the
edge of Russia at Vladivostok, then shipped the oil by train on the Trans-
Siberian Railway. Around the same time, Washington, intent on improving frazzled relations with its southern neighbor, quietly began allowing

a small amount of Mexican oil (handled by Davis) to enter the United States. The big companies stuck to their boycott.

Davis obtained refineries in Texas, from which he sent oil to Spain, nominally neutral but now in Franco's hands; from Spain the Texas-refined oil was clandestinely rerouted to Germany or used to refuel U-boats off Spain and Portugal. But the U.S. company Texaco and Standard held a near monopoly on this shady trade with the "neutrals," so Davis was disappointed to do little business in their ports.

As war in Europe curtailed profits, Davis looked for more ways to sell Mexican oil in the United States. By then Washington was becoming impatient with the blustering position of Standard and Shell, a stand that only benefited the Axis and appeared increasingly unpatriotic as U.S. involvement in the war came closer. Davis entered secret talks in New York with Mexican officials and Harry Sinclair, owner of Sinclair Oil, one of the smaller expropriated companies. Sinclair decided to break with the major companies and came to a separate agreement with Mexico, weakening the Big Oil boycott. By the end of 1940, Davis and other American buyers were purchasing more than 75 percent of total Mexican exports.

By this time, however, damage had been done to the Allies' cause. Germany and Italy procured 94 percent of Mexico's petroleum exports between the crucial months of March 1938 and September 1939. The Axis achieved a powerful head start on the war thanks to Mexican oil.

The oil gave Germany a jump on France and England, especially in the manufacture of fighter aircraft. The Reich had little hard currency to pay for the imported raw materials necessary to turn out tanks, ships, arms, and planes; by using a barter system with Mexico, trading machinery and other manufactured goods for oil, Hitler procured the vital petroleum supplies without spending the funds that went instead to the accelerated arms buildup. Mexican shipments provided the Reich with a six-month supply of oil at the start of the war, enabling Hitler's invasion of Poland in September 1939, which brought a still-unprepared Britain into the conflict. The oil also enabled the invasion of France the next spring. It filled Admiral Karl Doenitz's storage tanks to feed the fleets of marauding U-boats. For years Hitler's victories were fueled by the advantages that Mexican oil gave him early in the war.

•   •   •

On November 19, 1941, the long-protesting oil companies accepted Mexico's offer for their expropriated property. They realized that Mexico was not going to change its mind about oil nationalization and had found ways to market its petroleum without them, through William Rhodes Davis and others. The probability of U.S. entry into the war lent urgency to the resolution. Even Secretary of State Hull, who had hung on to the hard line favoring the companies longer than anyone else in the administration, became eager for a settlement given "world conditions and especially those of our hemisphere." The administration, not wanting to repeat the Mexico experience, pushed for agreements with other oil producers such as Colombia and Venezuela that would preempt unilateral expropriations.

After Pearl Harbor, Roosevelt encouraged Great Britain to renew its relations with Mexico, broken off when Shell lost ground in the nationalization. The times demanded alliances among democracies wherever they might be.

Roosevelt had long tried to convince Americans, especially political conservatives, that his Good Neighbor policy was not a free pass for Latin American extremists to confiscate property and take advantage of foreign businesses. He was required to make that argument less at home following Pearl Harbor, but he still had to impress Latin American countries with the Allies' friendship. Good relations with Mexico would show the others that rancor over economic imperialism was a thing of the past with Washington's nearest Latin neighbor.

On an April evening in 1943, President Roosevelt and Mexico's president Manuel Ávila Camacho sat side by side in high-backed, hand-carved chairs at a banquet table festooned with roses in the northern Mexican city of Monterrey. Ávila had succeeded Cárdenas in 1940 and declared war against the Axis in May 1942 after U-boats sank two Mexican tankers. The meeting with Roosevelt would help his popularity, Ávila hoped, which was flagging with wartime inflation and rumors of a military draft. Panic and demonstrations, especially in the countryside, had broken out with rumors that young Mexicans would be sent to die in foreign lands for someone else's war.

Back in 1909, when the first foreign oil companies were digging into

Mexican soil, U.S. president William Howard Taft and Mexican president Porfirio Díaz had met on the Texas–Mexico border at El Paso in "a veritable pageant of military splendor . . . and patriotic fervor," a Texas paper reported. On that occasion Taft demanded assurances of support for U.S. investments, and Díaz gave them. This time the presidential summit would be more give-and-take—a mark of how the war had shaken the bilateral relationship. Roosevelt and Ávila could dine like comrades knowing the oil dispute had been resolved. But they could not dine without worry.

A look at the newspapers during the week that Ávila and Roosevelt met shows what the Allies were up against: in North Africa, British shock troops fought hand-to-hand with German and Italian soldiers led by Reich field marshal Erwin Rommel, the Desert Fox; the Russians claimed Hitler was preparing to use poison gas, and the British threatened that if he did, London would launch massive gas attacks on Germany. On the day of the Monterrey meeting, Roosevelt announced that Japan had just executed several U.S. airmen captured the previous year in raids over Tokyo. Japan warned it would give future captured pilots a "one way ticket to hell."

Even so far from the battlefields, the atmosphere was full of war. Ávila was constantly reassuring the Mexican public he was sending no troops to fight, yet he saw himself as a wartime president. A stocky former army officer, Ávila had never left behind his fascination with military strategy and tactics. In the capital's presidential residence, Los Pinos, he ordered several war rooms arranged with detailed maps and model battlefields of World War II engagements, where he privately moved around figurines of soldiers.

Seated next to the U.S. president in Monterrey, Ávila might have regarded himself at a pinnacle of shared responsibility for the future of democracy. He pledged allegiance to Roosevelt's recent controversial demand in Casablanca for unconditional surrender of the Axis powers.

Yet the Mexican president kept certain decisions for himself. He declined to allow U.S. troops to be stationed in Mexico, as Washington desired. Neither would he accede to U.S. wishes to transfer Mexican Japanese— whether they were Mexican citizens or not—to concentration camps in the United States alongside Japanese American inmates. Instead, Ávila moved hundreds of families away from their homes near the U.S. border and the coasts into Guadalajara and Mexico City. The oilman Kiso Tsuru, the highly respected Matsumoto family, and other prominent Mexican Japanese helped to look out for the welfare of the displaced for the duration of the war. The families suffered from their forced dislocation inside Mexico, an episode largely unknown among the Mexican public. But almost seventy-five years later some elderly Japanese Mexicans still speak of Manuel Ávila Camacho as a champion who refused to send them to the American camps.

In Monterrey the presidents expressed satisfaction with their pact signed six months earlier, arranging for Mexico to send more than three hundred thousand workers to the United States to aid the wartime agricultural economy. U.S. growers faced a sudden and urgent need for manpower to replace men who went into the service. The Mexicans, often desperate for work, provided cheap labor. During the war, the bracero program was a vital source of assistance to the United States, helping to ensure an uninterrupted food supply for population and troops. Meant to be temporary, the program saw some 4.5 million Mexican workers take part until it ended in 1964.

Oil had brought the relationship between the neighboring countries to a point of crisis, and the exigencies of war spurred its resolution—but only after a delay that benefited the enemy. Roosevelt was determined that such calamity should not happen again. "We have all of us recognized the principle of independence," Roosevelt told his Mexican hosts. "It is time that we recognize also the privilege of interdependence—one upon another."

Roosevelt listened as the Mexican president recast the geographical proximity of the countries in a bright, positive light. Being so close to the United States was not necessarily a bad thing. Instead, the border between Mexico and the United States, unfortified and undefended, was a positive symbol.

"Geography has made of us a natural bridge of conciliation between the Latin and the Saxon cultures of the continent," Ávila said. "If there is any place where the thesis of the good neighborhood may be proved with efficacy, it is right here in the juxtaposition of these lands."

The war did not smooth differences between Washington and Mexico City forever. But no more would gunboats be dispatched to impose

U.S. will on its southern neighbor. Terms of trade would be hashed out over a table, not with a Big Stick.

As Roosevelt and Ávila met in Monterrey, Lázaro Cárdenas, who had chosen the middle-of-the-road Ávila as his party's candidate to succeed him, was serving as minister of defense and navy. William Rhodes Davis, the oilman who had made Cárdenas's hallmark reform—oil nationalization—viable at a critical moment, had left the stage.

The summer before Pearl Harbor found Davis in Houston, as hale and active as ever, tending to company business. At two o'clock in the morning on August 1, 1941, he stumbled down a corridor at the apartment he kept at the Lamar Hotel and knocked on the bedroom door of his longtime executive assistant, Erna Wehrle. Agitated and unnaturally talkative, Davis told her he was "really sick" and terribly thirsty. As Wehrle called Davis's local doctor, Davis went to the kitchen for water, returning back down the corridor once more to the door of her room. He stood there as she hung up the phone. Without a word, he collapsed on the floor, blood running from his mouth.

The official cause of Davis's death was given as "a sudden seizure of the heart." But it may have been murder. At age fifty-two, Davis had recently received a clean bill of health from his regular doctor. The description of his last moments appears to be inconsistent with coronary occlusion—"a sudden seizure of the heart"—and consistent instead with some kinds of poisoning, a biographer suggests, such as atropine (belladonna). Postmortem procedures were cursory; there was no autopsy, and the body was cremated. J. Edgar Hoover's FBI had discouraged further police investigation on a request from the British Security Coordination led by William Stephenson, "Intrepid."

Among BSC files is a record of Davis's business deals with the Nazis, including a project "to ship oil through Mexican charter vessels" to hidden fuel drops for U-boats on Atlantic and Caribbean islands. Davis had reached the end of his trail. The British intelligence file on the putative U-boat fuel-drop project closes tersely: "The swiftest way to put a stop to this scheme was to remove Davis from the scene."

3.

WHITE GOLD, THE STORY OF THE RUBBER SOLDIERS

The year is 1943. Deep in the Amazon jungle, a tapper makes a diagonal cut in the trunk of a rubber tree in the predawn darkness, when its sap flows most freely. During the day the milky latex travels down a ladder of older cuts to the base of the tree where it drips into a tin cup. Clean leaves have been placed on the forest floor to catch any precious bead that jumps from bark or cup.

In the green light of late afternoon, the tapper collects the milk in a bucket and carries it to a field station where it's shaped into oblongs and smoked over a fire of palm nuts until hard. Then, along with other tappers, he carries the rounded blocks on his back to a dock where they are loaded aboard a steamer that heads at top speed down the longest river in the world. The river widens to meet the rough Atlantic.

There in quick succession a German U-boat sinks the steamer, and a U.S. Navy ship dispatches the sub. The U.S. crew rescues survivors and pays fishermen to salvage the blocks. Officers secure the rubber onto another ship to continue its journey to the United States. Crewmen receive citations for their quick thinking, for salvaging a strategic material absolutely fundamental to winning the war.

More than fifty years later, on assignment in the Amazon, I trekked with rubber tappers in the stretch of jungle where they worked, rising in the chill before dawn, following a lantern beam along mushy trails to one *Hevea brasiliensis* tree after another. Diffuse light arrived with the morning, and the songs of presumably resplendent birds sounded deep in the canopy. The tappers, called *seringueiros*, made the same kind of artful cuts in the bark that their predecessors had made during the war. The process seemed timeless. Yet between 1942 and 1945, the fathers of some of these *seringueiros* worked under conditions of extreme urgency to produce rubber for the Allies.

The war ran on rubber, indispensable to manufacturing millions of tires for jeeps and trucks, to making gliders and PT boats. Some battleships required as many as twenty thousand rubber parts. Rubber went into thousands of items that meant life or death in the field. Tanks and airplanes needed gaskets, belts, hoses. Rubber was essential to lifeboats and oxygen masks, cameras, radar equipment, surgical gloves, cable wires.

> *There is probably no other inert substance which so excites the mind.*
>
> —CHARLES GOODYEAR, INVENTOR, 1838

More than a thousand years before Christ, the Mexican Gulf Coast civilization called the Olmecs—their name means "the Rubber People"—developed a sacred ball game that reenacted a contest between heroes and the lords of darkness at the beginning of the world. The Olmecs' daughter cultures, complex pre-Columbian societies such as the Maya and the Aztec, repeated the game for another thousand years in long, stone courts—their remnants can be seen today at sites from Arizona to Nicaragua. At the center of the ritual was the heavy, solid ball of rubber, made from the jungle tree whose milky fluid represented life forces—semen, blood.

Over the centuries, Europeans used latex from the Americas to waterproof shoes and stockings; but the substance they first called *caoutchouc* remained mostly a curiosity. In 1770, the British inventor Edward Nairne discovered that a lump of *caoutchouc* could rub away unwanted pencil marks, and he began to sell "rubber" erasers. Other inventors used rubber to make life preservers, bottles, mailbags, and raincoats. But the products went brittle in the cold and became sticky in the summer heat, when they did not melt down altogether into shapeless lumps.

In 1834, a would-be inventor named Charles Goodyear, just out of debtor's prison, was passing the New York outlet of a rubber products company when a life preserver in the window caught his eye. Believing he could improve its valve, Goodyear bought the preserver and developed his own version of a valve to inflate it. He took the invention back to show the store manager. Forget it, said the manager, the company wasn't in the market for valves, it might go out of business altogether. He showed Goodyear a pile of goods that had melted into a smelly glob. Rubber products just couldn't withstand extreme temperatures.

Goodyear began experimenting systematically and obsessively, often without a steady income, oblivious to his growing reputation as a madman. Eventually he developed a process that used heat to combine rubber with sulfur, hardening the rubber yet maintaining its elasticity. He patented the process in 1844, calling it "vulcanizing" after Vulcan, the Roman god of fire. Vulcanizing made rubber strong in all weather. Charles Goodyear was the object of adulation and accolades, but he did not have the business acumen to earn a living from his discovery. He was also afflicted by bad luck. He tried but failed to establish factories. Others infringed on his patent and he spent years in court fighting usurpers. He never made enough money to keep his family out of debt.

Nevertheless, vulcanized rubber was an invention whose time had come. A few years after Goodyear died, European and American inventors developed the internal combustion engine, and in 1886 two Germans, Karl Friedrich Benz and Gottlieb Daimler, patented the first motorcars. The stage was set for the world to roll into the twentieth century on tires of vulcanized rubber. Soon rubber cured by Goodyear's process would become a key strategic material in war.

God created war so Americans would learn geography.

—ATTRIBUTED TO MARK TWAIN

In the 1930s the U.S. Rubber Manufacturers Association and the financier Bernard Baruch, confidant of presidents, advised Roosevelt to stockpile rubber in the event of war. U.S. generals and admirals had begun to worry about hostile Japanese action in Asia as early as 1931, when Japan invaded Manchuria. Washington bartered surplus cotton for some British supplies, but stocks did not increase sufficiently to satisfy even growing U.S. domestic consumption—some thirty million cars were on the road. In case of war, Washington would not have enough rubber for both military and civilian needs.

Artificial rubber was not an answer for the United States and Britain. In 1940, only 1.2 percent of U.S. rubber was man-made, and the British had had little motivation to concoct the artificial product because their Asian colonies had produced a glut of natural rubber after World War I. Other countries were far more advanced. Russia began developing synthetic rubber using ethyl alcohol and petroleum after the October Revolution in 1917 to reduce dependency on the British and Dutch monopoly on world supplies. By 1940, the Soviet Union had the world's largest synthetic rubber industry. But Germany was catching up fast.

Without rubber-producing colonies abroad, Germany had deep incentives after World War I to develop the synthetic product. Prices for natural rubber fluctuated wildly, an unstable market for which neither government nor industry could plan. Utilities supervisors were reduced to insulating power and phone lines with tarred paper, for lack of rubber. In 1935, scientists at IG Farben began mass-producing the synthetic Buna-N, now known as NBR. By the end of the decade, the Reich was manufacturing seventy thousand tons of synthetic rubber a year, the United States a mere eight thousand.

Three months after Pearl Harbor, catastrophe hit the Allies' natural rubber pipeline. In February 1942, the Japanese occupied British Malaya, then moved on to the Dutch East Indies. At a stroke, the United States lost access to 90 percent of its global supply. The British retained some production in India and still held on to Ceylon, although the Japanese were advancing on the island. The total amount of rubber remaining to countries fighting the Axis—from South America, Mexico, and Africa—amounted to the equivalent of no more than two weeks of U.S. prewar consumption.

Where to get more?

The United States Department of Agriculture researchers found favorable areas of Latin America to grow *Hevea brasiliensis*, the most productive tree. Department operatives brought in seeds, established nurseries, worked with private landowners and on government properties in Costa Rica, Panama, and Guatemala. They distributed booklets with photos that showed step by step how to start a rubber plantation, the depth to which seeds should be planted, the distance between plants, at what height to graft and transplant. In Guatemala, where the biggest plantation in the region is still known as "Uncle Sam," the campaign gave life to a national rubber industry.

But *Hevea brasiliensis*, commonly called the Pará rubber tree, or just "rubber tree," takes five to seven years to grow. A shortage in the interim was certain to threaten Allied military success.

In September 1942, Bernard Baruch, as head of Roosevelt's Rubber Survey Committee, issued a report advocating the "urgent" acceleration of efforts to produce synthetic rubber, establishing more than fifty programs in various parts of the country. But that option would take time, too. Besides, synthetic rubber alone would never solve the crisis: the most promising processes required petroleum, itself a precious wartime commodity, and key items like tires required at least some wild rubber.

Baruch's committee recommended immediate measures to save tires (no new tires at all were manufactured during most of 1942): recapping, reducing the speed limit to thirty-five miles per hour, limiting annual use to five thousand miles per vehicle. "Carpooling" was encouraged, enabling passengers to comply with rationing, save money, and feel patriotic all at the same time. "When You Ride Alone You Ride With Hitler!" advised a government poster. In Britain the national Tyre Control authority instituted strong conservation measures and an efficient distribution system. A continued shortage in the United States, however, would have decisive effects on waging the war, according to Baruch's report. Left unresolved, the U.S. rubber crisis could lead to Allied defeat.

As factories converted to military production, the government asked citizens to turn in whatever they could spare for recycling: used tires, garden hoses, old raincoats. An illustrated poster indicated how much rubber was required for a gas mask (1.11 pounds), a life raft (17 to 100 pounds), a "scout car" (306 pounds), and a heavy bomber (1,825 pounds). Despite restrictions, scrap drives, and efforts to raise awareness about thrift, however, planners foresaw a fearsome shortfall represented in hard numbers: by 1944 the army alone would need 842,000 tons of rubber, but only about 631,000 would be available.

When Japan cut off Asian supplies, Washington determined that the most likely place within U.S. reach to find an immediate and stable rubber supply was the Amazon. Of eight South American countries that shared the basin of the great river and its high tributaries, only Brazil could provide wild rubber in required amounts—60 percent of the Amazon region lay within its borders.

But convincing Brazil that its jungles should be mined for the Allied cause would not be easy. In 1934, Germany had become Brazil's biggest trading partner, largely because of its purchase of coffee and cacao, and by the end of the decade German and Japanese demands for rubber were beginning to revive the dormant Brazilian industry. Rio was reluctant to harm its excellent market relations with the Reich. When the war began in 1939, Rio declared its neutrality; but squeezed by Washington, it stopped selling rubber to the Axis in 1940. Nevertheless, President Getúlio Vargas presided over a fascist-like state, and he was determined to take an independent political stand before the United States, the colossus of the north.

Short, portly, and vain, but affable and charismatic too, Vargas had run Brazil since 1930 with a combination of populism and an iron hand. He was an autocrat on the model of his contemporaries António Salazar of Portugal or Mussolini in Italy. In 1937, Vargas dissolved state legislatures and put a padlock on Parliament, shutting out lawmakers and ruling by decree. The Brazilian president was acutely aware of Washington's tradition of gunboat diplomacy, obstructing or overturning governments it didn't like, sometimes sending in the military to support U.S. business. Notwithstanding "Good Neighbor" promises, Vargas would not look good to other Latin leaders or segments of his own population if he seemed to bend to U.S. desires, especially for such a valuable commodity as rubber.

In Washington, however, military commanders had long been considering an invasion of northeast Brazil to establish a base for ships and planes in time of war, whether Vargas agreed or not. As early as 1938, the U.S. Department of War charged a joint commission with determining from what points an attack on the United States might come. The answers: South America, and the Panama Canal. U.S. planners established the southern limit of the nation's defense perimeter not on the U.S. border but on the hump of Brazil, the country with half of South America's territory and half its population. By 1939, protecting the bulge of Brazil against Axis aggression became the keystone of American military plans for defending the Atlantic front.

The hump of northeastern Brazil bulges like a gigantic fist into the Atlantic. Its outermost edge lies only eighteen hundred miles from West Africa, less than the distance between Los Angeles and Chicago. In 1939, concerned about Japanese belligerence in China and desiring an additional route to Asia besides the Pacific, the U.S. joint military command proposed establishing U.S. bases in northeast Brazil. The fist was an ideal staging ground for forces heading to French West Africa and the Far East beyond.

The U.S. timeline for enacting its plan became more pressing in June 1940 when Paris fell to the Nazis and French colonies in West Africa came under control of the collaborationist Vichy government. The Reich had established a virtual beachhead only a few hours' flight time from Brazil's northeast region, which was poor, ignored by politicians, and virtually unprotected. A May 1941 U.S. Army report read, "*Assumption*: That immediate and vigorous preparations are being made to extend Axis political, economic and military power to South America."

Most of Vargas's army was deployed to the extreme south of the country where it could keep an eye on Argentina, its southern neighbor; Rio suspected Argentine designs on Brazilian territory. The military also wanted to keep an eye on the million Germans in southern Brazil, whose loyalty it questioned. The northeast was an afterthought.

But not to the U.S. high command. Roosevelt ordered a contingency plan for speeding one hundred thousand U.S. troops to line the Brazilian coast from Belém to Rio de Janeiro. The Brazilians objected. Their own soldiers could defend the nation should the need arise. Nevertheless, immediately after Pearl Harbor, the U.S. military produced the "Joint Basic Plan for the Occupation of Northern Brazil [Joint], Serial 737 of 21 December 1941," calling for an amphibious landing to take key cities and ports. At the same time, the plan would secure the gateway region to the Amazon.

An armed confrontation appeared imminent. The secret operation's nickname: Plan Rubber.

Undersecretary of State Sumner Welles, the tireless and golden-tongued diplomat, convinced President Vargas to allow 150 U.S. Marines disguised as airplane mechanics onto facilities at Belém, Natal, and Recife. The Marines had orders to guarantee the safety and security of the airfields and transiting U.S. aircraft but to keep in mind that they were present by invitation. Vargas was still insisting on a neutral Brazil.

Yet even this apparently small concession to the Americans sparked fears of a counterblast against Vargas from Nazi sympathizers. If he fell, the Allies' situation would be even worse. In Washington, commanders pushed to execute Plan Rubber and invade Brazil's northeast. But Roosevelt resisted in favor of delicate diplomacy.

Meanwhile, the wily Vargas made his assessments and finally bet that the Allies would win the war. Brazil dropped its "neutrality" in January 1942, a move just short of declaring war. Fascist-leaning but pragmatic, and not an ideologue, Vargas envisioned an important postwar role in the world for Brazil if he cooperated with the Allies. He signed a landmark agreement called the Washington Accords, which took effect in May 1942. The armed invasion was off, but another kind of invasion was on.

The accords, officially named the Brazil–United States Political-Military Agreement, opened the door for one of the navy's biggest base-building projects in history. The Brazilian coast became dotted with air (in cooperation with Pan American Airlines) and ship bases vital to the antisubmarine campaign in the South Atlantic. Until the Allied landings in North Africa in late 1942, the agreement's air routes provided insurance against a German invasion of the New World. In 1943, the bases were vital to provisioning the Allied invasion of Sicily, which decisively took the fight against the Axis powers to Europe.

And although the cost was high, the agreement secured the strategic raw materials of the largest country in Latin America for the Allied cause.

A 1943 U.S. propaganda documentary made by the Office of War Information showed handsome, fit, young Brazilian men doing military training exercises, and crowds cheering President Vargas. The images flashed across the screen in a grand style that looked borrowed from Leni Riefenstahl's Nazi classic *Triumph of the Will*. Brazil's raw materials, the film told Americans, made the country "doubly valuable as an ally."

"These war factories in the United States use large quantities of Brazilian manganese, highest grade iron ore, zinc, nickel, and other minerals essential to the manufacture of tanks, machine guns, warships," said the narrator over shots of busy workers. "Bauxite from which the aluminum in our combat planes is made . . . the world's only source of high-grade crystal in substantial quantities so essential in the manufacture of electrical, optical, and precision instruments . . . one of the world's largest producers of industrial diamonds used in cutting the hard metals" for machine tools. "She can produce enough of the basic materials for making explosives to supply the entire world."

The alliance relieved anxiety over the U.S. rubber crisis, relief felt beyond U.S. borders. "Brazil's production of rubber alone may be a decisive factor in winning this war," said the film.

The massive rubber campaign envisioned in the Washington Accords also conveniently gave Vargas solutions to problems at home unrelated to the war, helping him to stay in power. The national rubber industry—second only to coffee in exports—had been flagging despite sales, but now was certain to take off again. And Vargas could kill two other birds with a single stone: by sending restive residents of the drought-ravaged northeast to collect rubber in the jungle, he could defuse that political time bomb while reinforcing claims to the Brazilian frontier, which neighboring countries disputed. For the Brazilian dictator, the campaign was a gift on a silver platter. He grandly named it *Batalha da Borracha*, the Battle for Rubber.

The ambitious Brazilian wartime campaign had two extraordinary predecessors: a great boom at the turn of the century and an expensive, megalomaniacal project by Henry Ford beginning in the 1920s that saw the creation of a Midwestern-looking town in the rainforest to produce rubber assembly-line style. Each remarkable preview foreshadowed the wartime "Battle," and each held lessons that planners ignored at their peril.

> *Roger warned [Negretti], pointing at the whip: If I see you use that on the Indians I'll personally turn you over . . .*
>
> *And Roger never saw him flog the porters; he only yelled at them so they would move faster or harassed them with curses and other insults when they dropped the "sausages" of rubber they carried on their shoulders and heads because their strength failed or they tripped . . .*
>
> *On the second day, an old woman suddenly fell down dead when she tried to climb a slope with seventy pounds of rubber on her back. Negretti, after confirming she was lifeless, quickly distributed the dead woman's two sausages among the other natives with a grimace of annoyance and a hoarse voice.*

> —MARIO VARGAS LLOSA, *THE DREAM OF THE CELT*

The Amazonian rubber fever of the late nineteenth century generated unprecedented prosperity. The rough Peruvian town of Iquitos, a deep-water port at the head of the Amazon system, grew into the world's largest city inaccessible by road. Four thousand miles east, where the river meets the Atlantic, the old sugar port of Belém turned into a thriving metropolis with wide boulevards and stately mansions. Between Iquitos and Belém, in the deepest heart of the rainforest, a river outpost called Manaus, a jungle wall at its back, grew to become one of the richest cities of its size in the world.

Even today, a visitor stepping out of the steamy heat into the city's Belle Époque opera house marvels at the display of wealth and elegance: cool stairs and columns of Carrara marble, plush seats imported from

Paris, Italian panels depicting scenes of drama and dance, a stage curtain painted to evoke the marriage of the nearby rivers Negro and Solimões as they join to form the Amazon. Fine glass chandeliers, seemingly innumerable, sparkle now, as they did in the 1890s to the astonishment of locals, with electric light.

Inland from Iquitos and Manaus, the rubber tappers who produced all this wealth led such miserable lives they had a nickname, the *flagelados* (whipped ones). Their bosses, affluent rubber barons, commanded a network of brutish overseers like "Negretti"—the real name of one of them—in the Vargas Llosa novel. The Peruvian Nobel Prize laureate based his depiction of the era of the *flagelados* on reports by the Irish-born British diplomat Roger Casement, who saw Negretti and his ilk in action.

In 1906, Casement's superiors sent him to investigate allegations of mistreatment in the homeland of the Putumayo Indians, a region variously claimed by Colombia, Ecuador, Brazil, and Peru where the woman in the novel fell under her burden of rubber "sausages." Casement's 165-page report said that henchmen went into the jungle to capture Indians for the rubber companies, some partly British owned. Not only were the tappers unpaid, but they became indebted for the tools and food they required, their wives and children subject to kidnapping and rape until the tapper returned with his assigned quota of rubber. The hostages, along with tappers blamed for infractions, were jailed in filthy stockades. They were "fathers, mothers, and children," Casement wrote, "and many cases were reported of parents dying thus, either from starvation or from wounds caused by flogging, while their offspring were attached alongside of them to watch in misery themselves the dying agonies of their parents."

Photos from the time show children with the marks of lashes on their backs and buttocks, emaciated men sitting on a bench in a cage, facing the camera, joined together by chains around their necks. The Indian population in the Peruvian region where Casement traveled plunged in the last years of the boom from fifty thousand in 1906 to eight thousand in 1911.

In the Brazilian Amazon, the process of getting rubber from tree to oceangoing ship involved a web of relationships called the *aviamento*

system, from the Portuguese word for "providing," that included patronage and debt peonage. Import-export houses in Belém and Manaus, the
major *aviadores* (those who facilitated the system), provided tools and
food on credit to river traders. The river traders in turn raised the prices
of the goods and delivered them on credit against future rubber deliveries to middlemen who controlled production for the owners of sprawling
estates.

At trading posts, the price of goods was inflated yet again and sold
to the *seringueiros* on credit. When tappers brought in the rubber they
collected, the middlemen and traders cheated them on its weight, and at
times charged a commission for handling it. The tappers rarely saw cash
and sank into perpetual debt. The rubber went to manufacturers in the
United States, Great Britain, Germany, and other industrialized countries.

When the British Foreign Office released Roger Casement's report,
public reaction was swift to condemn abuses and call for reform. It was
not respect for human rights that ended the boom, however, but economic
competition.

In 1876, an adventurer and naturalist named Henry Wickham surreptitiously sent *Hevea brasiliensis* seeds out of Brazil to the Royal Botani-
cal Gardens at Kew. The British, along with planters in their Southeast
Asia colonies, developed the seeds and young trees and established plantations. By 1912, the British controlled most of the world's rubber supply
from trim estates in Ceylon and Malaya, where they produced latex more
cheaply than the Amazon barons could do. The Dutch planted rubber in
their East Indies. In the Amazon, rubber fever cooled, and the wild trees
were left to sleep.

> *Fordlandia, an up-to-date town with all modern comforts, has
> been created in a wilderness that never had seen anything more
> pretentious than a thatched hut. Water is supplied under pressure
> after it has been thoroughly filtered to remove dangers of fever in-
> fection, and electric light illuminated bungalows in a region where
> such inventions are proof of the white man's magic.*

—"MODERN CITY RISES IN JUNGLE," *Chicago Tribune*, 1932

Henry Ford, one of the wealthiest men of all time, was sick and tired of the British world monopoly on rubber. In 1922, worried that a new production cap by colonial producers would lead to increasing prices, Ford looked to the Amazon. Having transformed global industry with the assembly-line method, Ford decided he must control the entire supply chain for making his cars, including the raw material for tires. Ford was also bent upon a civilizing mission, intending to export his ideas of clean living—he was a teetotaler and strict vegetarian—while creating his center of efficient American-style production in the jungle.

Ford obtained a concession for some four thousand square miles of jungle on the Tapajós River, one of more than a thousand tributaries that feed the Amazon. He trimmed the rainforest down to bare earth and sowed plantations with millions of trees. He laid out a miniature version of the kind of ordinary town that might have existed in the American Midwest in the years before the First World War. Managers from Detroit oversaw a diverse workforce: American technicians; laborers from Barbados; latex gatherers lured from jungle corners by better working conditions than the fraying *aviador* networks could provide; and three thousand laborers from the arid Brazilian northeast. As Fordlandia and its sister plantation towns grew over the years, new tappers arrived by boat at spanking wooden docks to a phantasmagorical sight, a slice of America transported whole to the Brazilian rainforest: neat bungalows, a hospital, a canteen, a powerhouse to keep the lights on and the sawmill running, a swimming pool.

Ford employees earned a living wage, in cash. Their wives didn't fish in the river and grind manioc as many once had done, but shopped in a market like women in cities. Discounted goods in company stores created consumers. Ford was transforming the Amazon. On the fringes of his holdings, shantytowns sprouted where workers went to brothels and bars forbidden in the Ford towns, and where they could eat familiar food, not the peaches, oatmeal, and soy-based meals Ford insisted upon serving in company dining halls. But the Michigan inventor seemed to have created a miracle in the jungle, replicating a successful American industrial operation complete with time clocks.

In 1940, Henry's son Edsel invited Getúlio Vargas to visit Fordlandia.

The first Brazilian president to travel to the Amazon, Vargas landed in a hydroplane downstream from Fordlandia at Belterra, which had become the showplace of Ford plantations, and he was formidably impressed. Vargas was a modernizer like Ford: he doubled Brazil's road network, multiplied its airports from a couple dozen to more than five hundred, and, with U.S. help, would launch the steel industry that spurred Brazil's postwar industrial boom. Vargas felt a kinship with the American industrialist. He saw before him what might be possible in the Amazon—modern-style development. At an elegant meal, dressed in a white tropical suit, Vargas stood under an arch of palm fronds before his entourage and addressed the American managers. Henry Ford, he said, had planted not only rubber but also "health, comfort and happiness."

Life at the Ford estates was not always as rosy as Vargas described. A decade earlier, workers had revolted against Ford's suffocating lifestyle impositions, his "civilizing" mission. They bristled at the enforcement of U.S. Prohibition laws in the middle of the Amazon and they resented seeing spinach—the classic American health food—on their plates and attending mandatory social functions such as dance lessons. They were frustrated by the strict eight-to-five schedule, with no concession to ferocious tropical downpours or the traditional break to avoid the worst of midday heat.

On December 20, 1930, simmering anger came to a head. Workers burned cars and pushed service vehicles into the river, torched buildings, and destroyed equipment. They smashed the time clocks. Reforms were made, and labor moved largely to the Belterra plantation. By the time of President Vargas's visit, rebellion was a thing of the past.

At home, Henry Ford crushed workers' attempts to unionize, and at a Michigan plant in 1932, he set goons loose on a protest march of more than three thousand laborers; five marchers died, nineteen were badly injured. An anti-Semite and a leader with his good friend Charles Lindbergh of the isolationist "America First" movement, Ford aired his views in a series of booklets titled *The International Jew, The World's Foremost Problem*. His newspaper, the *Dearborn Independent*, ran front-page stories exposing supposed Jewish plots and scandals, accusing the Jews of controlling the world's press. Ford denounced German Jewish financiers and accepted a medal with swastikas from the Reich.

What Vargas saw and admired in 1930, however, was only Ford's deliberately crafted society in the Amazon jungle. Before returning to Rio, he went on the radio in Manaus to praise Fordlandia as a pole of industrial development for the region, but he also extolled its social programs—high praise from a politician who advertised himself as "the Father of the Poor." He mirrored Ford's optimism about modern technology and faith in development projects on a large scale, even in the rainforest. The speech marked a milestone. Thereafter, Brazil saw its Amazon in a different way: no longer as a perennially sleepy frontier but as a region ripe for economic expansion.

Meanwhile, Fordlandia was offered to the wider world as an example of American can-do. When Walt Disney arrived in Rio in 1941 as one of Nelson Rockefeller's Goodwill Ambassadors, Rockefeller sent him to the jungle. "Among the present-day pioneers of the Amazon who are lighting the way for others to follow is Henry Ford," intones an authoritative voice speaking over a bright green map in Disney's 1944 documentary *The Amazon Awakens*. Roads, power plants, state-of-the-art machinery, schools, telephones—the film showed them all. Manicured golf links against a stunning rainforest backdrop. There was nothing, it seemed, that Ford's jungle world lacked.

Except dependable rubber production.

Growing the wild *Hevea brasiliensis* trees together plantation-style in the Amazon, a jungle version of Ford's assembly-line production method, does not work. Even as the Fordlandia model was being touted, its trees died by the hundreds of thousands. Leaf blight spread across their uppermost branches, jumping from the top of one tree to the next, devastating the canopy.

"The pests and the fungi and the blight that feed off of rubber are native to the Amazon," historian Greg Grandin has explained. "Basically, when you put trees close together in the Amazon, what you in effect do is create an incubator—but Ford insisted."

Could Henry Ford have combatted the destruction of his trees and made the plantation idea succeed, thus providing the rubber that would be needed for the war? With more workers, one argument goes, he might have carried on the intensive work necessary to fight the blight. But the old rubber patronage system still operated in places, and tappers were discouraged from taking Ford's jobs. And the word was out about unpleasant regimentation on Ford estates. Grandin, the historian, argues that Ford's cultural arrogance in trying to impose U.S. social and behavioral norms helped defeat efforts to recruit and keep laborers.

It may be that no number of workers under any conditions could have overcome the leaf blight. When *Hevea brasiliensis* trees grow relatively far apart amid a variety of other trees and vines in the wild, they resist pests. But the linear way Ford insisted on planting the trees together on cleared land allowed fungi, caterpillars, and other organisms to proliferate. (Outside the Amazon, the pests don't thrive enough to destroy rubber trees, even on plantations.) On his assembly lines, Ford tried to turn men into machines. In the Amazon, he tried to industrialize rubber production, but the trees weren't having it. Nature had the last word.

Even as Ford's vision was failing, U.S. war planners were identifying the Brazilian Amazon as the place to find rubber. One way or another, they must create another boom. Of course, a repetition of the abuses of workers that Roger Casement described would be intolerable. But Henry Ford's model would not work either.

An army of collectors would have to go into the wild to tap the trees where they grew naturally amid the diversity, and dangers, of the rainforest. And they must do it under the aegis of Getúlio Vargas.

The army of the Rubber Soldiers is a brave legion of our countrymen entering the jungle under a glorious banner of staunch patriotism to extract from the miraculous tree the precious latex that is so necessary for the Victory of the United Nations.

—BRAZILIAN NEWSPAPER, 1943

The rubber campaign rolled out in the largest rainforest on earth, which spreads over two million square miles, covering more than 40 percent of the South American continent. The Amazon's jungles and rivers are home to forty thousand species of plants and hundreds of mammals, including jaguars and giant anteaters; thousands more species of fish; birds, from scarlet macaws to gracile white herons; reptiles like the anaconda; creatures like the penis snake, which is not a snake but an amphibian; and frogs that live not on ponds but in trees. It is the richest system of life on the planet.

What the Amazon did not have was people. Even counting its port cities, the Brazilian Amazon's population density in 1942 was just over one person per square mile. The adjoining drought-plagued northeast served as a labor pool.

In Manaus, the U.S. Rubber Development Corporation (RDC), which answered to the U.S. Office of Economic Warfare, established headquarters in the opera house, the Teatro Amazonas, still elegant and spacious despite dust that had gathered in the decades since the rubber bust in 1912. Working in these unusual surroundings, RDC staff oversaw financing for Brazil's recruitment and transportation of migrant labor—Rio received a commission of US$100 per person, about US$1,700 in today's value. Program officers managed loans to the owners of estates where collectors harvested the raw material. Agronomists and other advisors calculated needs and progress. Personnel fanned out into the deepest corners of the jungle, developing transportation infrastructure networks.

Before the accords that gave Washington access to Brazil's raw materials, Nelson Rockefeller had attempted to get control of its rubber with a U.S.-dominated development corporation, aiming to open the region to investment by U.S. businesses. Vargas's economic advisor furiously complained that Rockefeller's idea was "American imperialism." Oil had just been discovered in the northeast Brazilian state of Bahia, and if the Standard Oil Company heir had his way, U.S. petroleum companies might begin to operate there, too.

Roosevelt stepped in to stop the Rockefeller effort, because he had a single goal in the Amazon: to get rubber. Instead of Rockefeller's plan,

Washington financed an independent Brazilian government economic development corporation directed overall by Brazilians. The RDC placed Rockefeller's Office of the Coordinator for Inter-American Affairs (CIAA) in charge of key branches of the campaign: sanitation and health, including malaria and yellow fever control, and transporting food.

Establishing RDC headquarters in the Teatro Amazonas, the monument to rubber baron excess during the first boom, was a matter of efficiency—plenty of space, near a major port—but symbolic, too. No longer would the Amazon's white gold, as it was called, its precious rubber, be managed by a traditional Amazonian elite of property owners. A central office of technocrats was now in charge.

Brazilian authorities, however, waged the Battle for Rubber like a military campaign. To draft laborers, Vargas created a Special Service for the Mobilization of Workers for the Amazon, known as "Semta" for its initials in Portuguese. Semta operatives sometimes dragooned unsuspecting young men at the point of a gun.

"I was in the field with my dad, and a soldier came and told me to get on the truck to go to war," eighty-three-year-old Lupércio Freire Maia told a Brazilian filmmaker in 2004. "I just wanted to ask my mother's blessing, but the soldier said he didn't have anything to do with that kind of business."

The roads, Maia said, were filled with men going to holding camps, miserable waystations short of clean water and basic sanitary facilities. Despite Vargas's insistence that Brazil was a "racial democracy," camp medics under the sway of the eugenics movement recorded the physical characteristics, biological types, and "racial" mixture of each conscript.

Most recruits volunteered, a free choice to the extent that desperately poor men leading hardscrabble lives might be considered free to choose. Vargas broke new ground in communication, reaching out to the masses directly with the modern tools of radio and films, presenting mobilization for the raw material as a patriotic campaign. Now tappers were no longer *flagelados*, the most miserable cogs in the rubber-making machine, but guardians of freedom and champions of national defense. Popular mass-market magazines like comic books portrayed migration to the jungle as a path to manhood and to more social status than might be found scratching the northeast's ungiving earth.

The Swiss artist Jean-Pierre Chabloz designed visual propaganda, and Semta circulated it far and wide. A typical Chabloz poster showed a map of Brazil in sepia with line drawings in black; soldiers along the coast, rifles ready, rubber tappers working at a clutch of trees representing the Amazon. "Each One to His Station!" the legend cried. In small letters in a corner were the words "For Victory," and a hand with fingers held up in a familiar wartime "V."

Vargas granted draft-age tappers deferment of military service for the two-year period of their contracts. As word spread that thousands of Brazilian soldiers would be shipping out to fight in Europe, many young men in the northeast decided it was better to sign up for the Amazon jungle, unknown as it was, than to be shot at on the Italian front. Sometimes families pushed the decision. "I enlisted as a Rubber Soldier because my mother cried a lot and didn't want me to join the Army," one rubber veteran recalled.

Meanwhile, Semta booklets and collaborating press cast Rubber Soldier enlistment as if it were a moral choice of the highest order. Northeasterners had an "obligation" to fight for world freedom "in the blessed lands of the Amazon." A Fortaleza newspaper exhorted, "It is time to guarantee for humanity the resources for the conquest of Freedom and the strangling of the Axis!"

Entire families enlisted because they thought it would help them survive. In the northeast, many lived on the verge of starvation, and Semta offered money to relocate. Semta propaganda and Chabloz's ubiquitous renderings presented the jungle as a lush and friendly place. "New Life in the Amazon" read one comely poster. In evocative color and soft light, a tapper cut the bark of a mighty tree near a homestead with a trim house made of logs. A woman hung fresh wash on a line as small domestic animals—pigs, chickens—ran about. "Amazon, the Land of the Future," another ad declared.

"My father was not interested in money," a seventy-four-year-old café owner named Vicência Bezerra da Costa told the Brazilian filmmaker Wolney Oliveira. "He wanted a place where there was water. Where planting might grow." Bezerra da Costa was thirteen when his father signed the family up, moving to the jungle with his wife and eight children. Vargas was populating the Amazon.

At staging camps outside Belém, Recife, and Manaus, recruits waited for transport for days or weeks, sometimes singing songs glorifying "Getúlio." Men and boys received uniform and kit: blue pants, white shirt, straw hat; a pair of canvas shoes with jute soles; a tin plate, mug, and eating utensils; a hammock; and a carton of cigarettes.

The journey by ship was tedious, with passengers generally confined belowdecks. The passage could also be dangerous. One day, Bezerra da Costa said, the crew ordered passengers to come topside with their life-jackets. In the pockets were water and hard biscuits for survival, as well as a cyanide capsule in case of a submarine attack and capture by the enemy. Minesweepers accompanied the ship. Bezerra da Costa's mother lifted the religious medals hanging from her neck and gripped them in her hands. "She didn't stop praying," he said. "We couldn't make a sound, or light a match."

The journey was no more comfortable when recruits transferred to local river transport. They traveled in steerage with livestock. Because of disorganization, they often went without food.

Vargas "enlisted" the Rubber Soldiers military-style, but at U.S. insistence the men carried labor contracts complete with identification photos. Once the workers were on remote estates, however, the old *aviamento* system, which had never been truly dismantled, took over, and few were treated as soldiers or contract laborers.

On the positive side, Brazilian government participation meant that estate lords no longer tortured tappers at will or chased them down with an armed posse when they escaped. Landowners who abused the tappers risked losing loans from the Brazilian Rubber Credit Bank, the RDC's counterpart in the campaign. But the tappers' lives remained harsh, and, as in Casement's day, letters from activist Catholic missionaries to authorities on behalf of collectors described dire conditions.

They lived in isolated jungle huts. Long hours left little time to grow their own food, and they suffered malnutrition. Trading-post operators overcharged for food and supplies bought on credit. The long-standing relationships that had governed rubber collecting since the nineteenth century were too deeply ingrained to be replaced overnight by government agencies or paper contracts. Tappers were supposed to receive 60 percent of the value of the raw material they delivered, but middlemen shortchanged them, and they went into debt. RDC staff members who reached remote estates reported anomalies, but neither Brazilians nor Americans had resources enough to police every corner of the region.

As if the difficult working conditions were not enough, arrivals from the northeast had no natural resistance to endemic diseases, unlike natives of the Amazon. Rockefeller's CIAA health and sanitation program became the basis for a Brazilian healthcare network, which included floating clinics on principal waterways and a nurses' training program. In the same way that Henry Ford provided free healthcare in his Amazon installations, conscious that ill workers meant impaired production, so too the RDC considered health and sanitation fundamental to its aim of producing large quantities of rubber in the shortest possible time.

But conditions overwhelmed intentions. Rockefeller's health unit distributed millions of free Atabrine tablets to treat malaria, but the pills didn't always reach their intended population. Corrupt locals skimmed deliveries to sell on the black market, often in cities. Middlemen charged for the tablets, and tappers usually did not have money. The innovative floating clinics were often too far away for *seringueiros* to reach without losing valuable work time. When a tapper's skin went the color of saffron from hepatitis, he often just drank lavender tea and hoped for the best.

"One day a branch blown by the wind hit me and I lost sight in this eye," seventy-nine-year-old Alfonso Pereira Pinto told Oliveira in 2004. "Later, I caught a sickness and lost my leg. When the war was over, I did not have the money to go home." Pinto stayed in Xapuri, in the western Amazon.

U.S. doctors and scientists brought in by Rockefeller undoubtedly saved lives. Learning from this experience with tropical diseases, they subsequently applied it to situations in Africa and the South Pacific where U.S. troops were stationed—GIs too had little immunity to endemic illnesses.

Despite Rockefeller's food program, however, which aimed to serve the entire northeast, tappers died from poor nutrition. Without roads from the food-producing south to the north, ships guarded by antisubmarine escorts carried provisions by sea to the mouth of the Amazon River; but outside the main network of tributaries, Brazilian government distribution was inadequate. In the fierce climate, food rotted in warehouses or arrived at destinations unfit to eat. Price regulations were ignored in the outlands, where transportation and resale depended on the old, firmly embedded *aviador* network.

Migrant tappers were most likely to survive if they brought families with them or formed unions with Indian women. While the head of the family collected latex, women and children cultivated food plots or gathered forest products for sale, such as brazil nuts in their heavy pods. Indigenous women in particular understood healing methods with medicinal plants, and traditional rainforest practices for avoiding dangerous animals.

In 1943, the United States received more rubber from Latin America, overwhelmingly from the Amazon, than from any other region on earth. In the other years from 1942 to 1945, the Brazil enterprise produced less latex than hoped for, about the same as African sources. Nevertheless, the Amazon's contribution helped keep the rubber crisis at bay until 1944, when synthetic rubber was produced in quantity.

Where the Battle for Rubber met defeat was partly because of the difficult terrain where it was fought. Estates were scattered amid a network of tributaries and waterways as complex as the system of veins and arteries of the human body. Geography itself made any orderly program difficult, let alone a campaign that unfolded on a frontier where state authorities were traditionally absent.

But human failings, too, contributed to disappointment. "Neither the Brazilian government nor the RDC was willing or able to expend the funds and human resources necessary to monitor and enforce their price controls at the rubber estates," wrote the Brazilian scholar Xenia Wilkinson.

Contemporary criticism came from a U.S. diplomat, Walter Walmsley, who toured the Amazon in 1943 and condemned wasteful spending, even graft, on the U.S. side of the program, lamenting the lack of understanding of tappers' conditions. "No darker picture exists anywhere of what in more progressive countries we choose to call corruption and exploitation," he wrote.

Through it all, Brazil prospered from the World War II rubber campaign far more than it had from the boom at the turn of the century, when rubber barons and import-export houses dealt more directly with New York and Liverpool than they did with Rio and São Paulo. The Washington Accords that governed wartime extraction earned income for the central government. And during the war, Vargas cemented his effort to make the Amazon part of the wider nation. Well into the twentieth century, elites had run vast swathes of territory as private fiefdoms; the Battle for Rubber brought the frontier under Rio's government control.

Of fifty-seven thousand Rubber Soldiers who labored between 1942 and 1945, thirty thousand died, whether from illnesses like malaria, yellow fever, and Chagas disease or from the bites and stings of serpents and scorpions; some drowned in rivers or were eaten by piranhas; others were mauled by jaguars. Of those who survived, some could not leave the Amazon because they remained indebted. Some did not know the war was over until a year or two after the armistices. Vargas, successful in starting the process of populating the Amazon, reneged on the pledge to return Rubber Soldiers to their homes. Many never received their promised pensions.

Military rulers who took over the Brazilian government in the 1960s had seen how the Americans built roads and established supply lines during the war. They continued Vargas's vision of the Amazon as a massive target for development, building more roads and dams. They moved the national capital closer to the rainforest, from Río to Brasília, and laid down a highway from the south, the Transamazonia, encouraging the influx of farmers, loggers, miners, ranchers.

In 1972, the NASA Landsat camera began sending pictures of the earth from outer space, giving an unprecedented view of how the Amazon region was shrinking. Stretches of green one week went brown the next.

The Brazilian rainforest was disappearing at the rate of an area the size of England, Scotland, and Wales, combined, every year. The Amazon basin alone provides a fifth of the world's fresh water, and it accounts for 40 percent of the earth's remaining rainforest; saving it became a global issue.

In the Amazon, the challenge was joined by old Rubber Soldiers themselves, as well as by younger tappers who invoked the spirit of Rubber Soldiers past.

In October 1985, 120 veteran Rubber Soldiers who still worked in the jungle joined their tapper sons and others in Brasília to demand pensions owed to veterans of the *Batalha da Borracha*. But they wanted more than just recompense. Their labor union in three Amazonian states of Brazil was organizing cooperatives to eliminate middlemen; they wanted support from other Brazilians, and security guaranteed by the state in their struggle. The demonstration was aimed to bring their issues into the public light. They sang patriotic songs from the war days: *"Long live the Brazilian soldier! Your product will be useful all over the world."*

By the late 1970s it was clear that extracting latex in the wild using the conservative ways of these local *seringueiros* was the most suitable production method in the Amazon. In the first rubber boom, tappers were *flagelados*, those who were whipped; during the war, as essential manpower for the Allies, they were "soldiers." In the 1980s, the decade that saw the six hottest years on record until that time, they called themselves "defenders of the forest."

Global environmental interest groups became allies of the modern rubber tappers, recognizing that extractive modes of production, along with demarcating indigenous territories to keep outsiders at bay, were part of a solution to save rainforests. The struggling Rubber Tappers Union suddenly had a seat at the table with international finance institutions considering aid and loans for Brazil.

A hefty, round-faced Rubber Soldier's son, Francisco "Chico" Mendes, articulate and seemingly indefatigable, became the movement's figurehead. There were no schools on the rubber estates; in his late teens, Chico had been educated by a tutor, an escaped political prisoner jailed for participating in the revolt of the charismatic Communist leader Luis

Carlos Prestes, the "Horseman of Hope." Chico's tutor led him to books and taught him how to find the Portuguese broadcasts of international news programs on the radio, advising him to count on the BBC for the most impartial coverage. He was also influenced by priests of the Liberation Theology movement, which interprets the gospel of Jesus with concern for liberation of the oppressed. A voracious reader, Chico became an organizer with a natural political skill to get people to reflect on their condition and to act.

Despite the putative protection of international connections and rising fame, or perhaps because of them, the unionized jungle workers made enemies of those who wanted land for themselves and who were linked to the old Amazon elite. "If a messenger came down from heaven and guaranteed that my death would strengthen our struggle, it would even be worth it," Chico told a friend. "But . . . rallies and lots of funerals won't save the Amazon. I want to live."

A gunman assassinated Chico Mendes on December 22, 1988, just outside his home.

Eight years after the activist's murder, during my assignment in the Amazon I went to the *seringal* where Chico Mendes had grown up and worked, in the municipality of Xapuri. I visited his grandmother, stayed at the wood-plank house of one of his cousins. Every day, well before dawn, Sebastiao Mendes, who was fifty-two, mechanically completed a morning ritual: he broke off a tiny piece of rubber from a ball of the raw stuff, lit it like a wick, and tossed it flaming onto a pile of wood in the stove, then put the coffee on. "You don't think about the cold," he said, "but about how hot it's going to get later."

We walked a trail soggy from overnight rain. Sebastiao Mendes etched a diagonal cut in a marked tree. He watched the white latex ooze, beginning its descent into the tin cup nailed to the trunk. He worked quickly and expertly alongside his son Antonio, who was eighteen. Throughout the morning they went from tree to tree, as each had done since childhood, half watching their strides for vines and exposed roots that could grab an ankle or twist a leg like a pretzel. They kept an eye out for stinging plants, rattlesnakes, and yellow-headed vipers.

"We trust to faith, because the snakes bite through your shoes," young Antonio said, grinning. In rubber-soled tennis shoes, he had it better than the tappers of his great-great-grandfather's day, who went barefoot or in thin sandals. He had it better than the tappers of his grandfather's Rubber Soldier generation, with their shoes of jute.

PART II

The Undesirables

4.

"WHERE THEY COULD NOT ENTER": JEWISH LIVES

On the small, dry island of Baltra in the Galapagos archipelago that soldiers called "The Rock," Saul Skolnick, a pipe-smoking American serviceman, loaded ordnance onto B-17s and B-29s. The airplanes patrolled the western entrance to the Panama Canal, watching for enemy subs. Had Skolnick been a pilot, his days might have been more exciting, but loading bombs was dull. Skolnick soon realized that there was not much after-work action either on the lonely island located more than five hundred miles off the Ecuadoran coast.

A cinema and a beer garden served 2,400 servicemen and 750 civilians, but you could only go to so many movies and drink so much beer. Off base, you could only shoot so many photos of basking land iguanas—Charles Darwin described them as having "a singularly stupid appearance"—or tame so many feral goats, a favorite hobby of some GIs. Even nature seemed to have been stingy with the island. The giant tortoises that made the bigger Galapagos Islands famous were absent on tiny Baltra. Darwin's legendary finches did not frequent the cactus and dry palo santo trees that grew in the red dust around the base.

To break the monotony, on a bright day in December 1943, Skolnick and some friends took one of the bombers on a joyride to Peru, seven

hundred miles east, to do some Christmas shopping for companions at
the base, some of whom gave Skolnick a few bucks to buy alpaca blankets.
Skolnick, barely into his twenties at the time, would remember that trip
for the rest of his life.

The plane landed at Talara, a U.S. installation newly built to protect
oil fields on the Peruvian coast. Skolnick and a buddy headed for the waterfront. They entered a shop wearing army air forces–issue short-sleeve
brown work shirts. From behind the counter a man looked squarely at
the name written on Skolnick's pocket and addressed the American in
Yiddish. The two carried on a lively bargaining session until Skolnick and
his astonished friend walked out laden with more blankets than they had
anticipated buying at a far lower price than they had expected to pay.

"Shit," said Skolnick's buddy, "I didn't know you spoke Spanish so
good."

The following spring, Saul Skolnick received an invitation from the
Talara merchant to return for a seder meal, and to bring friends. "The
shop owner was drawing on a Jewish Passover tradition of welcoming
the stranger," said Skolnick's son Paul, a retired broadcast journalist in
Los Angeles who heard the story many times from his father, who died
in 2002. "'Every unmarried Jewish woman in the country must have
been at that table,' he used to say. 'Here were a dozen nice-looking men,
and not one of them a Nazi.'"

The late Corporal Saul Skolnick, called by his son "a typical Brook-
lyn Jew," was surprised to find so many fellow Jews in a tiny town on an
overwhelmingly Catholic continent. "It opened his eyes," said Paul Skolnick. "He wondered, 'How did these Jews get here?'"

Unbeknownst then to Saul Skolnick as he sat with new friends at the
seder table in Peru, and still a surprise to many first-time visitors to Latin
America, Jews have been part of the hemisphere's living fabric since the
fifteenth century. In 1492, when Queen Isabel and King Ferdinand ended
centuries of Moslem rule in Spain and banished Jews from the country,
six Jewish crew members sailed with Columbus on his first voyage.

They were *conversos*, Jews who converted or appeared to convert to
avoid punishment. One of them, Rodrigo de Triana, was the first to sight

land. Columbus describes another, Luis de Torres, as "one who had been Jewish and who knew Hebrew and some Arabic." De Torres was the first to set foot upon the soil of the New World.

By banishing Jews and Moslems, the Iberian monarchs were performing a *limpieza de sangre*, a cleansing of the blood. They decided the cleansing should extend to the colonies too, so they forbade Jews and converts to the fourth generation to settle in their American lands. But determined travelers could always get exemption permits from corrupt officials, and sea captains could be bribed to land "New Christians" at secret inlets, such as south of Veracruz in Mexico, or on the Honduran coast, or in southern Chile.

The earliest Jewish arrivals in Latin America didn't suffer the same kind of shunning and denunciation from neighbors that they might have experienced in Europe. Possibly the shared difficulties of setting up lives in a new environment even acted as a kind of leveler, as it might in any frontier society. While Spain and Portugal ruled Latin American lands, however, Jews could not escape the long arm of the intolerant Catholic Church of the Iberian Peninsula.

On a pedestrian plaza near Avenida Juarez in Mexico City, the busy modern-day street that cuts into the heart of the capital's historic center, a steady flow of foot traffic swirls around outdoor cafés crowded with fashionably dressed patrons. Amid the bustle, a visitor might miss a small, bright yellow church set back from the street. But it is worth pausing to read the stone inscription on a pillar that faces the plaza: "In front of this was the burning place of the Inquisition, 1596–1771."

Established in Europe in the early twelfth century, the Roman Catholic tribunal used torture and execution to punish those it judged heretics. At first the Inquisition set its sights upon erring Catholics, then Protestants and Jews and social outcasts such as homosexuals. In the New World, the indigenous and African slaves might be brought before the court. In the end, however, just like the Holocaust, the Inquisition was aimed at Jews.

On the plaza in front of the stone pillar, the condemned of the Inquisition performed the auto-da-fé, a public confession of their crime of conscience. Many were imprisoned, although torture was less frequent than in Europe. From Mexico, the Inquisition governed nearby lands. A Portuguese-born Guatemalan, Nunes Pereira, died before the Mexican pillar for the crimes of "judaizing, heresy and apostasy." Accused heretics were brought to the tribunal in Lima from as far away as Bolivia and Ecuador, to Cartagena from Panama. "The reality was that every town in Spanish America was affected by the foundation of the Inquisition," a British scholar wrote.

Among ordinary New World Catholics, religious practice was not as fiercely intolerant as it was in Spain—neighbors knew that friends and other neighbors were Jews, but did not denounce them. Jews settled openly and built synagogues in Recife and other towns on the Brazilian coast as long as the Dutch held sway there, beginning in 1630. The region was free from the Inquisition until the Portuguese took it back in 1654 and tribunal authorities sent prisoners to Lisbon.

Over its two-hundred-year existence in Latin America, the Inquisition held about three thousand trials; probably a total of one hundred persons were killed. Sometimes the Inquisitors' motives were political—the Mexican independence hero and Catholic priest Miguel Hidalgo, charged before the tribunal and eventually found not guilty, said he would never have been accused had he not supported the liberation movement. But Jews, or targets branded as *conversos*, were nearly always vulnerable.

As Latin American countries broke away from Spain and Portugal in the early nineteenth century and the Inquisition disappeared from Latin America, a dramatic turnaround occurred: the newly independent nations began to accept Jews as immigrants.

Beginning in 1880, Sephardic Jews traveled to the most inaccessible jungles of Peru and Brazil. In improvised boats, they "navigated the waters of the Amazon and its tributaries in the incessant search for rubber and trade," wrote a Peruvian Jewish community leader almost a century later. In 1969, Yaacov Hasson visited descendants of the pioneers in Iquitos, at the Amazon headwaters. He reported that records and oral testimony showed that some of the earliest settlers had regarded the Amazon region as a possible utopia, and that they "identified their personal hopes with the prospect of a Jewish civilization here."

The crash of the rubber boom in 1912 dashed dreams in the Amazon, but Jewish pioneers were already settling elsewhere. As turn-of-the-century pogroms wracked imperial Russia and Constantinople, thousands looked to the vast expanses of Brazil and Argentina for refuge. The London-based Jewish Colonization Association, founded by the German banker and philanthropist Baron Maurice de Hirsch, obtained land and organized their travel. Russia was intransigent on its deplorable treatment of the Jews, and the fabulously wealthy de Hirsch saw emigration as their only hope.

In Russia, Jews were banned from professions and trades, including agriculture, but the Jewish Colonization Association purchased tens of thousands of acres near Buenos Aires to farm. Few of those who traveled with the colonization efforts had experience in the fields, but they joined the exodus anyway, looking for lives where they could practice their faith in freedom. In the Argentine province of Entre Rios, the colonization association planted miles of alfalfa, and settlers raised cattle. In the wilds of the New World, they worked in common, inspired by the same spirit of shared faith and work on the land that later gave rise to the kibbutzim in Israel. They would "keep their plows in good repair and watch the wheat grow like a vast green sheet," wrote the Lithuanian Argentine author Alberto Gerchunoff in 1914. "They kept the holy days and enjoyed the results of their labors."

Gerchunoff's landmark series of scenes taken from his life growing up in Entre Rios, *The Jewish Gauchos of the Pampas*, is dedicated to de Hirsch and considered the seminal work of Latin American Jewish literature. The small book reads like a paean to the enthusiasm and idealism of early settlers. In one vignette, new arrivals sing, "To the Argentine, We'll go—to sow; To live as friends and brothers, To be free!"

Beginning in 1904, the colonization association bought tens of thousands more acres in Brazil's southern province of Rio Grande do Sul, but after a couple of decades experiments there failed, partly because of the colonists' inexperience with farming. Some of the disaffected, and those who were simply worn out, became peddlers, often walking long distances to sell wares at shops, homes, ranches. Photos of the 1910s and 1920s show the typical Jewish peddler wearing a hat and tie but burdened from top to toe by a cargo of goods—a pack on his back filled with fabric and notions, pots and pans strapped across his chest, brooms in one hand, and a rake in the other.

Jews leaving the agricultural colonies gravitated to cities where they lived side by side with new arrivals who had disembarked at Veracruz in Mexico, Guatemala's Puerto Barrios, Cartagena in Colombia, Buenos Aires in Argentina, or Havana, Cuba. From Brazil's southernmost port, Rio Grande do Sul, they traveled to Uruguay and Paraguay. Others directly headed some two hundred miles north to the province's capital, Porto Alegre, where they lived in a shtetl-like neighborhood called Bom Fim.

There among shops, synagogues, professional offices, and vacant lots where youngsters gathered after school, the late 1930s and early 1940s passed in a microcosm of what Jews experienced, to greater and lesser degrees, throughout Latin countries.

> *Summer arrived and with it, Hanukah, the Festival of Lights. Joel and Nathan lit lights in remembrance of the Maccabees. After that would come Pesach and they would eat unleavened bread in re-membrance of the flight from Egypt, and then there would be Good Friday. And finally Holy Saturday, a day on which even the stones of Fernandez Vieira Street were filled with hatred for the Jews. The cinamomo trees would lower their branches to punish them, the fierce hound of Melâmpio would come in from the outskirts to pursue them with his barking. The goyim hunted down Jews throughout Bom Fim. They would be reconciled the next day and would play soccer in the field on Cauduro Avenue, but on Holy Saturday it was necessary to thrash at least one Jew.*
>
> —MOACYR SCLIAR, *The War in Bom Fim*

Hitler's rise spurred new Jewish migration, but just when refugees needed open doors most, Latin countries closed them. Radical rightist groups appeared in countries from Mexico to Argentina, sometimes supported by German Nazis but essentially homegrown, products of some of the same kind of forces that fed European fascism: economic depression, ultranationalism, fear of "outsiders" competing for jobs, suspicion of unfamiliar customs in an overwhelmingly Christian culture. Even in neighborhoods like Porto Alegre's Bom Fim, where Jews had lived for decades, anti-Semitism rose.

"At that time you couldn't open your mouth, you had to be quiet," said Sofia Wolff Carnos, who was born at one of Baron de Hirsch's agricultural colonies in 1909 and moved with her parents to Bom Fim. "Anyone who spoke out was condemned and persecuted."

Carnos's memories are among hundreds recorded by researchers from a Bom Fim synagogue in the 1980s. During her childhood in the 1910s and 1920s, Carnos said, girls who wanted to study at the good local school identified themselves as Germans, not Jews, because the school did not admit Jews. In the era of the fascist-friendly dictator Getúlio Vargas, anti-Semitism became ubiquitous.

"You couldn't speak Yiddish in the street," said Carnos. With her husband, a shopkeeper, Carnos collected clothing and supplies for aid packages and sent them to European Jews during the war. In Porto Alegre, she said, neighbors turned their backs on their own heritage. "People denied they were Jewish, not out of shame, but to save themselves" from harassment and from suspicion that they were communists.

An ultranationalist mass movement, Integralism (*Ação Integralista Brasileira*), drawing heavily from German and Italian Brazilians, became prominent in Porto Alegre, as elsewhere in the country. Because Vargas was competing with the well-established Brazilian Communist Party for the loyalty of workers, he tapped the fascist Integralists as a convenient base of support. People called them "Greens," or "Green Shirts" for their favorite attire.

"They just talked about exterminating the Jews," Carnos said. Residents expressed shock watching non-Jewish neighbors with whom they had grown up playing soccer in Scliar's "field on Cauduro Avenue" donning green shirts with the lightning-like Sigma patch. The symbol for a Greek letter (for a *hissing* sound), rendered in black on white with sharp edges, the Sigma was reminiscent of a swastika.

Today numerous synagogues remain in Bom Fim, but most Jews have moved out to other parts of the city, leaving the old neighborhood behind to gentrification, peppered with new cafés, Pilates studios, and gated houses. On a typical day, Osvaldo Aranha Avenue, which runs along the edge of the community and is now named for Vargas's foreign minister, carries seven lanes of traffic past towering palms. During the 1930s, however, the avenue was the scene of *Integralista* paramilitary parades. Marchers dressed in the green uniform raised their arms in a Nazi salute, like the followers of Hitler and Mussolini. They scuffled with Communists in street-corner battles.

Integralistas were not the only fascists in Brazil: "What seems much more serious to me . . . was a parallel movement . . . the descendants of Germans from the German colonies who, out of inherited patriotism (because it wasn't their own patriotism—they were Brazilians—it was the patriotism of fathers and grandfathers) accepted Nazism and the idea of Nazism," said Mauricio Rosemblatt, a Porto Alegre intellectual whose testimony is in the synagogue archives.

A million German Brazilians lived in southern Brazil in the 1930s, and German speakers to the second and third generation comprised as much as 50 percent of the population of some municipalities. Sometimes they used no Portuguese at all, their lives revolving around German churches, German schools, German social clubs. There were innumerable German associations for sports, gymnastics, shooting, and singing; for paramilitary training; Nazi clubs for boys, girls, and women, a veritable German world on Brazilian soil. To this day in the town of Joinville, where older residents remember the thrill of watching the *Graf Zeppelin* fly above rooftops in the 1930s, street signs in Portuguese also carry their former German names.

Most of the rest of Brazil was Roman Catholic, but in the German south residents attended Lutheran services led by German ministers. Most of the pastors were National Socialists, loyal to Hitler. In 1935, the head of the German Nazi party in Brazil, Hans Henning von Cossel, who lived in São Paulo, was amazed when he visited the southern city of Blumenau, which even today seems plucked from a European motherland with its German bakeries, blond children, and houses that look as if they come from Bavaria.

"Who could understand that sensation of finding in the heart of

South America a city where it's difficult to hear a word in Portuguese, and the houses recall a small city in central Germany, in which the shops and signs are in German?" von Cossel exulted. "Palms grow here and there, but seem out of place where even the few existing dark-skinned people speak German and seem like good 'Germans.'"

Among the good "Germans" in Brazil, Nazis were influential. When magazines published anti-Integralist or antifascist articles, the German or Italian embassies complained to publishers and authorities, and the issues were removed from the stands.

In Germany, Dr. Alexandre Preger had thought that the German people were "too well educated to pay attention" to Nazis, until April 1, 1933. An SS man posted a sign at Dr. Preger's practice: "Do not buy here, because the owner and attendant is Jewish." Preger sailed to Brazil, but even within the relative safety of the Jewish neighborhood of Bom Fim, he faced trouble.

In 1937, the ultranationalist Vargas forbade the use of foreign languages. "During the war we couldn't speak German, and I had to make sure the children didn't speak a word," Preger said.

When Vargas allied himself with England and the United States in 1942, Brazil slapped selective measures on residents with roots in Axis countries, over and above language restrictions. As a resident German, Dr. Preger's practice was placed on a commercial blacklist, and he was required to deliver regular payments to the Bank of Brazil. But his worst fear was that of going to jail. "For the Brazilians I was a German, for the police and all, born in Berlin. Not a Jew forcibly fled from Germany." Authorities threw Germans and German Jews into the same cells for violating the new laws.

Of all the anxieties Jews in Latin America suffered during the war, among the most painful was the lack of information about what was happening to loved ones in Europe. Everyone knew Jews were suffering, but details of repression were vague. Mail and telegrams didn't work, telephone calls were only a dream. Mordechay Bryk, a construction worker, came to Porto Alegre in 1935 at age sixteen and corresponded with his family in Poland until their letters stopped. Only in 1948 did Bryk find out that his parents, brother, and his brother's children were shot to death by a German-Ukranian patrol as the family huddled in a shelter in the woods—an eight-year-old girl hiding nearby was a witness.

Judith Scliar, an educator and widow of the novelist Moacyr Scliar, told me that throughout the war years her parents sent rice and flour from Porto Alegre to her mother's parents in Warsaw. But they too lost contact with each other. Her parents "had no idea of the death camps, the extermination that was going on," Scliar said. Later, they would discover that her grandparents died at a Nazi annihilation camp, Majdanek, in occupied Poland.

Until her death, Judith Scliar's mother lamented that she could not save her parents from their fate. But even if Latin American Jews might somehow extricate loved ones from Nazi hands, their relatives were unlikely to find shelter on Latin American soil. Countries restricted Jewish immigration, often secure in the notion that by doing so, they were only following the example of the United States, which imposed strict quotas on Jewish refugees. Washington's quota policy was shaped by xenophobia, anti-Semitism, worry about competition over jobs, and fears that Jews with close relatives in German-held lands could be blackmailed into working as agents for the Reich.

In both Latin America and the United States, immigration practice that discriminated against Jews was also shaped by a way of thinking that originated in England in the early twentieth century—eugenics. By the time of the war, belief in eugenics had spread throughout the world.

> It was a time when this theme was the topic of the hour; when eugenic babies . . . sprawled all over the illustrated papers; when the evolutionary fancy of Nietzsche was the new cry among the intellectuals . . .
>
> —G. K. CHESTERTON, Eugenics and Other Evils

Eugenics—the word comes from the Greek for "well born"—was a scientific and social movement that aimed to use laws of heredity as they were understood at the time to improve the human race. Widespread belief in eugenics contributed to the way that Jews fleeing fascism were shut out of Latin America, and to the way those already present were considered incapable of being assimilated into the greater society.

Today eugenics is considered a discredited pseudoscience, remembered mostly because of its association with racism and the ghastly Nazi drive to create a "pure" Aryan race. Originally, however, eugenics was considered an objective path to public health and social progress, and it influenced immigration practices in countries from the United States to Argentina. Its premise and sequel were widely accepted: human beings and the groups they belonged to varied "in their hereditary value," and social policies were best based on the perceived differences. Eugenics was forward-looking, respectable.

Brazilian eugenics, for one, was connected early to hygiene and sanitation. Medical professionals who embraced eugenics became public-health experts, advising against marriage between close relatives, advocating "constructive eugenics" such as prenatal care, sex education, and premarital exams for debilitating conditions, and encouraging only healthy couples to have children. Social reformers championed the movement—healthier and fitter individuals eventually would overcome social ills like poverty and "overpopulation," raising the quality of life on earth.

Soon enough, eugenics was also invoked to support prejudice and preconceptions, such as the imagined superiority of white people over those with darker skin. In Latin America, an extreme interpretation of "well born" led to hopes that eugenics would lead to the "whitening" of mixed populations. In Hitler's Europe, eugenics showed its darkest side of all, invoked to rid the Reich of all but healthy so-called Aryans. In 1940, the SS officer Walter Rauff, who would settle in Chile after the war, oversaw a fleet of air-sealed vans into which tubes delivered carbon monoxide to poison Polish children deemed mentally ill. Eventually the vans were used to eliminate 1.5 million Jews.

Nazi Germany took eugenics to extremes, but the United States was the first country to undertake eugenics-based sterilizations, and by the 1930s it had the most extensive such legislation outside the Reich. Under the Model Eugenic Sterilization Law, thirty-three U.S. states sterilized tens of thousands of individuals regarded as "socially inadequate," often mentally disabled, or deaf, blind, epileptic, or pregnant out of wedlock, regarding them as incapable of regulating their own reproduction. African American and Native American women were especially vulnerable.

In the rest of the continent, U.S. policy affected Latin Americans directly, and by example. Eugenic sterilizations began in Puerto Rico in 1936, and by 1960, when the program ended, a third of the territory's women had been sterilized. Eugenics-inspired sentiment that argued against "social inadequates" shaped the 1924 U.S. Immigration Act, restricting the entry of many who were desperate to flee Europe in the 1930s and 1940s, especially Jews and Italians. The act, which remained in force until 1964, did not recognize refugees fleeing for their lives, and completely excluded Asians. "America must remain American," said President Calvin Coolidge when he signed it.

Latin Americans were overwhelmingly Roman Catholic, and many still blamed Jews for the crucifixion of Jesus Christ, a belief the Church did not disavow until the 1960s. After the Russian Revolution of 1917, Jews were also suspected of being sympathetic to communism, of being "Bolsheviks." Eugenics provided a socially acceptable way of defining Jews as undesirables.

In Argentina, then as now home to most Latin American Jews, eugenists suggested that immigration take racial selection into account lest "non-Latin" newcomers damage the national identity. Such thinking was amenable to the powerful anti-Semitic political right, and the result was wartime laws that limited Jewish immigration. One of the most prominent and well-respected Brazilian eugenists, Renato Kehl, visited Germany in the early 1920s and returned as medical director of the Bayer pharmaceutical company with ideas about more radical "negative eugenics": undesirable individuals should be prevented from reproducing, "degenerates and criminals" sterilized. Influenced by work on heredity compiled by the U.S. Eugenics Record Office, Kehl constructed proposals for racial segregation and prohibiting immigrants considered inferior. As in other Latin countries, in Brazil the Catholic Church and contesting medical and social views stood as a brake against such extremes, but there were few brakes on views of Jews as the "other," a group of people resistant to assimilation.

The world seems to be divided into two parts—those places where the Jews cannot live and those where they cannot enter.

—CHAIM WEIZMANN, *Manchester Guardian*, MAY 23, 1936

Concerned with growing danger to displaced Eastern European Jews in Germany, Albert Einstein in 1930 supported a colonization project in Peru. The plan envisioned initially settling twenty thousand Jews, and eventually up to a million, on Peruvian land concessions.

"Maybe there truly is a possibility here to help a great part of the Jewish people find a healthy existence," wrote Einstein. To the scientist's dismay, influential Zionists bent upon a homeland in Palestine discouraged the project lest it split their movement. Whether such an ambitious Peruvian enterprise would have been successful or not is an open question, and any chance of such an escape valve would soon become moot.

In 1935, Germany's National Socialist government instituted the Nuremberg Statutes, a set of anti-Jewish laws that laid down a legal framework for the still-unimaginable mass killings to come, beginning with depriving Jews of citizenship. Most Jews who could did whatever possible to flee.

But they found no welcome in Latin America. In June 1937, for instance, the Brazilian Foreign Ministry issued a secret circular to its global consulates ordering diplomats to deny visas to persons of "Semitic origin." Publicly, President Vargas positioned himself as a champion of Brazil's special *brasilidade*, a shared identity composed of indigenous, African, and European roots that must bring all colors and classes together, forging a modern society. But discourse and immigration policy were two different things.

The secret circular and a new constitution with further restrictions amounted to a Jewish ban. Leaving *brasilidade* behind, regulations instead underscored a commitment to eugenics and whitening, the long-standing ideology that encouraged immigration of Western Europeans to "improve" the Brazilian "race." Eventually, the reasoning went, dark-skinned Brazilians would want to choose whiter mates, and darker-skinned

Brazilians would disappear. Jews—Semites—were not considered white. Without fear of reprisals, officials turned Jews away.

Despite similar attitudes in other Latin American capitals, brave individuals who held positions in their countries' diplomatic posts worked to save lives. In 1942, José Arturo Castellanos, an El Salvadoran army colonel, was serving in Geneva as consul general when a Transylvanian Jewish businessman, George Mandel, approached him and pleaded for identity papers for himself and his family. The Salvadoran diplomat appointed Mandel as "first secretary" to the consulate, a post that did not exist, and the two men began grinding out false Salvadoran passports, which they issued without charge to refugees. Castellanos is credited with saving from Nazi death camps some forty thousand Jews from Hungary, Czechoslovakia, Romania, Bulgaria, and Poland.

In Marseilles, Mexico's consul general Gilberto Bosques Saldívar rented a castle and a summer vacation camp and declared the properties Mexican territory under international law. There Bosques sheltered European Jews who reached the Mediterranean port city as well as Spanish Republican leaders fleeing Francisco Franco's fascist forces. Later referred to as "the Mexican Schindler," Bosques issued tens of thousands of visas, chartering ships to take refugees to African countries from which they sailed on to Mexico, Brazil, and Argentina. (Bosques and his family and forty members of the consular staff were arrested in 1943 and held by the Germans for a year near Bonn. Mexico City negotiated their release in a prisoner exchange.) Brazilian consulates in Europe generally rejected Jews based on the secret circular, but individual officers gave visas to petitioners on their own initiatives.

A few conscientious, risk-taking diplomats acting alone, however, could not solve the problem of resettling hundreds of thousands of Jews being forced out of the Reich. President Roosevelt may have had a personal desire to accept refugees, and Eleanor Roosevelt advocated strongly for them, but anti-Semitism among the U.S. political class, especially in Congress, argued against it. Isolationism—such as in the "America First" movement—was popular among a majority of Americans who believed in leaving Europe's problems to Europe. Yet American Jews and others pressured the president. In 1938, escape from the Reich, even though families must flee penniless, was still a possibility—if places could be found to receive them. Something must be done.

Ten days after Hitler's occupation of Austria in March 1938, Roosevelt called for an international meeting to consider solutions. For five beautiful days in July, representatives of thirty-two countries, nineteen of them from Latin America, and numerous nongovernmental organizations met at the splendid Hotel Royal at Évian-les-Bains on the blue and sparkling Lake Geneva.

From Berlin, Hitler sent a cynical message. "We . . . are ready to put all these criminals at the disposal of these countries," he said. "For all I care, even on luxury ships."

In the end, the heralded Évian Conference served as mere window dressing for expressions of global concern. Only a single country, the Dominican Republic, whose dictator Rafael Trujillo wanted to curry favor with Roosevelt and whiten his country's population, invited one hundred thousand Jews. Previously, Trujillo had accepted two thousand Spanish Republicans for the same reason. One of the Spanish refugees, with no false illusions, told an interviewer that "we are white and we can breed." However, by January 1940, when the program to bring in Jews began, submarine warfare and a shortage of space on Allied transport ships hampered emigration to the Dominican Republic. A few hundred Jews did arrive and set up an agricultural colony that continues to provide dairy products for much of the country.

Bolivia's delegation to Évian was led by the "the Andean Rockefeller," tin king Simón Iturri Patiño, La Paz's minister in France and one of the world's richest men. Patiño made no public commitment, but quietly over the next three years several thousand Jews entered Bolivia legally with the help of another hugely wealthy tin baron, Moritz Hochschild, born a German Jew. Other than the Dominican Republic's Trujillo, however, no government leader at Évian stepped up to the plate.

"NOBODY WANTS THEM," gloated a headline in the German newspaper *Völkischer Beobachter*. Speaking to the Reichstag the following January, Hitler said, "It is a shameful spectacle to see how the whole democratic world is oozing sympathy for the poor tormented Jewish people, but remains hard hearted and obdurate when it comes to helping them." Scholars have called Évian "Hitler's green light for genocide."

Despite restrictions, some eighty-four thousand Jewish immigrants managed to plea, cajole, or bribe their way into refuge in Latin America between 1933 and 1945, less than half the number admitted during the previous fifteen years. In Brazil, the elites who mandated immigration policy held two contradictory attitudes, both based on stereotypes. On one hand, feelings of anti-Semitism and eugenics-inspired prejudice worked against admitting Jews. On the other hand, a preconception existed that Jews were smart financial managers with capital who might develop the Brazilian economy. The belief that certain Jews could help Brazil moved authorities to grant some two thousand visas to German Jews in 1939.

In the New World, however, Jews fleeing fascism often became targets of the same suspicion that hounded them in Europe: a belief that they were ideologues of fascism's enemy, "Bolshevists," or communists.

In 1937 in Brazil, with his elective term of office about to expire, Getúlio Vargas hatched a communist conspiracy out of thin air and called it "Plan Cohen." He announced on the radio that perpetrators were about to take over the government. Two years before, in 1935, Vargas had launched a campaign of state terror against the leftist opposition, including Communists, which drove activists into an armed resistance that was quickly squelched. The Communist Party leader, Luís Carlos Prestes, had been tortured and jailed. Prestes's pregnant wife, Olga Benário Prestes, a Jew born in Munich, was identified by Brazilian diplomats working with the Gestapo and sent to Germany, where she was held at Ravensbrück concentration camp. She was removed to a state sanatorium and gassed in a euthanasia chamber in April 1942.

In 1937 Brazil, however, there was no communist plot, no "Plan Cohen." Yet Vargas manipulated the fiction to gain autocratic powers in what he called the Estado Novo, a "New State" with new legal tools against dissenters. To help maintain the regime, he stoked the always-present embers of anti-Semitism, casting Jews as a subversive fifth column in service of the Soviet Union.

Jews became widely and often irrationally targeted for surveillance, and even arrest. "The fact of an individual being Jewish or simply of Jewish origin would weigh negatively in the criteria of judgment of the Brazilian Political Police," historian Taciana Wiazovski has written. For Jews, it seemed simply that labor union membership, or knowing someone under investigation, or belonging to a Jewish organization, could justify the kind of scrutiny usually reserved for suspected criminals.

By the 1990s, authorities had dismantled the domestic spying organization of the São Paulo region, the Department of Political and Social Order (DEOPS); its archives, made public, revealed investigators' personal rancor against Jews and the kind of "evidence" they collected in the hunt for subversives. Documenting a request for a travel pass by Hildegard Boskovics, a secretary followed for nine years, an investigator's note said that she should be sent "to Hitler," since she is "an Israelite." In the case of Ernest Joske, an accountant followed for twelve years, incriminating evidence included stamps for donations to a relief society, International Red Aid—a kind of Red Cross established by the Communist International to provide assistance to political prisoners—and anti-Nazi, antifascist, and communist literature. Joske said he was anti-Nazi because he was Jewish, declaring he was Marxist in thought, which, of course, was not against the law.

After a 1932 raid on a center of Jewish organizations on Amazonas Street in São Paulo, a DEOPS file concluded that the clubs registered at the address, such as the Jewish Sport and Gymnastic Society and the Israelite Workers' Culture Center, were fronts for subversive activities. "The true character of these 'sport' and 'benevolent' organizations is but in truth only a well organized center of communist propaganda," said the file. Confiscated literature included periodicals from Buenos Aires and New York, in English, Yiddish, German, and Spanish, including *The Nation*, *The Soviet Russian Pictorial*, and *The Workers' Monthly*.

The infamous anti-Semitic screed published in Russia in 1903, *The Protocols of the Elders of Zion*, about an apocryphal Jewish plot to take over the world, circulated widely in Brazil in the 1930s and 1940s and influenced DEOPS operatives. The first step in the global takeover plot, according to the protocols, was the subversive education of youth. The children's monthly found on the Amazonas Avenue raid, *Pioner*, drew special attention—investigators reported it was meant "to pervert juveniles."

About three thousand miles north of Brazil, in the much smaller country of Guatemala, the stories of two refugees fleeing Hitler show how complex the journey to freedom could be for those who sought safety in Latin America. Even under Latin skies, Jews who escaped Hitler remained inexorably connected to the great tragedy of the Holocaust.

Ludwig Unger was thirty-five years old when he left his home in Hamburg in 1933. Tall, fit, with light hair and even, handsome features, Unger did not experience anti-Semitism while growing up in the cosmopolitan port city, nor had he felt it in his family's comfortable, upper-class circles or when he went to the Belgian front as a volunteer in the Kaiser's army. Fighting for Germany in World War I, Unger was wounded three times, captured, and interned for a while as a prisoner of war in England.

When Hitler became chancellor in 1933, he stood before massive crowds and delivered speeches charged with anti-Semitism and anticommunism. Nazi thugs beat Jews on the streets. Unger lost his job. Urged by his family, he crossed the sea to that exotic-sounding country, Guatemala, where an uncle ran an import business.

Ludwig Unger disembarked with a light suitcase at the Caribbean port of Puerto Barrios and boarded a train for the two-hundred-mile journey southwest to the busy capital, Guatemala City. There Ludwig became Luis, found work taking tickets at a movie palace, and soon managed a department store. Quietly affable, Unger easily made German and Guatemalan friends, and in 1936, he met and married a beautiful young Guatemalan Sephardic Jewish woman with the compelling name of Fortuna. He read the news of growing tension in Europe in local Spanish- and German-language newspapers. But Luis Unger lived thousands of miles away from Hitler now, and if fighting broke out in Europe, he would not be nearby. How could war reach him in the country called "The Land of Eternal Spring"?

The answers came one after another, each worse than the last.

In 1938, the *Auslandorganisation*, the foreign branch of the Nazi party, staged ships around the world so Germans abroad could vote to approve the *Anschluss*. A good friend of Luis Unger's made an excursion to Puerto Barrios, where he boarded a ship to cast his ballot. Using offshore polling places allowed the Germans to circumvent national laws prohibiting foreign elections. In Guatemala, families who went on the excursions to vote enjoyed a break from routines subsidized by Berlin, train rides, swimming off the ships (a second ship moored off Puerto San Jose on the Pacific), and picnics.

When Luis Unger's friend returned to Guatemala City, however, something had changed between them. "Listen," he said, "I can't be seen with you anymore." In his friend's office, a new photo of Adolf Hitler hung on the wall.

Unger felt "brutalized" according to his son David, a translator and novelist who lives in New York. Luis Unger spoke to his son of the broken friendship years later in words that showed it still stung. "He was speechless, he didn't see it coming."

Notices appeared in the German Embassy advising against associating with certain Jewish families, whether or not they had been neighbors for years. The unraveling of personal ties was just one sign of a deteriorating situation; it also became more difficult to bring over relatives.

President Ubico, the Guatemalan dictator who admired Mussolini, virtually closed the door on refugees from the Reich in 1938 when he cut the quota for German immigrants. He stood by when Nazis took control of Guatemalan German clubs and schools. Nevertheless, to the salvation of many, Ubico provided visas under the table in exchange for cash. Undoubtedly, he saved lives.

In the months before *Kristallnacht* in 1938, the mother of fifteen-year-old Hans Guggenheim was standing in a line to buy butter in Berlin when another Jewish woman said to her, "They are giving visas to Guatemala." Hans and his younger sister, Gaby, had already been sent to England; that night, their parents made a plan to write to a cousin whose family had moved to Guatemala in 1900 and ask him to obtain visas for them any way he could, so they too might escape. Once safely in Guatemala City, they went to President Ubico, who received visitors in a vast, pale green stone palace he had just built on the capital's central square. They paid money, and the Guggenheims left the president's offices with the promise of visas for their children.

At age ninety-three, sitting before tall windows in his multistory brick home in Boston, among pieces of fine art and artifacts collected over a lifetime, Hans Guggenheim recalled the excitement of that first trip across the Atlantic on a luxury liner. "Why cry bitter tears? I was barely eighteen and for me this was high adventure," he said. "There was a sub attack on the way to Cuba, and I ate frogs legs provençale for the first time."

Guggenheim, a painter and former professor of anthropology at the Massachusetts Institute of Technology, is writing a memoir covering the years "from fascism to Trump," and he remembers well the flowering beauty of the Guatemalan capital in the late 1930s and 1940s. Wealthy Jewish families lived in "large, elegant homes on the Reforma," a wide avenue, he said. In Berlin, the Nazis confiscated the family's assets, but in Guatemala they had a chance at life. His father soon owned a small factory that produced wrought-iron furniture in the capital, where Jewish life freely revolved around three synagogues—Ashkenazi, German, and Sephardi. At age twenty, the young artist had his first exhibition at the Club Guatemala, an exclusive downtown venue. He was at home. "We felt ourselves to be one hundred percent *guatemaltecos*," he said. "Probably there was someone around who didn't like Jews, but it wasn't institutionalized."

Guggenheim plainly calls Ubico, the Guatemalan dictator, a fascist. Nevertheless, in the capricious way of war, a figure that history defines as an ironfisted, self-centered ultrarightist is remembered by some as key to their survival. Guggenheim calls Ubico "a friend to the Jews."

"I wouldn't be here without him," he said. "He saved my parents' lives, and Gaby's life, and my life."

In 1939, Hans Guggenheim had a fine job downtown as an editorial artist at *La Prensa*, Guatemala's major daily. He did not know Luis Unger, who was about to begin work in the quartermaster's office of the U.S. air base under construction at the edge of the city. But just as Guggenheim felt safe in his new home, Luis Unger too was taking comfort in the midst of the growing bad news from Europe, knowing that his widowed mother was leaving Hamburg.

On May 13, Betty Unger and her sister, Gusti Hansen, set sail on the same kind of luxury liner that had brought Hans Guggenheim to Guatemala. They were headed for New York to join another sister, Julia, who had paid for their passage. Their passports were marked with a red "J" by the Reich, indicating they were Jewish. But they were fleeing toward freedom now, out of Hamburg bound for Havana. When they landed, the passengers—a third of them children whose parents awaited them—would disembark and stay in Cuba. Or, like Betty Unger and Gusti, they would arrange for transport to their final destination elsewhere in the Americas.

Many of the sisters' fellow passengers were professionals, lawyers, and doctors, forbidden to practice by the Nazis. Some had already been held in concentration camps. Max Loewe, a lawyer from Breslau, had been arrested on *Kristallnacht* and sent to Dachau, until he managed to secure a release and book tickets on the *St. Louis* for himself, his wife, and their fifteen-year-old daughter. The *St. Louis* trip was a "special voyage" whose financial details were overseen by the *Reichssicherheitshauptamt*, RSHA, the bureau for which Adolf Eichmann worked. The RSHA required everyone to pay for round-trip tickets, even though the refugees were traveling only one way. The German newspaper *Der Stürmer* crowed "GOOD RIDDANCE" when the ship sailed.

But Captain Gustav Schroeder ordered white-clad staff to treat passengers "like privileged tourists." Nazis among the ship's staff objected, almost to the point of mutiny, but Schroeder held his ground. It could not have been easy. Six Gestapo agents had infiltrated the crew. Their job on landing in Havana was to collect espionage documents from the *Abwehr* station, an outpost of the Reich's intelligence agency. Meanwhile, they were charged with keeping an eye on the captain.

Schroeder, a slight man with thirty-seven years' experience at sea, maintained his authority. He made sure that children were treated to swimming lessons in the deck pool and that adults enjoyed dances. He permitted passengers to throw a tablecloth over a bust of Hitler in the dining room and hold Friday night services. In photos from the voyage, men lounge easily in wooden deck chairs with blankets folded upon outstretched legs, women stand at the ship's rail in crisp white dresses as the breeze lifts their hair. Young boys look up at the camera, grinning as if they can barely contain their glee, free at sea with the run of the grand ship. Betty Unger and Gusti are there, appearing relaxed in a shaded seat on deck, dressed in flower-print organdy and shiny black Mary Janes, narrow-brim straw hats giving the middle-aged sisters a jaunty look.

As the *St. Louis* sailed toward Havana, Schroeder began to receive disquieting cables from the Hamburg-Amerika line main office.

23 MAY 1939: MAJORITY OF YOUR PASSENGERS IN CONTRAVENTION OF NEW CUBAN LAW 937 AND MAY NOT BE GIVEN PERMISSION TO DISEMBARK. SITUATION NOT COMPLETELY CLEAR BUT CRITICAL IF NOT RESOLVED BEFORE YOUR ARRIVAL IN HAVANA.

And from the shipping line's Cuba office:

26 MAY 1939 ANCHOR IN ROADSTEAD. DO NOT REPEAT NOT MAKE ANY ATTEMPT COME ALONGSIDE.

In Havana streets, Nazi demonstrations organized by the German Embassy protested the arrival of the refugees. On the *St. Louis*, rumors circulated around the decks that almost none of the passengers' landing permits were in order. The Cuban Immigration Service director, Manuel Benitez, was a charlatan and a thief. Benitez, a crony of future Cuban dictator Fulgencio Batista, whose protection he enjoyed, had been operating a visa racket, pocketing fees. President Federico Laredo Brú fired Benitez the day before the *St. Louis* was scheduled to dock, and canceled the transit visas Benitez issued—some say because the corrupt immigration chief failed to cut Laredo Brú in on the deal.

For days the sun rose over the *St. Louis*, anchored far from the docks of Havana. Except for thirty passengers who had received visas directly from the ministry—not from the conniving Benitez—no one was allowed to disembark. Some refugees became hysterical; women lifted their babies over the ship's rail and threatened to drop them if they were not allowed to get off. Depression possessed others. Max Loewe, the lawyer from Breslau who had survived *Kristallnacht* and Dachau, slit his wrists in view of other passengers and jumped into the sea. (A crew member dived in and grabbed Loewe and managed to place him half-dead on a launch to shore, where Loewe was hospitalized and survived, but his wife and daughter were forbidden to join him.) Captain Schroeder had selected a small number of passengers to act as liaisons with the others when the first troubling cables began to arrive. Now he assigned them to a suicide watch.

Betty Unger and Gusti waited aboard with the others, holding their "Benitezes"—the questioned transit visas had acquired a dark nickname. Schroeder cabled company headquarters, pleading intercession with diplomats. He went ashore with two Cuban attorneys to personally deliver a memorandum from the passengers to the Cuban president, but the president refused to see him. The American Jewish Joint Distribution Committee, a private U.S. benevolent association struggling to place refugees in safe havens, and other agencies lobbied frantically on shore, even offering money that was never enough for key officials.

Meanwhile, the *St. Louis* lay off Havana Harbor in tantalizing sight of the white buildings of the city. The tropical breeze blew softly, but passengers felt caught up in a vortex over which they had no control, the realization that freedom was slipping away. Some sold the last of family jewelry and other heirlooms to crewmen to pay for telegrams to President Roosevelt, to Cuban president Laredo Brú, even to the Cuban president's wife Leonor: "your woman's feelings give us hope . . ."

For three days, relatives of the passengers rowed or motored out to see their loved ones. From the small boats, the relatives shouted over the sound of the waves until, unbelievably, amid cries and lamentations, they watched the liner sail away.

Captain Schroeder did everything in his power to prevent returning his passengers to Europe, sending messages to a host of ports. But no country in the Americas would have them. Schroeder purposefully sailed the few miles north to Florida, and hugged the coast, hoping Washington would allow him to dock. But U.S. Coast Guard cutters forced the ship away. Returning across the Atlantic, he discussed running the *St. Louis* aground near Southampton, or setting a fire so passengers might escape and be rescued in British territory.

England, Denmark, Sweden, France, and Holland finally were persuaded to admit groups of the refugees. But the transit of the *St. Louis* goes down in history as a voyage of the doomed. Of the passengers, 254 were eventually taken prisoner in Europe and died in the extermination camps of the Nazi Reich.

Luis Unger would never see his mother again.

Betty and her sister Gusti disembarked in Amsterdam and lived quietly for three years in a small house in Groningen, a university city ninety miles northeast of the Dutch port. The last photo of them that David Unger has shows the two ladies sitting primly in wicker chairs on a wooden porch, wearing dark dresses, Betty with a high collar, Gusti in pearls. Their hands are folded on their laps, a bright sun lights their smiling faces. In 1942, Nazis and Dutch collaborators rounded up the Jews in Holland. The sisters died together in Nazi-occupied Poland at the Sobibór camp, where they were gassed.

Luis Unger found out from the Red Cross in 1947 about his mother's death. After the war, too, Hans Guggenheim and his family discovered that Hans's grandmother was gassed at Auschwitz. Soon after Hans and his sister had arrived safely in Guatemala, his parents had returned to President Ubico and asked for a visa for the grandmother, but Ubico turned them down.

"I suppose he thought, 'No, I've given them four visas, that's enough,'" said Guggenheim. "But he had no idea of what was going to happen, none of us did."

Sometimes it seems that Jews who lived through World War II in Latin America, and their descendants, carry the era in a way inseparable from thoughts of loved ones gone in the Shoah. Hans Guggenheim does not say he carries the old war with him, but he has begun art schools for children in countries affected by modern wars, in Mali and Guatemala. In 1995, he donated dozens of original Goya etchings, *The Disasters of War*, to a museum in Vietnam.

Even members of succeeding generations seem to maintain a connection with the war years that elders lived. Judith Scliar, born in Brazil, made a kind of pilgrimage to a new Jewish museum in Warsaw. The journey to the city from which her grandparents were taken, she said, affected her "deeply." On a balmy night in Bom Fim, Scliar gave a presentation to a packed synagogue about her Polish visit. Above us on a second floor in the synagogue's archive were the filing cabinets that held the wartime memories of the neighborhood's residents. On either side of me in the audience sat middle-aged women who told me their own stories of their parents' losses and migrations. I had the feeling that in Jewish communities like this one, wherever one might travel in Latin America, the war and its sequels still reverberated.

Marjorie Agosin's great-grandmothers escaped from Vienna and Odessa to Chile, where Agosin grew up. Agosin, a poet and literary scholar who teaches at Wellesley College, was born a full decade after the war, but seems to live steeped in the seemingly endless echo of the catastrophe. Her work as a poet and human rights activist resonates with what family and others experienced, in a fashion that connects the World War II era with the far-right state violence of her own generation in the 1970s and 1980s.

The Argentine military junta (1976–83) "tortured Jews under portraits of Hitler," Agosin wrote in *Dear Anne Frank*. Like Nazi genocide victims, those who were disappeared during the postwar Latin American dictatorships "did not have places of remembrance where they could be buried, and their families still do not know where to go visit them to remember them and to offer them life's gifts."

Sometimes the poet in Agosin seems to enter the very minds of those who came before her, on the journey from Europe to Latin America.

> *You walk the solemn avenues*
> *lined with rubber trees*
> *and the merchants*
> *with their figs and fresh fruit.*

Suddenly, you pause beneath the blazing sun
as if your wounded heart
were pulsing words
and you begin to say:
"One time in Vienna . . .
one time in Vienna"
and the angels of memory
arrive at your feet.

5.

NAZIS AND NOT NAZIS, IN THE LAND
OF THE WHITE BUTTERFLY

When Maya Sapper was a small girl, she loved to wander among the semi-tropical wonderland of trees and streams on the Guatemalan coffee plantation where she was born. The place was so far "in the boonies," she recalled many years later, that when her mother first came there as a young bride she cooked on a three-stone hearth like the women of the indigenous Q'eqchi' Maya, the original inhabitants of the mountainous region and for years the family's only neighbors. As Maya's father supervised her grandparents' vast holdings on horseback, her mother learned from the indigenous women the secrets of herbs and teas that might alleviate ailments, immersing herself in the new homeland so far from her native Germany. Young Maya, named for the Indian people her mother had come to admire, was born to the Guatemalan land in the same house as her father, never lived anywhere else nor dreamed she would ever live anywhere else.

"I remember once as a child, standing among the trees, with the light falling on the hanging vines, and seeing a huge white butterfly," recalled Maya when I visited her California seaside home. She had turned eighty-five and was sitting at a table in a small dining room, lifting her hands and spreading them wide at the memory. "Its wings were so white, almost transparent, just fluttering, and I said to myself, 'When I die, I want to be buried right here.'"

But it was the late 1930s, the war had started, and its ripples were about to shake the Sapper family's hardworking but idyllic existence. Beginning in 1942, a little-known U.S. program of political kidnapping swept up residents from Latin America, including Maya Sapper's father, Helmut, and brought them to the United States.

At a hemispheric conference in Rio de Janeiro in January 1942, U.S. assistant secretary of state Sumner Welles successfully pressured the Latin American republics to agree to take punishing measures against their residents with roots in Germany, Italy, and Japan. Nineteen countries complied, violating their own laws. The forced rendition policy that ensued also violated U.S. law. Mexico and Brazil uprooted entire communities and relocated them en masse within their own national borders, Colombia moved blacklisted men into hotels surrounded by guards. Fourteen other countries including Guatemala and Peru cooperated with U.S intelligence agents and diplomats and sent residents, not just Axis nationals but also native-born and naturalized citizens, to camps in the United States.

The captives did not suffer the conditions of inmates of Nazi death camps; but the isolated centers where they were held, sometimes for years, fit every definition of concentration camps, where large numbers of people, especially political prisoners or members of persecuted minorities, are deliberately imprisoned in a small area under difficult conditions, with limited recourse to law, or no recourse at all.

To justify the seizure and imprisonment of these civilians, the Roosevelt administration reached back through the centuries to a law passed during an undeclared naval war with France. In 1798, the Alien Enemies Act called for the arrest of nationals of countries at war with the United States as a measure to promote national security. A hundred and fifty years later, Roosevelt invoked the law against the Latin "aliens." To apply the Alien Enemies Act, however, it was necessary to get the individuals from Latin America into the United States. Almost immediately after Pearl Harbor, the captures began.

Some of those taken by force were shipped out as "repatriates" to Germany and Japan. Others became pawns in a game of exchange, traded by Washington for U.S. civilians held by the enemy. Still others, including entire families, existed in a limbo surrounded by barbed wire for years. Some of the U.S. camps that held the captives from Latin America did not close until December 1947, more than two years after the war ended.

The hidden snatch-and-imprison program foreshadowed the extraordinary rendition practices employed by the United States, with cooperating allies, in the "war on terror" after 9/11. Justified on the premise of rooting out the enemy wherever he may be, the shadowy World War II operation was aimed, its protagonists said, at ensuring national security at home. In fact, unreasoned fear drove the captures, combined with darker purposes: obtaining the pawns for prisoner exchanges, stifling commercial competition, and, in the case of ethnic Japanese captives, outright racism.

The kidnapping operation was kept from public view at the time and remains largely unknown even today. Yet it changed lives forever in the countries that agreed to cooperate by delivering their residents, even citizens, into U.S. hands. More than four thousand ethnic Germans like Helmut Sapper were taken by force from fifteen Latin countries and brought to camps at remote locations in the United States. The secretive program would tear Maya Sapper's father away and thrust her mother, her older brother Horst, and the rest of the family into years of uncertainty and loss.

Authorities also targeted more than two thousand ethnic Japanese, many of them women and children. Ethnic Italians were caught up, too, although to a lesser degree. The war against Italy ended in September 1943, and while two thousand Italian immigrants who lived in the United States were briefly interned in U.S. camps, President Roosevelt did not seem to regard Italians as a serious threat in North or South America. "I don't care about the Italians," he told Attorney General Francis Biddle in a discussion about interning aliens. "They are a lot of opera singers."

Allowing the "enemy aliens" to be taken away also caused losses to the Latin countries where they lived. It disrupted long-standing networks of commerce, social ties, and contributions to national cultures. The old ethnic communities would not be replicated in the same way after the war, when they were replicated at all. Maya Sapper's family in Guatemala was at the center of the storm.

•   •   •

By the time World War II started, the extended Sapper family was part of the German Guatemalan community of some thirteen thousand persons. The "Germans" had been contributing out of proportion to their numbers to the national economy, and to the country's store of knowledge about itself, for more than half a century. "The trajectory of the Sappers in Alta Verapaz is a living example of what some German immigrants achieved with their own efforts," wrote historian Regina Wagner. They started from the bottom, "without capital, but with dedication and an immense desire to create something solid to assure their existence."

Maya's grandfather Richard Sapper first came in 1884 to the green and humid region of Guatemala called Alta Verapaz, "True Peace." The name came from the sixteenth-century Dominican friar Bartolomé de las Casas, a historian and social reformer who convinced Spanish authorities that the province's Indians were best conquered by the cross, not the sword. Because Spanish soldiers did not enter as they did in the rest of the country, claiming land and upsetting traditions, settlers who arrived in the late nineteenth century found a pristine land peopled by Q'eqchi' Maya Indians, whose ways had changed little in five hundred years.

Like many other immigrants, Maya Sapper's grandfather had been drawn to Guatemala by glowing descriptions of the beauty of the land, and its potential for providing a living. Despite his youth, just twenty-two, Richard Sapper had already worked for German export businesses in Italy and Greece. Also like the hardiest of the planter pioneers—mostly German but a few French, English, and North Americans—Sapper spent months at a time traveling by horse and donkey or walking on the heels of native guides who hacked paths through virgin jungle, looking for suitable land for growing coffee. They measured tracts, slept rough, hunted and ate what they killed, cooked on open fires.

When Sapper discovered that his brother Karl, a recent graduate of Munich University in natural sciences, was suffering from a lung disorder, he invited him to cross the ocean and recuperate in the clear mountain air. Soon after Karl Sapper's arrival in 1888, the young naturalist employed his expertise in soils and geology as he, too, explored the region on foot, advising Richard on where to situate new plantations, or *fincas*. For the next twelve years, often accompanied by Q'eqchi' companions, sometimes funded by his brother Richard, Karl Sapper trod from Mexico's Isthmus of Tehuantepec to Panama, a "militant pedestrian" as one modern geographer called him, inveterately walking mountains and valleys to know them best, even when he might ride a mule or a horse. He recorded the lay of the land and its wildlife, and the agricultural customs of the native peoples he met. Much more intensely focused on Middle America than his famous forerunner of a century before, the Prussian naturalist and explorer of Latin America Alexander von Humboldt, Karl Sapper laid the foundations for Central America's modern mapmaking, and especially in Guatemala, for its physical and cultural geography to the present day.

By the time young Maya saw her unforgettable white butterfly on the plantation, her grandfather Richard had died, and the rest of the Sappers were living in alpine-style houses in command of hundreds of square miles of shiny-leafed trees. They were part of a family that had made cultural contributions to the country that would resound for decades. They produced some of the best coffee in the world.

Immigrant German coffee growers like the Sappers benefited from high world prices, but they also held tough when markets fluctuated. And they benefited from the late nineteenth-century policies of a Guatemalan government hungry for investment in agriculture and exports. New laws declared indigenous land virtually "without use," rendering it available for development by the newcomers. Even though Q'eqchi' Maya Indians had farmed corn and beans on their plots for subsistence living from time immemorial, they did not hold paper titles to the land; with the new policies many picked up their few belongings and walked through the jungle to new frontiers, but others stayed to continue farming their small traditional plots in exchange for employment with incoming European owners like the Sappers. The Germans, mindful of the benefits of a faithful labor force, generally treated the Q'eqchi' well and learned their language. Sometimes they married native women. When they had relationships with Q'eqchi' servants or mistresses, they might recognize the children of their unions.

Unlike absentee landowners who lived more comfortably in the capital while operating their holdings through majordomos, German coffee growers typically worked hard in place, hands-on. By 1890, two-thirds of the coffee production in the verdant north-central region came from land owned by Germans or German Guatemalans, most of it destined for the global coffee entrepôt, Hamburg. By the 1930s, their plantations in Alta Verapaz and on the Pacific coast provided some 80 percent of Guatemala's coffee, the principal export of Central America's largest country and biggest source of its foreign exchange. The Sappers expanded into processing locations, coffee exportation, a bank, and a string of plantations managed by Germans recruited from among friends and relatives in Europe. The names of the Sapper *fincas* resonated like a litany of prosperity: Cimama, Campur, Chirixquiche, Chajmayaic, Samox, Chajchucub . . .

The idea that a war being fought far away could mean catastrophe for her own sheltered existence never entered Maya Sapper's mind. More than seventy years later, sitting over tea in the room filled with coastal California light, she strained to put the pieces of that time in order. Her first hint of trouble on the horizon, she remembered, came in her mother's garden, blooming not only with roses but also with exotic specimens gathered from the nearby rainforest. "My mother must have had an inkling," she said. "One day she took her English friend around the garden and I heard her say, 'If something happens, please take care of my orchids.'"

As war loomed overseas, the Sapper children in Guatemala enjoyed riding their ponies or splashing in a square concrete pool on the plantation on the hottest days. At the same time they shared with their cousins in Europe aspects of a typical German upbringing. In the provincial capital, Coban, they attended the Colegio Aleman, one of hundreds of German schools in Latin America. From Mexico to Argentina, such a local German school might provide the best available education in town or city, adhering to the strictest German standards, with German teachers brought over to give classes in German to prepare youngsters for commerce or for the higher education they were meant to pursue in Europe. At Maya's Colegio Aleman, students also had to pass nationally required exams in Spanish, showing they were truly bilingual, with a grasp of national history and geography.

The colony that the Sappers called home was wealthy and productive, but it was only one marker of the influential German presence in Guatemala. To get products to port, planters built roads, which anyone might use. German companies built a railroad, an electrical grid, and a telephone network, which also served the general population. The Germans presented a contrast to Americans in Guatemala, for instance, who often came to take administrative positions in U.S.-controlled enterprises like the United Fruit Company and seldom ventured outside American-style compounds. Germans might love getting together in their *Vereine*, or societies, a seemingly infinite number of German sports clubs, beer-drinking clubs, volunteer fire brigades, mutual aid associations, and women's groups, but they also put down roots and threw themselves into the country's wider development because they saw its future as their own.

Germans in towns and cities ran a gamut of businesses whose signs hung proudly on shops. "Bornholt: Arrow Shirts, Stetson Hats, Fine Cashmeres"; "Topke: Ironmongery"; "Sommerkamp German Bakery: First Quality Pumpernickel, Pastries, Deliveries to Fincas." There were sausage makers, tea factories, breweries, tailors; purveyors of electrical appliances, camera equipment, and gramophones. Of thirteen businesses that sold farm and small-industry machinery in the capital, Guatemala City, in 1940, eight were German; most general merchandise and clothing stores were German as well. The capital's German Club, founded in 1890, was a social outpost for all of Central America, with annual *Carnaval* events and a calendar of galas including celebrations of "Octoberfest in Munich," "Fiesta of Sailors of San Pauli-Hamburg," "Winterfest in Garmisch Partenkirchen," and festivals named for wine harvests from the Danube to the Rhine.

German Guatemalans were an industrious, rooted immigrant community, with nostalgic ties to the past of their fathers. As the 1930s rolled forward, however, anyone who read *Deutsche Zeitung*, the Central American German-language newspaper, would sense a growing reflection of support for the ultranationalism of the Reich. Articles increasingly aimed to explain the development of Hitler's worldview and encouraged strict ties with the "fatherland." Columns lashed out at propaganda from U.S. news services that defamed the democratically elected Fuehrer. By mid-decade, *Deutsche Zeitung* was firmly in the hands of Nazi editors. As of 1936, all Guatemalans could tune their radios to news, chamber music, opera, and military band concerts direct from *Deutscher Rundfunk*, the

German government station. Even the Guatemalan national radio presented a "German Hour" with music and language classes.

The wave of pro-Nazi information and propaganda was partly a reflection of the global efforts of Reich minister of public enlightenment and propaganda Joseph Goebbels; but it also mirrored the views of the newest German immigrants. After Germany's defeat in World War I, more than one hundred thousand mostly young men came to Latin America searching for work, many carrying grievances at harsh treatment by the victorious Allies and admiration for the strong fist of Hitler. They were a world apart in their backgrounds from those whom historian Regina Wagner calls the *antiguos*—the older ones, men and women who arrived in Richard Sapper's earlier generation—and their children born in Guatemala like Maya Sapper's father, who never knew the defeated Germany. The *antiguos* had long practiced the tolerance for various points of view required in a new land. Friction rose between the *antiguos* and pro-Nazi newcomers, who were smaller in number but carried the force of attachment to a powerful movement.

Like many German Guatemalans who considered themselves Guatemalan, other Latin American communities with roots in Axis countries also had individuals who were perfectly assimilated, who might honor their forbears but considered themselves Brazilians, Bolivians, or Nicaraguans. And the communities had other persons who thought of themselves most as Germans, Italians, or Japanese abroad. The Axis "mother countries" encouraged loyalty even to the second and third generations, even outside their borders. German law considered ethnic Germans to be citizens of the Reich, period. Benito Mussolini (his parents named him after the Mexican reformer Benito Juarez) activated propaganda and cultural programs to maintain Italian identity abroad and spread Fascist beliefs. He aimed especially at the significant Italian population in Argentina. In Brazil, home to more Japanese than any place outside Japan, some of the emperor's "subjects" remained so fanatically loyal that when the war was over they refused to believe Tokyo had lost. Shindo Remei, an organization in São Paulo to which the most radical among them belonged, intimidated Japanese Brazilians who said the Allies won the war and attempted to sway ethnic Japanese in Peru. Members murdered at least twenty-three Japanese Brazilians.

Differences within such communities with roots in Axis countries were exemplified among the Germans in Guatemala City. In 1933, at the German Legation, members of the National Socialist German Workers Party (NSDAP) celebrated the Nazi National Work Day, extolling unity with the "homeland"; the popular German ambassador, an old-school imperial diplomat, gave a neutral-sounding address, but other speakers demanded allegiance to the party. Lutheran ministers newly arrived from Europe wove messages about the need to support the New Germany into their religious discourse. A fight ensued over the capital's Club Aleman, the German Club, with the Nazis attempting to take control of it from the *antiguos* in order to use the social heart of the once-unified community as a base for political organization. They took control of the Colegio Aleman, the German school, too, hanging photos of Hitler, and squeezed out Jewish children. The NSDAP opened its own "Association of Germans" that included Swiss, Dutch, and Austrian members—not just Germans but "racially" Germanic peoples—who greeted each other with a "Heil Hitler" salute. The party campaigned to collect money, clothing, and sacks of coffee for the Nazi *Winterhilfwerk* campaign to help poor Germans. Party associations hosted visiting German celebrities and lecturers, projected films and slide shows, and celebrated holidays such as the anniversary of Hitler's accession to power and the Fuehrer's birthday, creating a kind of cultural and gala calendar parallel to that of the *antiguos*.

Young Maya Sapper, enclosed by her family, was unaware of splits in the wider community, and only decades later when she found a trove of her mother's letters to an aunt in Europe would she realize what the family was going through in Germany. At that time in the late 1930s, she said, she thought her grandfather's vacation with them was "just a visit," a physician's long break to see his family. "In fact, he had troubles with Hitler, so he came to escape something—I don't know what," she said. Letters stopped arriving from Germany when the war began. Maya's mother, who "was not religious, but spiritual," stood under the moon and prayed in her way that those she loved would be kept safe from Allied bombs.

Maya Sapper was eleven when she began to feel the war directly. The family had moved from the countryside into Coban, the clean and pretty highland town that still bears vestiges of German touches in its architectural details, the names on its shops. "An American guy came checking out the school," she said, and soon after it closed. One morning Maya's mother woke the children saying, "We have to go to the penitentiary. They came with guns in the night and took your father."

The Guatemalan government, under the pro-fascist but expedience-minded dictator Jorge Ubico, who had benefited from U.S. support when he came into office, went along with Washington's program to physically remove key members of the German community, along with some who were not prominent at all. In many cases the United States did not recognize the difference between pro-Nazis and those who honored their ties to Germany but didn't like the Reich.

Washington's blanket suspicion of "aliens" in Latin America started early, and by 1938 officials were convinced of the threat of German and Japanese espionage, sabotage, and military operations throughout the region. U.S. secretary of state Cordell Hull called Axis penetration in Latin America a "real and imminent" danger that was "not limited to the possibility of military invasion." In Europe, Hitler had just taken possession of Austria and the German-speaking Sudetenland. The run-up to those events, Hull suggested, looked too much like what he believed was happening in the American hemisphere, where the Nazi threat was "acute in its indirect form of propaganda, penetration, organizing political parties, buying some adherents, and black-mailing others." At the Eighth International Conference of American States in Lima, Peru, the United States, Mexico, and Central and South America agreed to joint action to defend the states of the region from outside attack.

Guatemala declared war on the Axis on December 11, 1941, four days after the Japanese bombed Pearl Harbor. In January 1942, ninety-six businesses, shops, newspapers, a local railroad, and sixty-seven *fincas* belonging to ethnic Germans were placed on the U.S. State Department's Declared List of Blocked Nationals, a unilateral blacklist made up without consultation with the countries where the businesses operated, aiming at blocking "Axis funds" in Latin America. In July, 117 men from

Guatemala joined hundreds of men, women, and children from other Latin countries who would be deported to Germany in the next years, sometimes on miserable voyages with buckets for toilets and limited permission to leave quarters for air.

President Jorge Ubico was an unlikely partner for the U.S. program. As an army officer, Ubico had been governor of Alta Verapaz, knew the Germans there well, and often professed his admiration for them. Fond of wearing military regalia with plenty of gold leaves on his hats, Ubico took over the government in 1931 and became known as Central America's Napoleon for his dictatorial ways and haughty demeanor. A strongman who ruled with the help of a vicious secret police, Ubico admired Hitler and Mussolini. In this he was like leaders in Chile and Argentina—Chile sent its military to train in Germany, Argentina to Italy. Fascist regimes with their passion for order promised a model for the progress and stability lacking in many parts of Latin America, and legal fascist political parties grew. The populist Brazilian dictator Getúlio Vargas governed with his own version of fascism in the biggest country of the hemisphere.

But Guatemalan president Jorge Ubico was nothing if not opportunistic. He hid his personal leanings, and soon watched the U.S. Air Force begin construction on a coveted airport that remains the nation's international air depot to this day. He expropriated the *fincas* representing vast tracts of the country's most productive lands, turning some of them into state property, selling others. He took Helmut Sapper's land.

Why did the Americans want Helmut Sapper? Not only was he born in Guatemala, not Germany, but he did not participate in the 1938 shipboard voting held to approve the *Anschluss*. He was a known antifascist. At an event where others pledged readiness to fight for the Reich, he stood to declare that he was "not a supporter of the doctrines of Hitler." And why did the Americans fail to release him for months after the war ended? The answer throws light on an underlying rationale for the capture of many Latin American Germans: Washington wanted to eliminate economic competition from the most formidable non-Latin business network south of the Rio Grande, clearing the way for U.S. firms.

The U.S. Embassy in Guatemala City called Sapper and four others "the most important internees in the United States." In a postwar dispatch to the State Department, the diplomats argued the five men should be prevented from returning to Guatemala not because they posed a political threat—Germany had lost the war months before—but because they were so important among German Guatemalan businessmen. Sapper was the baron of the Alta Verapaz coffee plantations and connected businesses. The Nottebohm brothers, Karl—who considered himself a "pure Guatemalan," as the embassy cable itself reported—and Kurt, were also prominent businessmen and bankers, and, like Sapper, Guatemala-born. They were so wealthy that their family compound occupied an entire city block in the capital. Another of the "most important internees"—note that the embassy dispatch does not say "most dangerous"—was Hermann Kaltwasser, whose business sign in Guatemala City read: KALTWASSER: CHEMICAL AND PHARMACEUTICAL PRODUCTS, VETERINARY MEDICINE. Kaltwasser had been in Guatemala since 1914, and U.S. agents admitted they could find "no evidence" that he collaborated with Nazis, even indirectly. "Nevertheless, he was one of the main outlets of German products in Guatemala," said the dispatch. The fifth man, Martin Knoetzsch, the Nottebohm's general manager, had signed a public declaration to protest the Nazi party takeover of the Colegio Aleman. Knoetzch had delivered a list of Nazi party members to the Guatemalan government as an act of loyalty to his adopted country, another fact known to the diplomats.

The U.S. Embassy warned Washington that the return of the men to their families in Guatemala "should be resisted on grounds of their economic importance, although reliable evidence of undesirable political activities is lacking." Historian Max Paul Friedman wrote that the case shows how the U.S. capture and deportation policy evolved from being "an undertaking primarily motivated by the need to ensure security against subversion into a long-term project of permanently weakening German economic competition in a region long claimed as 'America's backyard.'" Latin American authorities willingly deported "owners of property that was easier to seize when there was no one left behind to defend it."

In highlands Coban, on the morning Maya's mother announced that their father had been arrested, the family walked from home across town to the jail, where they found others they knew already in the visiting room. Police took the prisoners to Guatemala City, a day's drive away.

"My mother packed us into a car and followed him to the capital," Maya remembered. They rented a room at a downtown hotel. For a few days, Helmut Sapper was allowed to visit, sometimes to stay overnight, as long as he reported back to police every day, until January 19, 1943. "Then, without warning, they took them. Later we found out it was in a plane with windows covered so they couldn't see out."

Weeks later the family discovered that Helmut Sapper was being held with other prisoners at the Kenedy Alien Detention Center in southeast Texas. Named for Mifflin Kenedy, a nineteenth-century entrepreneur, the town was once known as Six Shooter Junction—bar patrons on the main street near the rail line entertained themselves by jocularly firing at passing trains. Texas Rangers mounted on horses, lassos in hand, met the first internees as they stepped from the train.

In Guatemala, the government froze the bank accounts of the captured men and seized their assets. In a show of loyalty, workers on the Sapper plantations collected the gasoline ration coupons that still arrived for the now-silent machinery and passed them quietly to Maya's mother, who sold them to buy food for the children. "Kind people" gave them clothing, or a chicken, but shock remained. In the hotel rooms in Guatemala City, Maya convinced her mother to let her sleep in her father's pajamas. "I knew he was gone," she said. "I just wanted to be hugged by his skin."

Maya's brother Horst, barely a teenager, had learned about machines on the plantations and now began repairing cars and motorcycles to help support the family. Letters arrived from Helmut at Camp Kenedy with holes in them where U.S. censors had snipped out words or phrases. He hung his things on a nail, he wrote, worked in a kitchen, and it was always very hot. "Don't go to Germany," one letter said. With the Nottebohm brothers, Kaltwasser, and Knoetzsch, Helmut Sapper said he was fighting his circumstances. "We are going to sue," he wrote. The men charged they were being unlawfully detained, and in a habeas corpus challenge they demanded to know the charges on which they were imprisoned, or be set free.

After three years at Camp Kenedy, Helmut Sapper won his case and returned to Guatemala on December 24, 1945, giving his family their best Christmas in memory. With home and property gone, however, there was no way to pick up life where he had left it. He sold kitchen gadgets and cheap cameras from Germany door-to-door. Young Horst's repair business was thriving, and, taking a risk, he joined with his father in a venture to import motorcycles—they could offer guaranteed maintenance. Eventually Maya's siblings presided over a lucrative German import agency. Helmut Sapper, however, remained embittered.

When Maya was a nursing student in Canada, she fell in love with a young American doctor who flew to Guatemala to ask Helmut for his daughter's hand in marriage. Sapper refused. He said he didn't want his grandchildren growing up speaking English. (The couple eloped.) Maya returned to Guatemala when her father died in 1972, but she was not there when her beloved brother Horst was brutally murdered by un-known assailants in 1981, in the midst of Guatemala's internal war.

I asked Maya whether she, too, carried the kind of resentment that had made her father bitter.

No, she said, but she did take a stark lesson from what he went through. "There are times when you have to prove your innocence, in-stead of having someone prove your guilt," she said.

"The Americans didn't want business in the American continent to go on with Germans," she said. "They were in charge of the continent, the way they saw it."

Maya Sapper stepped from the room and returned with miniature albums filled with sepia-toned photos. There was her father Helmut seated with his children at home, a relaxed look on his young face. There was Maya as a girl standing outdoors in a light-colored frock before a steep-roofed house in Alta Verapaz.

Maya walked me through her garden to leave, toward a wooden gate. An overwhelming perfume of roses stopped me, the kind of deep, rich perfume you rarely find in roses today, the flowers peach-colored, volup-tuous. "They were my mother's," she said.

6.

IN INCA COUNTRY, CAPTURING "JAPANESE"

Throughout 1940 and 1941, Japan had evinced great interest in Latin America as a possible trading partner, and the guardians of the security of the United States viewed the burgeoning Japanese presence in the region with considerable suspicion. They began to weave a web of contingency plans for Latin America.

—P. SCOTT CORBETT, *Quiet Passages: The Exchange of Civilians between the United States and Japan during the Second World War*

The U.S. forced rendition and removal program swept more than two thousand ethnic Japanese from their homes in Latin America and brought them to concentration camps in the United States. The given justification for this mass abduction was to prevent a fifth column from sabotaging the Allies. But the real reasons went deeper.

Like Germany, Japan maintained intense interest in Latin America as a market and as a source of raw materials—Japan was second only to the United States as an importer of Peru's primary export crop, cotton, for instance. Just as the wartime U.S. blacklist struck at German-owned firms in Latin America, prohibiting them to do business, the Allies wanted to restrain competing Japanese enterprises to clear the way for the friendliest possible postwar trade. And Latin governments were ready to take over the blacklisted businesses.

Racial prejudice was key—the same prejudice that drove the U.S. wartime imprisonment of 120,000 U.S. Japanese residents, two-thirds of them born in the United States, without charges or evidence of wrongdoing. Governments in Latin America could see that Washington was incarcerating its own "Japanese," although they did not need to look to the north for lessons in racial bias. Latin politicians and elites often saw themselves as European—white—despite a mixed heritage with black and indigenous populations. In policy and inclination, many were comfortable with discrimination, if not hostility, against Asians.

The most important reason of all for capturing ethnic Japanese out of Latin America, however, was that the United States urgently needed "Japanese" individuals to exchange for Americans held prisoner in Asia. Washington needed trade bait.

During the war, the imperial Japanese interned some 12,100 American men, women, and children: 6,000 in China, 5,000 in the Philippines, and 1,100 in Japan. Some were diplomats who might be exchanged for other diplomats, one for one, in traditional fashion. Most, however, were businesspeople or other Americans who had decided to make their homes in Asia. The numbers included missionaries whose churches had not moved them out in a timely way, despite State Department warnings that hostilities were imminent. Or they had decided to take the chance to stay since they did not feel directly threatened. Once war started, diplomats and other high-value prisoners were among the first to be exchanged; but for U.S. authorities it was intolerable to think that thousands of other U.S. citizens and their families might endure imprisonment or worse at enemy hands. A way must be created to trade for them and bring them home.

Japanese residents in the United States and Japanese Americans were not an option to use for the trades. Even penned up in remote camps, they had more rights as U.S. citizens and legal residents than Latin American "Japanese" brought to the United States as illegal aliens. The captives from Latin countries would come under the control of the U.S. State Department's Special War Problems Division charged with the prisoner exchanges.

The State Department created the division in 1939 "to handle special problems arising out of the disturbed conditions in Europe, such as aiding in the repatriation of American citizens." By July 1942, its prisoner exchange program, which came to be called "Quiet Passages," had effectively cleared Europe of the American civilians who wanted to come home. The Quiet Passages with the Japanese were more protracted. They were complicated by a shortage of transport, overlapping responsibilities among U.S. government agencies, and the shortfall in eligible "Japanese"— such as employees of Japanese government agencies or Japanese citizens who wanted to be repatriated—to trade for the Americans. Secretary of State Cordell Hull thought the use of ethnic Japanese captives from Latin America such an excellent idea that he suggested not stopping at a few, but virtually cleansing the continent. He encouraged President Roosevelt to continue "our efforts to remove all the Japanese from these American Republic countries for internment in the United States."

More than any other country, Peru collaborated with Washington in sending away its residents of Japanese ancestry. Successful entrepreneurs and social leaders were taken from a thriving community of thirty thousand. Of the twenty-two hundred Japanese sent to the United States from Latin America, about eighteen hundred came from Peru. Many were the best and brightest of the community.

FBI agents, diplomats, and U.S. military intelligence personnel looked for Peruvian Japanese who might be security risks. Not everyone on the hunt was fluent in Spanish. Sometimes denunciations were accepted at face value from suspicious neighbors or business rivals. Peruvian Japanese say that FBI agents combed newspapers to make their arrest lists, seeking men who played important roles in Japanese cultural, trade, and self-help groups, even noting who attended social events. When detectives brought in the suspected subversives, there was little recourse to the law, although local officials were not above bribery to free a suspect if the price was right.

Of all the U.S. Embassy posts in Latin America, Lima may have been the only one where a diplomat with command of both Japanese and Spanish was assigned to scrutinize the Japanese community. John K. Emmerson, a native of Canon City, Colorado, had attended the Sorbonne and served ambassadors in Tokyo and Taipei before coming to Peru in February 1942. As third secretary of the U.S. Embassy, he wrote, his brief was "First, the expulsion of the leaders of the Japanese colony; Second, the control of their movements and activities; and Third, measures to counteract Axis propaganda."

In looking for "dangerous" Japanese, Emmerson engaged the help of a Chinese Embassy functionary. In the provinces, he looked for informers among local Peruvian Chinese whose ancestral home was at war with Japan, and who were often commercial competitors with Peruvian Japanese. Emmerson's assessment that Peru's Japanese were "dangerous, well organized, and intensely patriotic [for Japan]" supported the State Department's effort to eliminate an ethnic minority that Lima was glad to be rid of.

The Peruvians were so eager to expel their Japanese that diplomats had to turn down many of their suggestions. Nevertheless, it is worth asking whether, for all his expertise, the embassy's point man in Lima had been swept up in the fervor to find subversives where they did not exist.

After twenty months at the job, John Emmerson seemed to take a step back. He questioned whether the "Japanese colony" was indeed a threat. He wrote a hundred-page report that, among other observations, charged Peruvian officials with graft in connection with the deportations. The report was shelved, "for the sake of the kind of international harmony that avoids unpleasant truths," wrote historian C. Harvey Gardiner. Thirty-five years after he left Lima, Emmerson wrote of the Peruvian Japanese: "During my period of service in the embassy, we found no reliable evidence of planned or contemplated acts of sabotage, subversion, or espionage."

On Emmerson's watch, nevertheless, Peruvian Japanese "believed to be dangerous" were shipped out of the country, and others were prohibited from traveling, their telephones disconnected, schools closed, property confiscated.

Chuhei Shimomura, who owned a small import company, was arrested without charge, and there was no hearing. More than seventy years later, Flor de Maria Shimomura remembers visiting her father at Lima's forbidding Panoptico prison in 1943. A few days after his daughter's visit, with a thousand other prisoners, Chuhei Shimomura boarded the oil-fired steamer *Etolin*, seconded from the Alaska Packers' Association, newly painted with the word DIPLOMATE starboard and port.

"We went to the dock to see if they might have mercy," Flor de Maria said. But no one was released. Her brother Carlos said the picture of that day *"queda gravado,"* remains engraved in the mind. With their mother, they watched the ship "until it disappeared."

In the United States, Breckinridge Long, a confidant of President Roosevelt and chief of the Special Division, suspected that the Justice Department would object to thousands of persons being imprisoned on U.S. soil without due process. He tried unsuccessfully to convince the War Department to take over responsibility for the Latin American captives, and they remained in State Department custody. Long was right about Justice Department concerns: Attorney General Francis Biddle asked Secretary of State Hull to consider hearings for the prisoners when they came to U.S. soil, "similar to those given to alien enemies of the United States to determine whether they should be strictly confined." The Justice Department also desired to have one of its representatives present in Lima to "review the facts" as individuals were being arrested, "to avoid the task of detaining persons who are not dangerous."

But Secretary of State Hull didn't like the ideas. The embassy was carefully managing the process, he said. Biddle folded. The war was raging, concern for "due process" a casualty.

The wartime crisis of the Peruvian Japanese is virtually unknown outside Peru, and memory of their experience is largely disappearing or ignored inside the country. But those who remember portray a dark and complex moment, not only in the modern history of the Andean land but also in the history of U.S. allegiance to its own principles.

My family slept behind me, piled close
Like a tribe camped at some ruinous place
Then I placed my tongue on the wall
To leave a humid mark before we left

—JOSÉ WATANABE, FROM "WALL," IN *Flags behind the Fog*
(*Banderas detrás de la niebla*)

Luxury cruise ships sailing the Pacific today tie up at Callao, Peru's major port, and passengers depart for the museums and colonial center of nearby Lima, lush with history, old gold, and the ornate marble tombs of Spanish conquerors. Or they board minibuses to the airport, where they fly to Cuzco, two miles high in the Andes, gateway to Machu Picchu, the breathtaking fifteenth-century citadel capital of the Incas. They usually skip the port city of Callao itself, the center of Japanese life in prewar Peru, because now it carries a reputation for drug-gang violence after dark.

Walk Callao's streets by day, however, and you find a bustling city where *chalacos*—the nickname for local residents—go about their business with spirit. Long-distance trucks pull away from the docks and drive along streets filled with small shops and *chifas*, eateries that dish up Peruvian-Chinese fusion food. Young men dare to cross traffic pushing a wooden cart filled with plucked chickens, ready for market. On the byways near a busy business street called Calle Sucre, it is not hard to imagine the neighborhood the way it looked when Cesar Tsuneshige was born here in 1935.

"There was one Japanese shop after another," said Tsuneshige, a veterinarian. His father Makoto was a neighborhood doctor. Tsuneshige exudes energy, walks tall, and was impeccably dressed in suit and tie as he showed me around the place he still lives. "This is where the beer factory stood, and here was the milk shop."

In the first decades of the twentieth century, Japanese immigrants came on mostly rural labor contracts but often headed for Lima or Callao as soon as they could. They may have been working on cotton plantations or fleeing cruel overseers in Amazonian rubber camps. Whatever their path, in Callao they found a community where hard work could help them survive and often prosper.

A newcomer might set up first as a barber with only comb and scissors, placing a chair on a street corner. (By 1924, Japanese outnumbered Peruvian barbers three to one.) Or he might run deliveries for a general merchandise "bazaar," working first for room and board but perhaps— and this often happened—becoming proprietor of a store with its name painted on an awning. Walking about Callao with Tsuneshige allowed me to see its prewar past. I felt as if I were reading an urban palimpsest, where traces of what came before still seeped through.

"And this was my old school," Tsuneshige said. A door silently opened in the long white metal wall.

"I saw you waiting," said a doorman.

Across an open playground, kites in the shape of golden carp fluttered from the roof against a cloudless blue sky. The schoolyard had been dirt when Tsuneshige was young, but it was paved now, marked with numbered yellow circles where children were drilled to gather in case of earthquake. "When we came to school we stopped and bowed toward the *Dirección*, out of respect," he said, indicating the director's office. Inside, Tsuneshige mused on the years from 1942 to 1944 when his mates disappeared from the schoolyard. "They took the families away, and I never saw them again," he said.

The school director, a Peruvian who carries "not a drop of Japanese blood" as he told me later, entered and bowed deeply, Japanese style. "It remains our custom," he said. Just 8 percent of four hundred current students "are what you might call 'Japanese,'" he said.

"So much changed in our lives during the war," Tsuneshige said. His father escaped capture when a neighbor warned the family with hand signals from across the street that unknown men in plain clothes—detectives—were at the door. "He climbed a floor and jumped into the yard where he kept the gamecocks," then fled.

This school had been saved from government takeover by the same kind of quick thinking. When Peru declared war on Japan, word came that authorities had taken control of the Lima Nikko, the big Japanese-owned academy in the capital ten miles away. Directors at Tsuneshige's school hurriedly transferred ownership to a Peruvian staff member. When detectives arrived, the new owner-director introduced students and staff as "my clients." Schools like this one were a centerpiece of prewar Peruvian Japanese life, symbolizing roots in a new land, but also harking back to the homeland, which was retreating ever farther away in the older generation's memory.

Parents like Tsuneshige's father and his good friend Iwaichi Naganuma, who owned a laundry on Calle Sucre, founded the school. On a wall hung

black-and-white photos of directors who had served in continuous succession since 1926. Tsuneshige walked up to the wall and pointed one
by one to pictures of the school directors who had been deported to U.S.
concentration camps. They started with Iwaichi Naganuma, known in Peru
by his Spanish name, Luis, thin-faced, serious, with frameless glasses
and a trim mustache.

In 2016, Naganuma's sons, Kazushige, Kazuharu, and Kazumu, came to
my home in San Francisco, where they now live. In Peru they also had
Spanish names, and when they began school in the States their older sister
Kiyo gave them English names their teachers could easily pronounce:
Jimmy, George, and Tony. Today, however, they prefer to use the full
Japanese names their parents gave them at birth.

Kazushige, the oldest, told me he had retired from work at the Japanese Tea Garden in Golden Gate Park; Kazuharu had also retired, from a
job at a printing firm; and Kazumu, the youngest at age seventy-six, was
a graphic designer and active soccer coach. Kazushige and Kazuharu had
memories of many scenes of their childhoods, and over the years their
sister Kiyo, who died in 2012, had filled in certain details. It was clear the
brothers, the only survivors of seven siblings, wanted to keep the family
story alive.

The first time detectives knocked, Kazushige said, his father ran from
a back door and repaired to the mountains outside Lima with their eldest
brother, who was fifteen, because their father was afraid the youth would
be arrested too. They hid for days, then returned. The scene repeated itself until FBI agents finally entered the house and stayed, so Naganuma
gave himself up. Agents ordered him to report to the docks at Callao to
board a U.S. Army transport, with his family if desired—the Peruvian
government wanted to get rid of as many Japanese as possible. Parents
and children packed a single trunk. Little did they know that their story
would be that of almost all captured Peruvian Japanese, permanent exile
from home. Peru would not take its "Japanese" back.

The Naganumas told me their father had come from Japan to Peru in
1910 on an agricultural labor contract and sent home for a picture bride.
Iwaichi met their mother Isoka for the first time as she disembarked from

her ship; without words, he wrapped a watch around her wrist as a wedding gift. Kazuharu remembered the family's Callao house with its attached commercial laundry on Calle Sucre, "all hand wash, with big paddles and metal tanks and clothes and sheets hanging outside and a sewing room to make repairs."

In the 1930s, the lives of the couple, Iwaichi and Isoka—who often went by a Spanish name, Maria—were filled with work at the laundry, with children, and with tragedy, too. Their three-year-old boy, Guillermo, "swallowed a pin," perhaps a straight pin picked up from the laundry floor or a decorative pin twisted off his cap, and choked on it. The Naganumas' friend Dr. Makoto Tsuneshige, Cesar Tsuneshige's father, could not save him.

To hear them tell their story, the Naganuma boys thrived in the streets of prewar Callao. Spanish was the language of play. They celebrated Peruvian holidays as well as *undōkai*, traditional Japanese sports festivals. "We had a big yard," remembered Kazuharu. "A garden, dogs, cats, chickens." Their father built a music studio. "I used to watch people dancing, mostly legs through the lower half of a swinging door, because I was still small." Once a week Dr. Tsuneshige's wife gave lessons to the Naganuma sisters on the Japanese *koto*, an instrument like a zither. When Kazushige was lucky, his sisters might take him along to the movies, to see a Western like *Santa Fe Trail* with Errol Flynn and Ronald Reagan.

Once he saw an animated feature that made fun of Japanese, with a General Tojo–like figure wearing big black-rimmed glasses, "with buck teeth" and other stereotypical features (perhaps *You're a Sap, Mr. Jap*, from Paramount). "I went home and talked about it, but I wasn't offended," Kazushige said. "I was thinking of it as a Peruvian kid."

In 1947, the Naganumas, bedraggled and impoverished, suffering from tuberculosis, were released from the U.S. Justice Department concentration camp in Crystal City, Texas. The only one to return to Peru, briefly in 2016, has been Kazushige, to pick up the ashes of his brother who had died from swallowing a pin. During all those decades, Cesar Tsuneshige's family had tended the tomb of the toddler Guillermo. In California, Kazushige, Kazuharu, and Kazumu had the ashes of their brother interred in the grave of their parents. The young Guillermo's Japanese name, Kazuaki, was already on the tombstone. Their father had ordered it engraved, thinking until the end of the son he had left behind in Peru.

Before the Naganuma brothers left my house, Kazumu brought out a framed photo of his family standing under the sun in Crystal City where they had been incarcerated. The boys wore short pants and suspenders, their older sisters dressed in white. Their father wore large glasses, as he had in the picture on the wall at the Callao school. Their mother had pinned a flower on her jacket.

They were throwing stones. I had to help push my sister up the ladder to another floor—she was eight months pregnant. While they were downstairs looting the bakery, we hid.

—CHEIKO KAMISATO, ON THE 1940 ANTI-JAPANESE RIOTS IN PERU

The groundwork for Peruvian collaboration with the U.S. capture program was laid with growing Peruvian nationalism and racial animosity, with political opportunism and economic pressure worsened by the Great Depression. Many Japanese in Peru struggled economically, but others—and these were noticed the most—were prosperous. By 1940, they owned 15 percent of the country's major export production, cotton, a crop that could be grown on small parcels affordable for first-time entrepreneurs; a few companies became very large. Japanese enterprises were scattered throughout the country, not just in Japanese neighborhoods, and they served a wide clientele. The Naganuma laundry, for example, had the business of the Peruvian naval academy in Callao, with its steady flow of sheets and linens to be washed and ironed, a small commercial gold mine. Peruvian Japanese monopolized the barber trade, shirt making, watch and clock shops, bakeries. Sidestepping banks, they preferred to use a community savings and loan system called *tanomoshiko* (reliable group) that depended on a code of honor for timely repayment, and they were unlikely to go into debt.

Success bred envy. In the 1930s, Peruvians accused "outsiders" of taking jobs. A whispering campaign grew. Newspapers published alarmist stories charging that Japanese dairies adulterated milk, their shops

sold shoddy goods. Rising militarism in Japan spawned more vague, in-
flammatory articles claiming that local Japanese were agents for imperial reach, spies, a fifth column preparing an invasion of Peru with caches
of hidden weapons. "Japanese" could be in league with native Peruvian
Indians scheming to reclaim what was lost to them with the Spanish
conquest.

The most paranoid wondered what the Japanese were saying when
they talked, or what they printed in Japanese characters. What had begun as handwritten sheets posted in barbershops, giving news of community and homeland, had long since expanded into mimeographed
flyers, and finally into a host of newspapers and magazines.

The Japanese were outsiders in ways different from Germans and
Italians. They were not European. Newspapers warned against the "yellow peril." Public intellectuals advised that immigration should be limited
to those who would improve "the race." Anti-Asian prejudice followed
long-standing disrespect for Chinese, who had replaced black slaves eman-
cipated in 1852; slaves and the Chinese had worked in rubber and sugar,
just as the Japanese did when they came at the turn of the century. In the
1920s and 1930s, laws limited Japanese immigration and curtailed, or even
rescinded, civil rights and citizenship of naturalized or Peruvian-born
Japanese. The laws were politically popular, but the circle was vicious:
Peruvian Japanese kept to themselves more as chances to mix and assimi-
late slipped away.

On May 13, 1940, an anti-Japanese march by teenage students in
Lima sparked rioting from the capital to small cities. Neighbors, thugs,
and supporters of President Manuel Prado, who had made no secret of
wanting to see a Peru without Japanese, trashed hundreds of businesses
and homes. A mob invaded the house of Hijime Kikshi, who owned four
thousand acres of cotton, and looted until a policeman showed up to an-
nounce laconically, "There's nothing more here." Timorous Chinese merchants hung the Chinese flag from their shops with signs that read in
Spanish, "We are not Japanese."

Some defended their Japanese neighbors. "When the mob came to
my mother's dress shop, the neighbors came quickly, one hundred percent
Peruvians," recalled Carlos Shimomura. "The butcher stood in the door

with his cleaver, the vegetable seller with a stake. They put up the Peruvian flag." The shop was spared. Elsewhere, however, decent people closed their doors. Ten Japanese died, and hundreds more were injured. Police only stood by.

Eleven days later an 8.5 earthquake shook Lima and Callao. Buildings fell, including houses called *quincha*, made of cane and plaster and considered earthquake-proof. Walls of the cathedral crumbled around exquisite chapels and the black marble figures guarding the tomb of Francisco Pizarro, conqueror of Peru. In all, 179 people died, 3,500 were injured.

To the astonishment of the Japanese, Peruvians came humbly to their doors or stopped them in the streets to plead forgiveness for the riots that preceded the earthquake, taking the natural disaster as punishment from heaven. "Please Lord, I did nothing bad to the Japanese!" a woman was heard saying.

But the Japanese felt no satisfaction at the turn of events. The riots, tolerated if not encouraged by the government, meant a line had been crossed. Peruvian Japanese knew they could not count on support, or even protection, in their own country.

The riots didn't touch peaceful, semitropical Chiclayo, a city founded by sixteenth-century Spanish missionaries ten miles from the sea, the hub of trade roads to jungle and highlands five hundred miles north of Lima. "My father always told me when he was leaving on a trip for business when he would be coming home, so I would know how long he would be gone," his daughter Libia Maoki remembered. When detectives rounded up her father and other Japanese men from Chiclayo, along with a few Germans, Libia watched the truck drive away, and this time she would not know when he would return.

Whenever she and I met to talk in a coffee shop in a suburban strip mall south of Sacramento, Libia Maoki maintained a coolness and attention to detail of the kind likely required for the job from which she had retired, overseeing charters for a long-distance bus company. In 1914, Victor Maoki started a small café and opened a general merchandise shop for workers on a cotton plantation called Hacienda Tuman, she said. A photo of the time, still dear to his daughter, shows him dressed in a suit, tie, and waistcoat, a kerchief in the breast pocket of his jacket, dark eyes looking out from behind rimless glasses. In a day when convention mandated serious looks in pictures, there is the hint of a smile on his lips. Maoki traveled back to Japan to find a wife and married Hitomi, a nurse.

Hitomi Maoki was "shocked at how primitive everything was in Peru." She took the name Elena, and as the family grew with children she looked for ways to help expand business. She cut shirts from white cotton and sold them to laborers. When Victor's brother brought a contraption from Japan for making *senbei*, rice crackers, she created molds to stamp the top of the snacks with images of Charlie Chaplin, including bowler hat and mustache, and sold them. Libia pulled homemade taffy from a nail while her mother cut it to pieces and wrapped them in paper, distributing them to shops. Business expanded to downtown Chiclayo with a tire-repair shop, a wise investment at a time when cars were hitting roads still largely unpaved.

Some Japanese immigrants dreamed of saving money to return prosperous to Japan, but Victor Maoki planted himself firmly in the New World. "Father always said we should live like Peruvians," said Libia. "He gave us Spanish names. To him it was important even that we worship like them." He baptized his children as Catholics, and they made their First Communions. He organized construction of a school "with walls painted white, the classrooms open, airy, with maybe sixty children," remembered Libia's sister Blanca. "In Peru they were preparing us to be leaders. So it's really too bad they got rid of us."

The Maoki shops, even modest in size and far from the capital, might have been prize enough to draw attention from greedy authorities. Yet thousands of other Peruvian Japanese were not kidnapped, even when their businesses were put on the U.S. blacklist and confiscated. Why, then, take a man like Victor Maoki?

Maoki was the one who made the long trips to Lima to request donations of bricks from the Japanese Embassy to build the school. When someone in the community died, he handled paperwork and made funeral arrangements. Three of Maoki's children had died at tender ages and were buried in the local cemetery, but the remains of non-Christians, including many Japanese, were forbidden in the hallowed ground; so he obtained land on a corner of the hacienda as a dignified graveyard for those who might rest nowhere else. On a low hill he erected a sixteen-foot-high cross facing the Pacific, in homage to immigrants who arrived on the first voyages from Japan in 1899 and 1903.

A month after he was trucked away, a letter from Panama from Maoki arrived. A flattened portulaca flower, a moss rose, dropped from its folds. He had not forgotten his daughter Blanca's twelfth birthday. He had lost twenty pounds, he wrote, and become very thin.

There are no accounts of physical resistance recorded among captives at the time of deportation. But there was defiance. Men ran to avoid capture, like Dr. Makoto Tsuneshige and the father of the Naganuma brothers. When Victor Maoki was taken, he stood stoically with other prisoners in the back of the truck, as if they wanted to leave unbowed. "They said 'Banzai,'" an all-purpose cheer meant to lift spirits, said Libia. "And they began to sing." In the southern city of Ica, friendly police warned Seiichi Higashide of possible arrest by agents from the capital, and he spent six months entombed in a room he excavated under a floor of his house, a six-by-nine-foot secret living space equipped with only a tatami mat to sleep on, a shortwave radio, a desk, and a chair.

Higashide, a teacher who had come to own a high-end dry goods shop and presided over a businessmen's association, emerged from his hiding place when there was no more news of arrests and he thought the danger was over. But on the evening of January, 6, 1944, after a lakeside Sunday picnic with his family where they went sand skiing among the dunes, five armed men entered his house. What the thirty-five-year-old immigrant from Hokkaido had spent fifteen years building in his adopted country was about to be destroyed.

In a 1993 memoir, *Adios to Tears*, Higashide wrote that he was held at Ica police headquarters overnight but refused to be transferred to Lima in a filthy paddy wagon. He was allowed to hire a taxi—with a police detective as passenger—for the journey to the capital three hundred miles north. He stopped at a photographer's studio en route for a portrait to send to his family if he should not return. In the picture, a handsome, sad-faced man in suit and tie stares into the camera. Later, when American soldiers carrying rifles with fixed bayonets ordered him to strip naked for inspection, Higashide held on to one thought: he had committed no crime.

Most of those captured from Latin America traveled by sea, often in old civilian workhorse ships taken over by the U.S. Army. From Peru, voyages began in Callao or the oil-exporting port of Talara, the westernmost point on the South American continent.

Talara was important for a reason beyond its port; the British International Petroleum Company (later BP Oil) had been operating there for decades, extracting crude from nearby fields. In an agreement between Washington and Lima, engineers had just expanded facilities around the company airstrip to base U.S. aircraft. Deportees transiting at Talara witnessed the busy comings and goings of ships and aircraft, a welcome sight to Higashide's group of frightened, exhausted captives, who had traveled the six hundred miles from Lima over two and a half days in the back of an open truck, "like simple freight under the blazing desert sun." Rumor had it that they were being taken to a mountainous area where they would be massacred. "Matters were so confused by that time, it would not have been strange if that had actually happened," Higashide wrote. "The procedures and discipline of the Peruvian authorities had deteriorated to that point." Another captive said U.S. soldiers pushed his group onto the ship at the point of bayonets.

Nevertheless, some remember moments of grace at Talara. After a journey during which guards failed to provide sufficient food, Augusto Kage's father told him that ambulant vendors on the dock gave captives fruit from their trays. Kashiro Hayashi told his son Thomas that a U.S. soldier noticed he was limping oddly and ordered him to halt. The soldier discovered the contraband pen Hayashi had hidden in his shoe. "Please let me keep it," Hayashi pleaded. "I must write to my family." He kept the pen.

On the voyages out of Peru, forbidden from leaving the dank, stinking holds of the ships in which they rocked, prisoners assumed they were headed north toward the United States. But without sight of the sun or stars they could not know for sure. Higashide's ship slowed and stopped too soon. Hot air entered the hold, and speculation ran rampant. Where were they?

When the steel hatch lifted, the captives climbed a metal ladder and walked weak-kneed from confinement onto the deck. Disoriented by the light, Higashide made out a blur of palms. "It must be Panama!" he said.

> *We are the hostages*
> *Damn it, take us any place . . .*
> *Bear it, bear it, the raindrops whisper*

—AREQUIPA MERCHANT TAIJIRO TOCHIO, "SONG OF FAREWELL"

The first captives to arrive in the U.S. Canal Zone, shortly after the attack on Pearl Harbor, were met by jeering U.S. soldiers waving rifles. On shore, they received orders to construct their own toilet facilities. They cleared trees and brush in the tropical forest, providing free labor for construction of a U.S. military camp. They were forbidden to pause or ask for water; guards sometimes beat or kicked them, or jabbed them with bayonets.

When Seiichi Higashide's ship docked on February 1, 1944, things had not changed much. A U.S. officer dictated a list of rules in fluent Spanish and warned of severe punishment for infractions. Awakened at 5:00 a.m. every day, the men from Peru dressed in double time and ran out to formation, where they stood at attention to watch the Stars and Stripes go up and recite as ordered, as well as they could, the Pledge of Allegiance.

Bewildered and unaccustomed to the heat, insects, and rain, Higashide and his twenty-eight companions, including at least five naturalized Peruvians and two persons born in Peru, cleared underbrush all day with hatchets and machetes. The task was alien to most like Higashide, who "had handled only a pen or abacus in my work." The captives wore ill-fitting army-issue boots and fatigues that were too big for them. "I wished that the F.B.I. chief, who often spoke of the Japanese fifth column, could see this sad sight," Higashide wrote. It was "pitiful" to watch the older men strain at their work. Painful blisters bubbled on everyone's hands, and "when those broke and settled, new blisters again grew back over those barely healed blisters."

Their uncompensated labor violated the Geneva Conventions, the internationally accepted rules regarding noncombatants during armed conflict. But the captives were unaware of their rights, and the Americans were unwilling to tender them.

Higashide recorded the thoughts he had at night when he returned to the bunkhouse. From the time he was a small child, he had read "many books" about the United States. "I had felt that America was an ideal country that should be taken as a model for the whole world. Why, then, had that country moved to take such unacceptable measures? Where was the spirit of individual rights and justice that had filled the Declaration of Independence and the U.S. Constitution?"

A year after Victor Maoki was taken, his destitute wife Elena applied to the Spanish diplomatic mission that represented Japanese interests, begging to be reunited with her husband. "I heard that they did not want to use people residing in the United States for prisoner exchanges," she told her daughters, referring to interned Japanese Americans. "Instead they wanted to use the people arrested in Peru."

U.S. authorities called the decision of wives to join their imprisoned husbands "voluntary." But the conditions into which the kidnappings had thrust families, and the idea they might never see loved ones again, beg the question of just how much free will was involved.

After his father was taken, Augusto Kage worked to help his siblings and his mother, who was not Japanese but Peruvian, until "we were begging like mendicants." Agents who came to their isolated farm to arrest his father had said he posed a risk because they lived too close to the oil works at Talara, three days away by mule. Two years later his mother said, "If we're going to suffer here alone, let's go suffer there, and we will suffer together." Without belongings to pack, they were taken with only the clothes they wore, to a bleak stretch of Texas desert named for artesian wells long gone dry.

7.

INMATES, A FAMILY AFFAIR

*When we were passing through the Panama Canal, we could not
see outside because the windows were all blacked out.*

—KAMI KAMISATO, TWENTY-FOUR-YEAR RESIDENT OF PERU

The transports from Latin America followed a pattern. As the captives
boarded ships, officials demanded they turn over their passports, so they
would land in the United States as undocumented aliens, subject to arrest. Men were held belowdecks, while women and children squeezed
into shared cabins with bunk beds. Starr Gurcke, an American married
to a German resident of Costa Rica, reached her cabin on the U.S. Army
transport *Pueblo* with the couple's two little girls in tow and found its
bunks had been claimed. They spent the three-week trip on a stained bare
mattress on the floor in the muggy air—opening portholes was forbidden. In close quarters passengers developed fevers and coughs or blistering
sores that crusted dry and yellow.

Sometimes women were charged with cleaning toilets and other facilities. On the first transport from Peru, which carried only men, U.S.
guards ordered prisoners to launder the guards' clothing; on landing, all

had to sign papers attesting that they had been well treated afloat. Such forced labor violated international conventions meant to protect prisoners of war, but the only recorded objector—a man who refused to wash a guard's clothing—was sent to the brig.

Ships sailing through the Panama Canal to New Orleans braved waters where German U-boats prowled. The Naganuma brothers remember evacuation drills against possible submarine attacks; no attacks took place, but for children, any break in the confinement and routine was welcome. Mixed with relief at the drills, nevertheless, was the frightening memory of "soldiers with Tommy guns" on guard around the clock.

Mothers scrambled full-time to keep a semblance of order and comfort for the children at sea. When Starr Gurcke realized she had lost her purse, she futilely searched the decks for a comb she might buy to comb her children's hair. A sailor stopped and challenged her; she tearfully explained, and the sailor gave her the comb from his pocket. Overwhelmed by the generous gesture, she retreated crying back to the cabin. Angelica Higashide watched in horror as American guards threw her baby's milk overboard, can by can, and did not respond to her protests in Spanish; fortunately, a Filipino kitchen worker took pity and found her some milk every day for the rest of the trip.

Whether ships landed at New Orleans or San Pedro, California, the FBI handled interrogations and officially informed the passengers that they were under arrest for traveling without proper documents. The maneuver was "contrived" and "Machiavellian," wrote scholar Jerre Mangione. During the war, Mangione served as a special assistant to the Immigration and Naturalization Service (INS) commissioner and as the Justice Department's public relations director for the INS, and his brief included visiting inmates from Latin America at some twenty INS camps. One camp commander told him, "Only in wartime could we get away with such fancy skullduggery."

Captives and families were made to strip as attendants sprayed them with DDT. Adults were separated by gender, but children were not; the experience of shedding their clothes in front of strangers, then being covered with the white powder left females, especially, of all ages feeling humiliated. From San Pedro or New Orleans, trains departed for the trip to Crystal City, a center of the U.S. prisoner exchange program.

The train to Crystal City hurtled along as if it were traversing the wider world without being part of it, the windows of its cars blacked out. Inside, parents and children from Latin America huddled together, not knowing what might be next. Most were ethnic Japanese, but some were German, and some were neither, like the Peruvian mother of Augusto Kage, or Starr Gurcke, who had been born in California. Rumors had it that the passengers were destined for hard labor. Some feared worse.

Isoka Naganuma, surrounded by her children in the train car, "thought that it was the end of the family." Libia Maoki's mother looked around at two daughters and a son, at an adopted older daughter and her husband and infant, and was "convinced our family was headed for its doom."

Passengers on the darkened trains were already unnerved in the aftermath of removals from their homes. When Werner Gurcke's business appeared on the blacklist—he imported buttons, umbrellas, and Hamilton watches—his wife Starr put the shop in her name in a last-ditch attempt to save the family income. On the grounds of "several reports . . . from a source generally reliable," according to the G-men's notes on his case, Werner was thrown into a jail specially built for men the FBI called "dangerous." Werner Gurcke didn't belong to any party, but often such small businessmen were targeted on the basis of commercial, not ideological, activity. Both the FBI and the State Department were careful to make it appear as if the initiative for arrests came from local authorities.

While Werner Gurcke was in prison, police arrested Starr one night in December 1942 as she was putting the girls to bed. She was only "a sort of American citizen," said the notes on her case, and should be "sent to concentration camp with her husband." Police took mother and daughters to a holding center at the German Club, which was filled with other dazed women and children. There in happier times Starr and Werner had dined and watched movies or played tennis. Now the once-crystalline swimming pool reeked with foul odor—it was the only place to rinse diapers. In January, at night so fewer eyes might see, Costa Rican guards took the women and children from the club and the men from the jail by bus and train to the Pacific port of Puntarenas. After hours of stomach-churning travel, attendants provided children with canned milk, which many promptly vomited up.

At least after debarking from the SS *Pueblo* and being interrogated by the FBI in San Pedro, California, the Gurcke family was together on the train. Other women and children hoped to see husbands and fathers taken from them months or even years before. From camps in Santa Fe, New Mexico, from Kenedy and elsewhere, their men were on the way to join them, riding their own trains to Crystal City.

NOTICE TO THE INTERNEES FROM LATIN AMERICA

Question: *By what authority am I being held in custody?*
Answer: *You are being held in custody under the authority of the Alien Enemy Act (Sections 4067 4070 of the Revised Statutes of the United States) which gives the President of the United States power to confine and deport natives or citizens of an enemy country in time of war.*

—UNDATED TYPEWRITTEN MEMORANDUM POSTED TO BULLETIN BOARD,
CRYSTAL CITY DETENTION STATION

The trains squealed to a stop at a station 120 miles south of San Antonio, 30 miles from the Mexican border, where passengers boarded buses whose windows were not blacked out. The captives' first sight of their surroundings might have seemed phantasmagorical, endless vistas of shrub and sand. In the small town of Crystal City (population six thousand), the self-styled "Spinach Capital of the World," a life-sized statue of Popeye the Sailor Man stood, smoking a pipe, arm muscles bulging. More shrub, cactus. So lonely did the land appear to the first European to set eyes upon it, the sixteenth-century Spanish trader and faith healer Álvar Núñez Cabeza de Vaca, that he called the place the "Desert of the Dead." Five miles outside town, the U.S. Immigration and Naturalization Service had taken over a Farm Security Administration camp previously used to house Mexican migrant workers. The buses drove through a gate onto the 290-acre site, now surrounded by wire fencing ten feet high and marked with six looming guard towers.

Sometimes the Japanese Peruvians already inside gathered to welcome new arrivals, singing, alleviating the fear of women like Elena Maoki. Families were separated by ethnicity and housed each in a section of the camp—Japanese, German, and Italian—in single-family bungalows, or duplexes and triplexes with shared showers. Visitors and inmates remarked on the better quality of housing for the Germans, but the Japanese did not complain. Elena Maoki said, "They gave us a place with a common bathroom with our neighbors, but I wasn't worried, because they were all from Peru."

Opened in late 1942, Crystal City's mostly wood-frame huts were set upon stretches of dirt that swirled viciously in the wind. Biting red ants and stinging scorpions were all around, and dwellings lacked insulation against sweltering summers and frigid winters. Nevertheless, the pleasant scent of sage in bloom or of orange and lemon trees might waft through the streets. One of the jobs for pay available to internees was construction work in the camp, and soon houses with newer materials appeared. Captives planted gardens and vegetable plots with seeds they ordered from Sears and Roebuck catalogues.

As time passed, the place might have been mistaken for a suburban subdivision, except for the armed guards who walked the streets and manned the watchtowers. Every resident was aware that the penalty for attempting to escape was death. And strict regimentation meant that no one would confuse Crystal City for a settlement of free people. Whistles sounded three times a day for mandatory roll call. Censors read mail coming in and going out; inmates were limited to writing a maximum of two letters and one postcard a week, although as Christmas approached, cards from the War Prisoners Association with a picture of a Christmas tree were handed out for mailing.

Once the Latin Americans came to Crystal City, they became prisoners of war. The U.S. Justice Department's INS that ran the camp, the only one for Latin American families, was beholden to abide by international treaties meant to guarantee decent conditions: the First Geneva Convention of 1894 that established the principle of proper treatment for noncombatants during wartime and the 1907 Hague Convention stipulating the right to humane treatment, to sufficient food and medical care, and to keep personal effects. Prisoners, said the treaties, must not be treated as convicts or made to work on jobs of a military nature, and labor must be compensated.

Even beyond international treaties however, the State Department's Special War Problems Division had a very pragmatic reason for ensuring that a camp like Crystal City was decent and livable. The division in charge of the prisoner exchanges was convinced that imperial Japan would operate on the principle of "reciprocity." Mistreatment of prisoners in the United States, including the Latin American "Japanese," would be met with reprisals against U.S. prisoners in Japanese captivity, it was believed, and conversely, good treatment would help ensure the same for Americans in Japanese hands. "From the very beginning of the war until the final surrender, the Special Division operated on the theory that the Japanese government kept a score card of sorts and meted out reprisals for deemed injustices to Japanese nationals," wrote P. Scott Corbett, a scholar of the prisoner exchanges.

The problem the Special Division faced was grave. More prisoners were urgently needed to exchange for American prisoners under Japanese control. But the Quiet Passages operation would not go swiftly. Transport was in short supply because ships were in demand for the war effort. Staff labored over time-consuming interchanges with the Japanese, who wanted to be sure certain nationals were included on the prisoner exchange lists, just as Washington did. Overlapping duties with other government agencies and rivalries that went with them troubled the program. Even at its smoothest, the Quiet Passages were extremely complex, involving coordination of eighteen different agencies, from Customs to the Foreign Funds Control Office, and sometimes the Air Transport Command. Two exchanges involving thousands were successfully completed by 1943; for the rest of the war, the Special Problems Division struggled to arrange more. Meanwhile, side by side with some Japanese American detainees from the United States, the men, women, and children from Latin America had to make a life within the fenced perimeter of Crystal City.

The sun shines practically every day of the year.

—NARRATOR, U.S. DEPARTMENT OF JUSTICE FILM, 1945,

ON THE ALIEN ENEMY DETENTION FACILITY, CRYSTAL CITY, TEXAS

Ironically, although a prison, Crystal City offered bright possibilities for the young, easing the trauma of being torn from home. Kazushige Naganuma enjoyed his job delivering blocks of ice. "If I had said it to my father at the time, he would have flattened me, but for me it was a paradise." After the anti-Japanese riots of 1940 in Peru, the Naganumas kept their children home in an excess of caution, "cooped up with the cook and the nanny," as Kazushige said. At Crystal City, things were different.

The Naganuma boys attended a school taught in Japanese. At first, the language switch was difficult for children who spoke mostly Spanish, but they adjusted; many who were in the camp for being "Japanese" first learned the language at Crystal City. There was a school for German speakers, which Starr and Werner Gurcke's eldest daughter Heidi attended, and English-curriculum grammar and high schools accredited by the State of Texas for Japanese American youth, its teachers inmates from Hawaii. There were sports teams and cheerleaders, Boy Scouts and mimeographed school newspapers.

"Sugar cane and grapefruit grew wild, so I would grab a fruit from a tree in the grove or broke off a stick of sugarcane," said Kazuharu Naganuma.

During summers the temperature could hit 115 degrees, and parents had to wrap protective cloths around iron bedframes lest children burn themselves. But everyone could cool off together in a 250-foot-wide circular pool built by the prisoners on a swamp drained and cleared of snakes. A German internee surveyed the site and an Italian Honduran inmate, the civil engineer Elmo Gaetano Zannoni, designed the pool; camp administrators emphasized its use as an irrigation reservoir for fruit trees when requesting construction funds from the INS. Youngsters like the Naganuma brothers roamed as they wished, as long as they did not approach the dreaded fence. Elena Maoki remembered with warmth that the camp provided "everything for children," even judo classes and sumo wrestling.

Under the surface, however, the knowledge that they were prisoners never left inmates, even the young. "I was indifferent to the fence," Libia Maoki said, but the guards were another matter. "The machine guns pointing at us scared me." Libia's older sister Blanca knew their lives were no longer their own. "Before, we were more or less on top of the world, but at this point we just had to bow to everyone, it seemed." In Peru, their father's business had flourished; they had household help and a driver. Now their extended family was in line to be exchanged for prisoners held by the Japanese—to go to Japan, where they had never lived.

For young and old, life in Crystal City held elements of the surreal. Latin American youngsters and mixed Japanese Peruvian couples spoke Spanish among themselves, but the Japanese school, with its courses and events in Japanese history and customs, was aimed at preparing inmates for life in Japan. To call their looming journey "repatriation" was to use the word in an Orwellian way—many were slated to go to a country they had never known or had purposely left decades before to settle in the Americas. Some had brought mementos of their Catholic faith from their Latin American homes (Libia Maoki carried a small crucifix). But the presence of numerous Buddhist clergy set the religious tone for the "Japanese" inmates. Because they were more likely than Japanese Christians to maintain the language, perform traditional rituals, and stay connected with events in Japan, Buddhists were considered a risk to the United States. After Pearl Harbor, when the FBI listed groups deserving scrutiny with the designations "A," "B," or "C," with "A"—with which Buddhists were labeled—highest risk, Buddhist clergy were rated "A1," the label for the most urgent threat to national security.

The camp at Crystal City held four thousand captives in 1944. Awareness that the Japanese were watching—the reciprocity principle—and the international mandates helped to ensure decent conditions. International Red Cross observers, charged with monitoring concentration camps in many countries during the war, visited often. And inmates generally encountered goodwill among camp administrators and civilian employees.

If they wished, men and women could work up to eight hours a day at ten cents an hour. Each group—German, Latin American Japanese, American Japanese, and the few Italians—produced its own newspaper and elected its own "council" to represent it before camp authorities.

At her house in Santa Cruz, California, Starr and Werner Gurcke's daughter Heidi Gurcke Donald showed me "coins" of pressed paper used as scrip—they looked like casino tokens—to pay captives like her father, who worked in the mattress-making shop and the camp maintenance department. In a camp store, special food items and other products were available for the scrip. Besides pay for jobs, adults received $5.25 a month, children age six to thirteen $4.00, and even two- to five-year-olds received an allowance worth $1.25. A photo from Crystal City showed Starr and Werner, with tight smiles, holding the girls in their pinafores, their shiny blonde hair bobbed alike.

There were not enough jobs to keep everyone busy, but parents did not burden their children with adult worries. "What it seemed everyone expressed was *gaman*," Kazumu Naganuma said, using a Japanese term for dignified forbearance in the face of what is nearly unbearable. "Be patient, do the best with what you've got."

Nevertheless, many men especially became downhearted with what Germans called *Gitterkrankheit*, fence sickness. Some showed signs of depression. Their property had been confiscated, their assets were frozen if not gone completely, their sentences had no fixed end. Being captive inside the fence undermined a man's status as the head of the family. Children wondered what adults had done wrong to land them in a desert prison, treated like criminals. A Department of Justice film meant to showcase the place as a model camp features an attendant in white pushing a man in a wheelchair as the narrator says, "Ills were often imaginary, traced to detention, the fence, the loss of freedom."

The camp hospital—doctors were inmates—treated "malaise" and multiple cases of "threatened abortions." Some suicide-watch reports were recorded, including on two Japanese Peruvian mothers whose daughters, ages thirteen and eleven, drowned in a tragic accident in the pool.

In 1993, when Kashiro Hayashi was ninety-eight, he told his son Thomas that he still remembered the sensation of constant oppression, relieved only when he carried the dead on burial detail. Inmates bore coffins to a cemetery outside the fence. "It's not good to leave with a dead person and feel free," Hayashi told his son. "But that feeling of freedom is something I could never forget."

And there were shadows of the greater conflict that fell over Crystal City. Many inmates like the Gurckes steered clear of Germans who were obviously pro-Nazi, like Fritz Kuhn, called "the most infamous Nazi in the world," the former strutting leader of the German American Bund. At the Stringtown, Oklahoma, camp, the first arrivals—mostly hard-core Hitler sympathizers—elected a Nazi from Costa Rica, Ingo Kalinowski, as their spokesman, and Kalinowski hoarded Red Cross packages from Germany for his friends. In some camps, fights broke out between the minority pro-Nazi populations—estimates range from 3 to 15 percent of German prisoners—and others.

Jews—they numbered about eighty from Latin America in various camps—suffered "extreme mental anguish," as William Heinemann, a German Jew arrested in Panama and sent to Stringtown, put it. The prisoner exchanges were not always voluntary; Jews feared they might be traded for American prisoners of war and sent to German death camps. To protect them from Nazi sympathizers, authorities eventually transferred Jews who felt threatened to a special camp in Algiers, Louisiana.

After the war, some captives remained at Crystal City for more than two years; the bureaucracy to free them worked more slowly than the program that had imprisoned them. Seabrook Farms, a company that produced frozen and canned vegetables, offered work to inmates in its New Jersey installations for twelve-hour shifts at fifty cents an hour (thirty-five cents for women) at a time when military prisoners of war on private contracts received eighty cents an hour and rations. The inmates from Crystal City were given one day off every two weeks, no sick leave, no paid holidays. "Even for that time, these working conditions were considered to be severe," wrote Seiichi Higashide, who took a Seabrook job along with his wife and two hundred other inmates paroled to work in the plant. They replaced German prisoners of war. The job did not constitute bondage, but descriptions portray a life of unrelenting toil, unlikely to draw anyone but the desperate who sought escape from the place they lived as prisoners.

Others were able to obtain sponsors that allowed them to live elsewhere in the United States on parole, as long as they reported regularly to local authorities. For some the requirement lasted into the late 1940s. A Shinto priest and community leader in San Francisco sponsored the Naganuma family. The brothers, speaking English with a Spanish accent and looking Japanese, said new friends doubted their story when they shared it. "They would say, 'That could not have happened—how could they get away with it?'" said Kazumu Naganuma. "People don't believe it happened, it's not in the books."

From inside Crystal City, or later on "parole," some began the difficult pursuit to obtain legal status in the United States, even as they felt they were not wanted. In a scenario that resonates with Kafkaesque absurdity, U.S. authorities officially regarded the captives as illegal aliens for having entered the United States without visas or documents.

Some inmates took a different tack. Twenty-four Germans from Latin America launched a legal challenge to avoid being forcibly removed to the ruins of the Reich. The lawsuit in June 1945 argued that they were not subject to the removal measure as enemy aliens since the United States was no longer at war. They lost the case.

In 1945, most Peruvian Japanese wanted to return to their homes, but Lima, having partially cleansed itself of an unwanted minority, refused to take them back. And with homes and livelihoods gone they had little to go back to. Long deprived of radios and newspapers from outside, they generally knew only that the war was over. Hundreds volunteered for, or passively accepted, deportation to Japan, where they hoped to find extended families.

On December 11, the SS *Matsonia* carried twenty-four hundred passengers to Japan, including six hundred Japanese Peruvians from Crystal City. Only on arrival at the port of Yokosuka in Tokyo Bay did they truly understand that Japan had lost the war. Boatmen on sampans called out begging for fruit or cigarettes. On the dock, rows of women dressed in white robes bowed continuously while crying *"Sumimasen"*—"I'm so sorry"—in apology to the arriving passengers they saw as compatriots.

That night in a temporary barracks, where dead bodies were stacked in one corner—there was no gas for vehicles to take them away—shaken families planned trips to towns where they thought they might be taken in. Carmen Higa Mochizuki, a young teenager from Peru who didn't speak Japanese, watched her mother become virtually enslaved by resentful relatives on Okinawa. The island was a vast, wasted tract following the fighting earlier in the year, when almost half the population of three hundred thousand died.

Libia Maoki's family narrowly escaped the voyage to Japan when her father Victor was hospitalized with severe gout. However, the family's adoptive daughter and her husband, their toddler and newborn baby—the baby was a Texan, like 250 others born in Crystal City—did sail. Weeks later the daughter wrote to say that she had to comb fields for wild grasses to boil for food. The infant died, she said, from hunger.

The kidnap program leaves a legacy of questions about the behavior of a democracy in war. When and for how long can an authority deprive people of liberty without trial, let alone without charges? What right does a government have to reach outside its borders to snatch putative enemies? What role do race and other kinds of prejudice play in determining who is perceived as the enemy? The FBI would never disclose the evidence behind a prisoner's capture, so a captive could not face his accuser or offer a defense.

Some of the deepest legacies of the program are carried in the minds and hearts of those who lived through them. This personal legacy will die with the program's survivors, but while they are alive it often continues to simmer, or burn in their thoughts; each in his or her own way is affected every day by its consequences. Let one story stand for the rest.

When Chuhei Shimomura sailed away from Callao in 1943, his wife Victoria searched for something comforting to say to her children through her tears. "Your father is leaving. He will come back to you," she said. There was truth, and no truth at all, in her words.

A month later Chuhei wrote from Panama; in 2016, his son Carlos showed me the letter at his house in Callao. The envelope was stamped "Detained Alien" and "Examined." Inside, thin paper, elegant Spanish script. "How was my daughter's birthday? I was holding her photo and crying all through the night."

Carlos and his sister Flor de Maria, both now in their late seventies, spent hours showing me family photos and letters like the one from Panama. Carlos, an engineer specializing in fisheries, stood more than he sat, sometimes going to a shelf to pull out a folder or reaching over to the computer keyboard to bring up an image. Flor de Maria, recently retired from teaching Spanish literature at the National University of San Marcos, the oldest (established 1551) in the continental Americas, was quicker to laugh or sigh than her brother; she was a warm presence. I had met with them in the café at the Peruvian Japanese Cultural Center in downtown Lima, where they insisted I come to Carlos's house. His SUV possessed motion sensors all around that performed loudly in the chaotic Lima traffic. It was a relief to reach the home in a quiet neighborhood, to enter past a pond with a live turtle and climb narrow stairs to the orderly office.

A photo of their mother Victoria as a lovely young woman reflected her Japanese and Peruvian parentage. On Chuhei's birthday in 1937, Victoria presented him with a ring engraved on its face with his initials entwined, *CS*. The couple lived happily in Callao, where Chuhei's small import business grew until it appeared on the blacklist in 1942.

He resigned himself to capture—he had seen it happen to other Peruvian Japanese *comerciantes* whose businesses appeared on the list. On the day he expected the detectives, Chuhei Shimomura prepared a small suitcase and sat down to wait.

"He did not hide," Flor de Maria said, wonder still in her voice.

"He was samurai," said Carlos, referring to the onetime military aristocracy of Japan that was effectively gone by the 1870s, before his father was born. Carlos showed me his own business card, printed with a flowerlike symbol of samurai heritage.

Brother and sister told their story tag-team style, each filling in details. "These things should not be kept hidden, they have to be understood," said Flor, placing more letters before me. From Camp Kenedy, Chuhei wrote to his wife, "What will be the future for you and for my children?"

Chuhei wanted to request family unification, possible through the

Spanish diplomatic mission, but Victoria's mother had taken in the family and persuaded her that a concentration camp was no place for small children. U.S. authorities ordered Chuhei sent to Japan in exchange for an American prisoner. Victoria sent him a black-and-white studio photo. Before a wall painted to look like a refined drawing room, she sits gazing into the camera, lush black hair framing her face. She is wearing pearls and a dress coat, holding gloves and a purse on her lap, ankles crossed demurely above open-toed high heels. Carlos stands looking unsure, one hand holding his mother's. Flor de Maria stares from under a cloth bonnet, a small bag on a shoulder strap draped grown-up style across her coat.

"This is the last letter I shall write on this voyage," wrote Chuhei on October 21, 1943, aboard the MS *Gripsholm*, a Swedish ocean liner chartered by the U.S. Special War Problems Division. The ship had entered the port of Goa, India, where the exchange would take place, and he expected to be boarded on a Japanese ship bound for Yokohama. "Take care of your health. Don't take on heavy work. The war will not last long."

When time passed with no news, mother and children frequented the U.S. Embassy. "They treated us with indifference, as if to say, 'How annoying, how tiresome these people are,'" said Flor de Maria. "Finally, someone said, 'Señora, I'm sorry, your husband died in the war.'"

As adolescents, Carlos and Flor de Maria tutored other students to help their mother. Victoria remarried, but the man she hoped might provide support treated her badly, and they parted. "I heard her crying at night," said Flor.

In 1976, when Carlos and Flor de Maria were in their late thirties and Victoria past middle age, a bombshell fell on their lives. In the course of Carlos Shimomura's work at a government ministry, a businessman recognized his surname. He said he had known Carlos's father in Peru before the war, and knew him now in Japan. Carlos dined with the businessman at a Lima restaurant, "and for the first time in my life, I ate Japanese food." Soon a package arrived with a letter in his father's unmistakable Spanish script.

"He sent me this ring," said Carlos. He was wearing the ring his mother once gave his father as a birthday gift. "Look at how clear the initials still are," said Flor. *CS*, father and son, Chuhei and Carlos Shimomura.

"This ring carries much memory," Chuhei had written, the first communication with his son in more than thirty years. "I can never in my life forget that time, the flower of my youth . . . Do not take it off."

In 1942, when Chuhei Shimomura reached Japan, the imperial military sent him to serve in the occupied Philippines. By the time the intermediary put him in touch with Carlos, Chuhei had become a wealthy owner of portside warehousing facilities, living in his ancestral home with a Japanese wife and two sons. A few months after the ring arrived in the mail, Carlos went to meet his father at the Lima airport.

"From the moment he appeared in the door of the airplane, I said, 'There is my father.'" At Flor de Maria's house, where she had prepared a meal, their mother was waiting. "We all greeted each other," Carlos said, as if the moment had been touched with formality. "Then my father sat down and cried. I had never seen a man cry like that."

Chuhei Shimomura would stay in Peru for several days, but that first evening he made his good-byes quickly, unable even to wait for the meal, not able to talk. He asked his son to take him to the nearby neighborhood where they had all lived as a family. The two men stood outside their old house. It was eleven o'clock at night.

"Look, it's all just the same as it was, all the same!" Chuhei said. They gazed at the house for a while. "Son, do you know the song 'Caminito'?" Of course Carlos did. And together they sang the tango composed in Argentina and known throughout Latin America. *"Little path that time has erased . . . I live in sadness . . ."*

When one of their half brothers wrote to them of Chuhei's death in 1984, including with the letter a photo of his Buddhist funeral, Carlos and Flor had a Mass said in Lima. But the rupture that came with the family's experience of political kidnapping during the war had marked them in ways that could not be erased.

"My mother and my aunts told me that as a child I was always looking for my father," Flor de Maria said. Her brother's house sat on the flight path for Lima's airport, and the last planes of the evening seemed close above our heads as they descended for landing, making a roaring chamber around her words. It impressed me that, seventy years after the fact, the estimable professor looked bereft when she spoke of those years.

"They said I looked for him in rooms of the house. 'What time is Daddy coming?'"

Carlos weighed in, as if to calm the strong feelings of the conversation. "*Bueno*, they are the lessons of life," he said. But Flor would not be quieted.

"For thirty-six years, to need my father, every day of my life . . ." It occurred to me that even though Flor de Maria Shimomura had never spent a moment breathing stale air in the hold of a swaying ship, had never spent years surrounded by barbed wire or looked up to see guns pointed at her, she, too, had led a life captive to the kidnap program. As long as witnesses such as these were alive, I thought, we might still have a chance to hear of historical mistakes made in the name of national security, in a war remembered as honorable. But when they are gone?

Carlos and Flor de Maria Shimomura drove me through the streets of Callao to Lima, choosing a route along the sea. On one side, cliffs loomed; on the other side, lines of white foam caught headlights from the road as waves rose and broke. The emotions of the last hours had spent themselves, and brother and sister began to sing, upbeat songs from their mother's homeland in northern Peru and the melancholic but comforting tango, "Caminito," about the familiar "little path" once walked with such joy and love.

"Don't tell her if she passes by again . . . that my tears watered your soil . . ."

PART III

The Illusionists

New films broke with the Hollywood pulp tradition of featuring rough Hispanic characters in backwaters. The message: Latin Americans are worthy allies in the coming war. "DOWN ARGENTINE WAY"

Pan Am was the "chosen instrument" — designated carrier — for the U.S. government in wartime. It's featured in this Hollywood extravaganza.

Harold Seroy, Wikimedia Commons

"You too – Go to the Amazon" the government recruiting poster reads, to tap vital rubber for the Allies.
Serviço Especial de Mobilização para a Amazônia

Home-grown rightists like these Brazilian Integralists shared the "Roman salute" with Nazis and Italian Fascists.
Arquivo Histórico de Joinville

Iwaichi and Isoka Naganuma's children were born in Peru and baptized Catholics, with Spanish names and prominent Peruvian godparents. All were taken to a U.S. camp for "enemy aliens."
Courtesy of Naganuma family.

Heidi (left) and Ingrid Gurcke were born in Costa Rica to an American mother and German father. Ingrid stopped talking for their entire first year in a U.S. camp for "enemy aliens."

Courtesy Heidi Gurcke Donald

Heidi Gurcke Donald spent her early years surrounded by armed guards at the Crystal City concentration camp in Texas.
Mary Jo McConahay

Starr Pait married Werner Gurcke, a German, in Starr's California home, and then they moved to Costa Rica. The FBI said she was only "a sort of American citizen" and should be "sent to concentration camp with her husband."
Courtesy Heidi Gurcke Donald

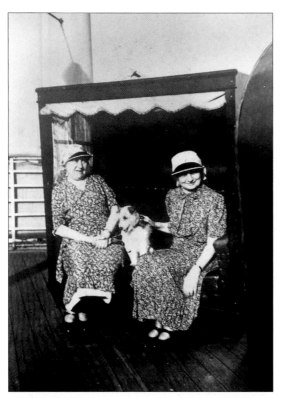

Sisters Gusti Collin and Betty Unger aboard the Jewish refugee ship *St. Louis* en route to Cuba in 1939. The Cubans turned the ship away. So did every other country in the Americas, including the United States.
Courtesy David Unger

U.S. authorities rounded up ethnic Japanese in Panama and placed them in Canal Zone tent camps. *AP Photo*

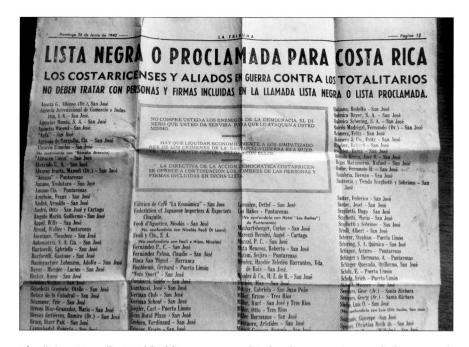

The "Lista Negra"—FBI blacklists—appeared in local papers. No proof of enemy collaboration was necessary. People sometimes accused others to deflect suspicion from themselves or curry favor with authorities.

Courtesy Heidi Gurcke Donald

"Brazil is Present in the Fields of Europe!" An expeditionary force of 25,000 Brazilians fought alongside the Allies in decisive battles for Italy.

O Globo, Rio de Janeiro

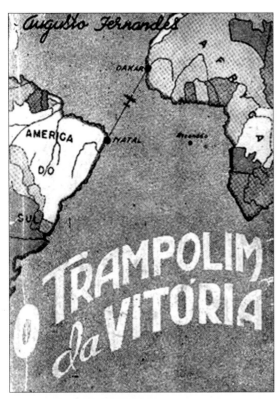

By 1943 U.S. naval and air bases proliferated in the region. Natal, just 1800 miles from the coast of Africa, was "The Trampoline to Victory."

Trampolim da Vitória. *Augusto Fernandes*

German spy Hilde Krueger enjoyed Mexican night life, here with (left) Cantinflas — Mario Moreno — and Spanish bullfighter Manuel Laureano Rodríguez Sánchez, Manolete. *Juan Guzmán, Fundación Televisa*

8.

SEDUCTION

The Nazi intellectual imperialism of ideas is just as serious a threat as the possibility of a military invasion.

—NELSON ROCKEFELLER, U.S. COORDINATOR OF

INTER-AMERICAN AFFAIRS, 1940

Young Nelson Rockefeller looked out over the extensive holdings that spread around his ranch in Venezuela, where the family oil business was well entrenched. Not yet thirty, Nelson directed a subsidiary of Standard Oil of New Jersey and controlled vast reserves in the country. Rockefeller was already an aficionado of Latin American art, a proclivity he received from his mother, Abby. And he did his best to speak Spanish.

On his 1939 visit to Venezuela, Rockefeller decided that the best way to preserve the status quo that allowed companies like his to prosper in Latin America was good public relations with host nations. But with war on the horizon, the image of the United States, its commercial interests, and its people were being challenged in these very places where Rockefeller not only had business, but for which he was developing affection.

When he returned to New York, the ambitious young man prepared a short memo with colleagues from other family businesses, the Chase Manhattan Bank and the Rockefeller Center, and had it delivered to President Roosevelt. Nazi propaganda and its infiltration into Latin America media must be fought, the memo said, fire with fire. The outcome of the three-page paper was the creation of the Office of the Coordinator of Inter-American Affairs (CIAA), which became known as the Rockefeller Office for its director—Nelson Rockefeller. The CIAA's mission: economic and psychological warfare in Latin America.

Working with the FBI, the Rockefeller Office contributed to blacklists the names of companies suspected of aiding the enemy or simply owned by ethnic Germans, Japanese, and Italians, cutting off their trade with the United States. After Pearl Harbor, the Rockefeller's CIAA was the engine behind an all-out propaganda blitz.

Even before the United States entered the war, Rockefeller hired staff in New York and key Latin cities for the CIAA. At first, said one former staff member, "almost all our efforts were directed into organizing the pro-Western elites of Venezuela and Brazil into a private network of influence." Soon, however, they set their sights on the wider population.

The Italians and especially the Reich through Minister of Propaganda and Public Enlightenment Joseph Goebbels were providing stories, including opinion pieces in Spanish and Portuguese—even signed "By Adolf Hitler"—for regional publications. With steady flows of money, sometimes out of Rockefeller's own pocket, the CIAA was determined to overcome the Reich's head start in spreading its own version of the truth.

Rockefeller reached out to Henry Luce of *Time* magazine, radio broadcasting companies, film studios, and producers of U.S. products from Lux Soap to Coca-Cola, making sure the Treasury Department gave an exemption for the advertising costs of corporations that worked with him. Advertising from these U.S. companies through the CIAA soon reached 40 percent of the total advertising revenue of radio stations and newspapers in Latin America, virtually supporting the media that took the ads, impressing readers and listeners with the pleasures and products that came along with the American way of life. Rockefeller mobilized a staff of twelve hundred journalists, ad men, and public-opinion experts, such as future pollster George Gallup.

The slick magazine *On Guard*, a typical CIAA offering, was based on the model of Henry Luce's *Life* magazine, featuring pictures by the world's best photographers. With the cover banner "For the Defense of the Americas," *On Guard* soon outsold the Reich-subsidized magazine that aimed at the same general audience. A typical issue of *On Guard* in Portuguese featured photos of battle-ready Mexicans drilling in Baja California and U.S. Army guards on watch at a seaside fort in Puerto Rico. An article talks about the "slavery" conditions of the occupied French and shows churches going up in flames at the hands of Germans—photos certain to strike fear into the hearts of pious Latin Catholics.

Rockefeller's most audacious counterpropaganda weapon, however, was unabashed glitz. He recruited Hollywood stars such as Rita Hayworth, Errol Flynn, Bing Crosby, and Douglas Fairbanks Jr. as "Goodwill Ambassadors." They hobnobbed across the continent with government officials and the social upper crust, appeared on radio, and gave interviews. George Balanchine and the American Ballet Caravan performed in Latin American cities for five months, premiering two productions that would become known as masterpieces: the *Concerto Barocco* and *Ballet Imperial* (Tchaikovsky Piano Concerto No. 2). Aaron Copland visited fellow composers in Mexico, Colombia, Peru, Brazil, and Argentina and oversaw public performances of his ballet *Billy the Kid*, which treats the bandit as an antihero and reprises cowboy songs. Waldo Frank, a socialist novelist and literary critic who wrote for the *New Yorker* and the *New Republic*, gave public lectures and interviews. Frank was arguably better known in Latin America than in the United States for his book *Our America* (1919), in which he explores a vision of North and South America united across ethnicities and geography to fulfill a common progressive destiny. As a Goodwill Ambassador, Frank endeared himself to the region when he opened lectures saying, "I come here to learn."

Nevertheless, a look at the lines outside cinemas in busy downtown Latin capitals showed Rockefeller that he might reap the highest return for investment and reach the most people by combining Goodwill Ambassadors with the most magical medium of the time—movies. For years Latin countries had railed at the cinema stereotypes Hollywood used to portray people who lived south of the Rio Grande as "bad hombres," greasers, slick Latin lovers who lose the girl to American he-men, women who were voluptuous but brainless, gunslingers, and some wizards who knew about witchcraft and potions. Instead, Good Neighbor films would portray Latin Americans as who they were, building a bridge between the Latin movie-loving public and U.S. audiences.

The CIAA embarked on a program of seduction by celluloid. Rockefeller reached out to Hollywood through John Hay Whitney, a refined millionaire from one of New York's best families and chief of the CIAA's Motion Picture Division. Together, "Jock" Whitney and Rockefeller recruited two paragons of American creativity as Goodwill Ambassadors to Latin America: Walt Disney and Orson Welles.

In the case of Welles, the appointment would be catastrophic. In the case of Walt Disney, however, it worked spectacularly well.

While half of this world is being forced to shout "Heil Hitler," our answer is to say, "Saludos Amigos."

—WALT DISNEY ON A HOLLYWOOD RADIO PROGRAM, DECEMBER 12, 1942

Brazilians knew Mr. Walt Disney before he ever set foot in South America—he was the father of Mickey Mouse. Mickey's appeal cut through politics. Word had it that George V, the king of England, wouldn't go to a movie exhibition unless one of Mickey's cartoons was also on the bill; Mussolini loved *Topolino*; FDR requested that a Mickey Mouse cartoon be included when he screened movies for guests in an upstairs hall of the White House. Disney feigned puzzlement and sounded aggrieved when he heard that the Fuehrer was not a fan.

"Imagine that!" he wrote in a magazine article. "Well Mickey is going to save Mr. A. Hitler from drowning or something some day . . . Then won't Mr. A. Hitler be ashamed."

In fact, Goebbels thought *Snow White and the Seven Dwarfs* was a "masterpiece," and once gave *Der Führer* a Christmas package containing eighteen Mickey Mouse cartoons; Hitler was "pleased to no end," Goebbels wrote in his diary. Goebbels' censors in the German Ministry of Propaganda did ban some Disney films, such as *The Barnyard Battle*, judging it "offensive to national dignity." (*Barnyard* portrayed an army of mice fighting cats wearing German army helmets.) But Disney cartoons ran in German movie theaters even as Hitler ranted against imported foreign cultural products. And the German public loved their *Mickey Maus*.

Mickey represented an image of Americans that Nelson Rockefeller wanted to promote. The Mouse lived in a small town not unlike those found in early twentieth-century Kansas and Missouri where Disney grew up. He invented can-do solutions to vexing problems, such as using Pluto's wagging tail as a windshield wiper in a storm. And anyone might relate to Mickey's dilemmas. Take the inevitable appearance of ants, squirrels, and dancing flies that devour *The Picnic* when Mickey and Minnie are distracted, or the menagerie of buzzing, humming, and crawling insects in *Mickey's Garden* that only grow larger when they come into contact with bug spray. Disney films and comics peppered the globe in thirty-seven languages. Their very existence was good propaganda.

Best of all, as a person Walt Disney was the kind of Goodwill Ambassador who stood for values that harked back to an imagined simple "all-American" past. Born in Chicago and brought up on a farm, Disney moved to California at age twenty-one, but in a way he never left the Midwest. He kept its Heartland habits of friendliness and plain living. His worldview was not overly preoccupied with cultural relativity or political engagement. Young Walt grew up poor, worked newspaper routes and lunchtime jobs, and didn't go to college. But he was more apt to attribute his underprivileged boyhood to his father's lack of ambition to rise above harsh circumstances than he was to blame the economic and political system in which his family lived. By the time he was forty, he was wealthy and influential. You would hear no critique of America's faults from Walt Disney. "There's enough ugliness and cynicism in the world without me adding to it," he said.

Disney was also a consummate businessman. His Walt Disney Studios was the Google or Apple of its day, operating on the cutting edge of technological advances. Boyishly athletic, although often found with a cigarette in hand, Disney agreed to come to Latin America, but he did not agree with Rockefeller's idea of a typical Goodwill tour. He wouldn't meet mayors and presidents or attend formal events, and he insisted upon bringing along a team to work on film ideas. He was already on his way to being a billionaire, but more than anything Walt Disney was a workaholic who once said, "We don't make movies to make money, we make money to make more movies."

That was all fine with Rockefeller and Jock Whitney. They agreed to underwrite expenses for the traveling film team that Disney and his people came to call El Grupo: the boss, his wife Lillian, fifteen writers and artists. Rockefeller also agreed to back two films from the trip for up to $50,000 each. Thus in August 1941, after a two-day air journey (no night flying) from Los Angeles to Miami to the Bahamas to Belém, El Grupo's Clipper set down upon the blue waters of Rio's Guanabara Bay.

The members of El Grupo strolled among crowds in the Brazilian capital and roamed tropical gardens, rode horseback on Argentine ranches, floated in the balsa boats of Lake Titicaca on the border between Bolivia and Peru. At night in Rio, they went dancing at the elegant Urca Casino with its stunning view of the bay, where they could dine on French cuisine served upon Limoges porcelain and drink from Czech crystal. By day they worked hard, thinking film with pencils and pads in hand; at the same time, they made themselves available to locals they met. A picture from *Life* magazine shows Disney behind his handheld camera shooting beachgoers while lying flat on his stomach—fully clothed—on the strand in Copacabana. In another shot, Mary Blair, a twenty-nine-year-old artist from Oklahoma, carves out an image of Mickey Mouse for onlookers from damp sand. One fine day on the terrace of the luxurious Alvear Palace Hotel in Buenos Aires, Disney donned his hat to mime the steps of the traditional *zamba* with dancers who arrived to show how it was done; footage by another member of El Grupo shows Walt light-footed and adept, the dance's signature white scarf in hand as accordionists play and artists around him try their luck with the steps.

Disney's warning that he wouldn't meet local lights evaporated. He good-naturedly played the role of popular guest at galas, nightclubs, and events in his honor. Everywhere they went, El Grupo sketched and took notes, photographed, and recorded the music they heard—samba on Rio streets, the urban tango and rural *zamba* in Argentina, the *cueca*, the panpipes and wooden flutes of Chile and Peru. Disney was unable or unwilling to learn enough Spanish or Portuguese to converse with those he met in the street, but he had other ways to communicate. He stood on his head for a gathered crowd or posed for pictures, sometimes surrounded by children.

"Walt Disney is far more successful as an enterprise and as a person than we could have dreamed," wrote Jock Whitney in a report to Rockefeller in New York. "His public demeanor is flawless. He is unruffled by adulation and pressure—just signs every autograph and keeps smiling."

The era of what political scientists would later call "soft power"— using means other than brute force, such as communications, to bring countries into alignment with diplomatic goals—had truly begun. Disney's journey also influenced his growing creative enterprise.

Before the Goodwill tour, Walt Disney had rarely set foot outside the United States, and few others in the group were well traveled. South America hit them like a sensual avalanche with its vibrant colors, lush foliage, and new rhythms in music and dance. Disney constantly recorded what he saw with a small sixteen-millimeter camera—the pictures show his artists on beaches, in traditional markets, covering their sketch pads with images of exotic plants and birds, and with renderings of details of Latin life they were seeing for the first time. They noted the way rural Peruvian women carried their babies wrapped on their backs; the way mounted Argentine gauchos hurled their traditional throwing weapons, called *bolas*—weights attached to the end of leather cords—and watched them fly through the air. Wooly Andean llamas were a new animal to them—they watched the creatures sprint and fall captured, legs tangled up in the *bolas*.

Latin America changed the eye of Disney Studios, a shift personified in the artist Mary Blair, who would shape the distinctive look of Disney for the next twenty years, from feature films to the Disneyland theme parks. Mary Blair's watercolors of the late 1930s showed dark, stormy skies or huge trees washed gray and black; in one of her first Disney works, concepts for a tale about a dog that would become *Lady and the Tramp*, Christmas shoppers walk heads down in the cold, huddled inside thick coats. They would be her last work of the kind.

Blair was tall and blonde and stood out for her appearance wherever she went on the Latin America tour, wearing wide-brimmed hats against the sun and fashionable skirts and jackets she sewed herself. Yet she was able to blend in, too, in a way, exhibiting unhurried interest in people around her. The proof is in the intimacy of the images she captured—local people carrying baskets of chickens and flowers on their heads, or waiting for customers in timeless patience before a selection of fruit spread on the ground in a village market. The new light in South America and rush of fresh impressions transformed Mary Blair's art forever, marking future Disney movies from *Cinderella* to *Peter Pan*. Intense, often dissonant colors—the kind seen in native Latin American costume—now came together vividly to tell the Studios' stories, beginning with the films that would come from the Latin America trip, *Saludos Amigos* and *The Three Caballeros*.

"Disney saw it happen before his eyes and instinctively understood that Blair's assertive art was in sync with the changing times and future projects," a commentator wrote. Her work was "modern." After the South America journey, the kind of softer-hued, fairy-tale art that inspired *Snow White and the Seven Dwarfs* (1937) was "out." Instead, "bold graphics, stylization and surrealism were in." The continent's color and vivacity would imprint the look of Disney images carried in the minds of generations.

For Rockefeller, Goodwill Ambassador Walt Disney left a good personal impression. He drew huge crowds when he opened *Fantasia* in Montevideo and Rio; he talked to hundreds of schoolchildren. Radio and the printed press had only good things to say, except for the Buenos Aires Nazi newspaper *El Pampero,* which groused that Jewish names were on the roster of El Grupo and editorialized against an alien "invasion." Now Rockefeller must wait for the films, but they would not come quickly. Within days of El Grupo's return to its Burbank studio, Pearl Harbor was bombed.

In Burbank, artists and writers worked on the first Latin American opus, *Saludos Amigos*, while frenetically producing films for the war effort. On December 8, 1941, Disney flew to Washington with storyboards for the first of hundreds of public-service animation products ranging from encouragement to pay taxes to collecting kitchen fat—in one short, Pluto patriotically gives up his beloved bacon grease for use in glycerine-powered torpedoes and depth charges. A 1943 Academy Award winner, *Der Fuerher's Face*, created to sell war bonds, showed how brainwashing worked: a frazzled Donald Duck is a reluctant Nazi, overwhelmed by demands of jobs for the Reich and by the effort of constantly saluting *Heil Hitler!* A cutaway of his skull shows his brain changing. In the end, Donald awakes from his totalitarian nightmare to hug the Statue of Liberty.

As the Walt Disney studios worked on *Saludos Amigos* and a documentary called *South of the Border with Disney*—perhaps the first of the now-familiar "making of" genre of documentaries—teams were also producing training films for U.S. civilians and the military. They carried titles as dry as *Four Methods of Flush Riveting* or as exciting as *Stop That Tank!*, about how to use the Boys brand antitank rifle. (Soldiers fire at Nazi tanks that blow up in a frenzy of noise and bright color; Hitler's tank ends in Hell, where he blusters to Satan about the unfairness of the new weapon.) At a time when U.S. companies like U.S. Steel and the Ford Motor Company reaped windfalls from war business, Disney declined to make a profit from the government films, which amounted to 93 percent of the Studios' production from 1942 to 1945.

In February 1943, Disney finally saw the U.S. release of the film made from the journey for Rockefeller, *Saludos Amigos*, a paean to Pan-Americanism that quickly became a box office hit. The forty-two-minute travelogue engaged viewers not only with its images and storytelling but also for its new combination of documentary live action and animation, a technique the studio would later use for films such as *Song of the South* and *Mary Poppins*. Disney had wanted to do a story for each country on the Latin American trip, but Rockefeller insisted instead on a single sweeping film, so *Saludos Amigos* takes its storyline from El Grupo's journey: artists and writers go off to tour corners of South America, their impressions on sketch pads melding into animations. In the first of four segments, Donald Duck is a stereotypical tourist who dons native dress and tries to charm a llama with a flute as he has seen a boy in a market do, with hilarious results; in the second, a small airplane with an ebullient personality crosses the Andes by marshaling all the gumption of *The*

Little Engine That Could, braving a ferocious storm and monstrous mountain to deliver the mail; in the third sequence, Goofy, a cowboy of the
American West, is transported over a map to the Argentine *pampas*, where
he becomes a gaucho, proving in the Pan-American spirit how much
alike we are north and south.

In the grand finale of *Saludos Amigos,* Donald Duck meets his match
in a cigar-chomping parrot named José (Joe) Carioca—a *carioca* is a Rio
native—who demonstrates the sights and sounds of his hometown with
Brazilian panache. A famous samba song, "Brazil" by Ary Barroso, forms
the soundtrack, sensuous and lively. Called *"Aquarela do Brasil"* in Portuguese ("Watercolor of Brazil"), the music drives images of magical quality: as a paintbrush sweeps the screen, blue watercolor drips luxuriously
to become a waterfall, flowers turn into flamingos, palm trees into green-
feathered parrots. The brush drips black and a huge bunch of bananas is
transformed into a flying flock of yellow-billed toucans. In a bow of respect to the continent, *Saludos Amigos* was the first Hollywood film to
open in Latin America before it opened in the United States. In a review,
James Agee called the film a shameful attempt at "self-interested, belated
integration," but audiences north and south loved it. Countries that were
not featured, such as Venezuela and Cuba, howled in complaint to the
State Department.

In February 1945, Disney released his second major film from the
trip, a musical called *The Three Caballeros,* in which animated characters—
Donald Duck, Joe Carioca from Brazil, and Pancho Pistoles of Mexico—
interact with live dancers. The formidable birds—Pancho is a red
rooster—get along famously, a metaphor for Good Neighbors. "We're three
caballeros, three gay caballeros," they sing. "They say we're birds of a
feather." Donald receives birthday gifts from "friends in Latin America"—
a film projector, a book that opens to a sojourn in Brazil, and a piñata—
sparking travels to Bahia in Brazil rendered in Mary Blair's strong
magenta and gold, and to Patzcuaro, Veracruz, and Tehuantepec in Mexico, where the caballeros watch traditional dances. Donald falls for gor-
geous Latin women, but his approaches are charmingly dissuaded,
recalling the phrase Agee once used to typify a Disney trademark: "sex-
less sexiness." American audiences hear, many probably for the first

time, stellar musical talent from south of the border: the Mexican Dora Luz sings an English version ("You Belong to My Heart") of the classic *"Solamente una vez"* by the legendary composer Agustin Lara, and Aurora Miranda, sister of Carmen, lights up the screen in a production number singing *"Você já foi à Bahia?"* ("Have You Been to Bahia?").

Stereotypes do not disappear in *The Three Caballeros*—they are presented as silly and harmless. Pancho Pistoles is not the "greaser" Latino of pre–Good Neighbor Hollywood, but he does pack two revolvers that he shoots off for effect. Jose Carioca is not an exotic Brazilian familiar with dark arts, but he does show Donald how to use "black magic"— some fancy finger moves—to restore Donald's stature after he shrinks to enter the birthday book. Far from a continent of danger and superstition, Latin America in *Saludos Amigos* and *The Three Caballeros* is a stunningly beautiful region whose inhabitants have much in common with each other and with the United States. The films' documentary images, animated characters, and captivating sounds made the Good Neighbor policy attractive and enticing.

Walt Disney's teams never pointed cameras at the poverty of people whose beauty and culture they exalted; it was not the side of the region Rockefeller wanted to show. That does not mean Disney or Rockefeller, or groups such as the American Red Cross, ignored the power of film to educate people about how to better their lot—even though the education did not challenge the political and economic structures that caused the poverty in the first place.

The CIAA's Health and Medical Unit enlisted Disney in its campaign to reach residents of inner-city neighborhoods and the countryside with messages about improving nutrition, sanitation, and efficient farming. The division drew from multiple producers to distribute films on behalf of Latin American governments and service organizations, but Disney's contributions, with titles such as *How Disease Travels*, *Cleanliness Brings Health*, and *The Winged Scourge* (how mosquitoes spread malaria), were especially effective because they reached viewers while entertaining. In *The Winged Scourge*, the mosquitoes' wings beat with the music in the style of *Fantasia*. Snow White's Seven Dwarfs put up window screens in an example of collective action. The CIAA's teams forded streams and braved dust storms to reach remote villages where they played the films in public squares, employing the same kind of sound trucks that the Bayer Company was using to exhibit German propaganda films in Brazil. They showed the films in police stations and hospitals, sometimes up to eight thousand times a month. Some spectators had never seen a film before. They might comment aloud as the picture ran, and applaud enthusiastically at the end.

The American public was happy to see the Disney full-length features at theaters, but questions arose among members of Congress about why U.S. taxpayers should be paying for other movies to improve the well-being of indigent people a continent away. Vague allusions to the Good Neighbor policy were not a sufficient, or candid, answer. The chief of the CIAA Medical and Health Unit, Maurice Feuerlicht, explained to one important constituency, U.S. educators, that "for strategic reasons the other American republics are important to our security." Films about improving health and agriculture were not just about their Latin audiences but "helping our selves in a justifiably selfish way." The Allies depended on Latin America for rubber, quartz crystal, quinine, bismuth, iodine, and foods that sustained and healed the troops, Feuerlicht wrote in a teachers' journal, the *Educational Screen*, in 1943. "Hence, the health of our southern neighbors is a powerful weapon in our own behalf." He called the films "our modern medicine show." Over the course of the war, they played to four million Latin Americans.

> *If you want a happy ending, that depends, of course, on where you stop your story.*

> —ORSON WELLES, SCRIPT, *The Brass Ring*

The propaganda mandate of the CIAA was to contrast the Allies' democracies with the totalitarianism exemplified by the Reich. In recruiting Orson Welles, Rockefeller's original idea was to use the radio star's deep baritone voice and significant oratorical skills to give speeches about individual freedom—radio reached wide in Latin America, even to the illiterate who were beyond the draw of the written press. The host of the *Mercury Theatre on the Air* seemed a perfect choice.

Orson Welles had taken to the stage at age nineteen, a strapping six-footer with jet-black hair and a talent for miming accents and dialects. At barely twenty, he was playing the mysterious radio serial hero "The Shadow," who possessed the "power to cloud men's minds so they could not see him."

To maintain the show's mystery, Welles played The Shadow anonymously, but he became a household name when he produced the radio series called *The Mercury Theatre on the Air*. He chose dramas for their effectiveness on the airwaves—the first was Bram Stoker's *Dracula*—and in 1938 he ran the most notorious Halloween radio program in history, his adaptation of the 1897 novel *War of the Worlds* by H. G. Wells. The show drew so much attention that the program attracted the commercial sponsorship of the Campbell's Soup Company, and Welles brought in stars whose names read like a who's who of the era's most celebrated performers: Katharine Hepburn, Laurence Olivier, Helen Hayes, Margaret Sullivan, Burgess Meredith, Joan Bennett, Lionel Barrymore.

President Roosevelt and Rockefeller wanted the propaganda of the CIAA to flow north and south, underscoring the concept of common ideals throughout the Americas. In Orson Welles, Rockefeller saw an orator who would give not only public lectures but also radio addresses heard in Latin America and the United States. His words would carry far, and they would be irresistible.

By the time Welles was packing to board the Pan Am Clipper to South America in early 1942, however, something had changed in his public profile. He was still the most recognizable voice on radio, but now he was also a famous, innovative cinema director. His first major film, *Citizen Kane*, was being hailed as the greatest ever made. *Kane*'s central character, a barely disguised version of yellow-journalism mogul William Randolph Hearst, played by Welles, was unforgettable. Welles's treatment of the Hearst character was unremittingly scathing; Hearst tried to have the film's negative destroyed, forbade his chain of newspapers from giving it reviews or ad space, threatened blackmail. Meanwhile, word of mouth celebrated *Citizen Kane* all the way to Latin America.

After the film opened in New York in May 1941, Jock Whitney met among the warm breezes of Rio de Janeiro with Lourival Fontes, the powerful and Machiavellian chief of Brazil's Department of Press and Propaganda. The wily Fontes saw a way to get some propaganda of his own from the CIAA's operation. Yes, the speeches and radio performances of Mr. Orson Welles would be welcome. But why not have the famous director make a film for all the world to see featuring Rio's legendary Mardi Gras carnival, the city's annual extravaganza of dance, song, and wild costumes, a production that would serve the purpose of introducing Brazil to Americans? And not incidentally, bring tourists to Brazil? Fine, said Whitney. Rockefeller agreed.

Welles stalled because he didn't want to leave the editing of his second film, *The Magnificent Ambersons*, in the hands of others, and also because he was developing a new project, *The Story of Jazz*, with Louis Armstrong and Duke Ellington. But Rockefeller and Whitney both owned chunks of Welles's studio, RKO, so in a way they were his bosses. And since Welles was under contract to RKO, Rockefeller strong-armed the studio into backing a South American film by the director to the tune of $300,000, another point of pressure. On December 20, 1941, with Americans still in shock over Pearl Harbor, Whitney sent Welles a pointed telegram. "Personally believe you would make great contribution to hemisphere solidarity with this project. Regards."

Years later Welles drolly told filmmaker Peter Bogdanovich: "I had been given to understand it was my duty." In fact, Welles was a patriot, and he considered the assignment a wartime contribution. He was also a personal friend of President Roosevelt, who once told Welles that he considered him "the second greatest actor in America"—after himself. In his farewell speech as host of *The Mercury Theatre on the Air*, Welles informed his listeners that he was going "to the ends of the earth as we know it."

What happened next has been the subject of controversy by film buffs and scholars for more than seventy years. Either the much-expected Pan-American film, which Welles titled *It's All True*, was never completed because Orson Welles self-destructed, drank too much, worked in disorganized fashion. Or it was never finished because he delved too deeply into his subject, was too true to his ideals, and found himself sabotaged by Rockefeller and RKO.

What is certain is that even as he worked on the would-be opus, Orson Welles embraced his mission as a roving ambassador for Pan-Americanism. "I come to Brazil hoping to reveal it both to those who judge it badly and to those who do not yet know it," he told reporters on arrival in Rio.

In a series called "Hello Americans," Welles shared the microphone with Brazilian celebrity entertainers like Carmen Miranda and Sebastião Bernardes de Souza Prata, a beloved actor, comedian, singer, and composer popularly known as Grande Otelo. "Hello Americans" went out over shortwave to the United States on the NBC Blue Network, predecessor of ABC and home of popular broadcasters such as Lowell Thomas and Walter Winchell. On April 18, 1942, Welles played master of ceremonies at a gala birthday celebration for President Vargas hosted by U.S. ambassador Jefferson Caffery at the glamorous Urca Casino.

"This is Orson Welles, speaking from South America, from Rio de Janeiro, in the United States of Brazil," he intoned for the U.S. radio audience and distinguished local guests, standing handsome and vigorous at the microphone in a white tuxedo. He suggested that borders were fluid, addressing "friends from Maine to Manaus, from São Paulo to Chicago, Rio to San Francisco . . . over a hundred stations in North America and most of the stations in Brazil." When he arrived in Rio, Welles had proudly told news reporters that he had been conceived in Brazil when his parents were on their honeymoon. Now on the radio, after the orchestra played *"Tudo É Brasil"* in fox-trot rhythm, Welles translated the title. "All is Brazil," he said, then added in a voice laced with emotion, "Oh! My Brazil."

Welles also sent the message that Americans had much to learn from southern neighbors. On a show with Carmen Miranda, he delivered a discussion of native instruments, demonstrating the rasping and percussive sounds of shells and drums. On the Vargas birthday party show, he sprinkled in Portuguese words and introduced audiences north of the equator to the new music that was driving the film he was shooting. "If you mix two words, 'music' and 'Brazil,' and stir well, you will get samba," he said. "And if you mix in some Brazilians, you will get the samba dance."

Welles had not been keen on the Mardi Gras movie idea hatched by Jock Whitney and the Brazilian minister of press and propaganda. But music changed his mind. "I went groaning with horror at the thought of making a film about carnival," Welles told Bogdanovich. "As it turned out I became fascinated with samba."

Captivated by the moving music, Welles frequented the Urca Casino, befriending Grande Otelo and other Afro-Brazilian musicians and artists performing there. He became hungry for knowledge about the country and hired researchers to provide him with information on subjects from mining to native costumes to slave revolts. When he had to leave Rio for Buenos Aires to accept an award for *Citizen Kane* and give an inaugural address to the newborn Argentine Academy of Motion Picture Arts and Sciences, he made the trip short. Back in Rio, he lectured on subjects from Shakespeare to the use of poetry in playwriting. He partied with the Rio business and social elites, charmed the wives of diplomats and Vargas's daughter, Ella. "AMERICAN LEGEND LOVES BRAZIL, AND BRAZILIANS LOVE MR. ORSON WELLES," read a typical newspaper headline. If Welles and Rockefeller had stopped there, the tale would have had a happy ending.

The movie Welles envisioned about Latin America, however, *It's All True*, exploded his relationship with Rockefeller and went to the heart of questioning exactly what a Goodwill Ambassador was supposed to do. Neither Disney nor Welles took a penny for the job, although they were giving up income they might be earning at home, so they were not beholden to Rockefeller for compensation. But how closely they were bound to the CIAA's interpretation of good propaganda was an open question.

Orson Welles wanted to make a film that would elicit feelings that people both north and south might share, using real events, a Pan-American epic to demonstrate common dreams and emotions, a spur to mutual understanding. Where could he start?

Before coming to Brazil, Welles had begun a film called *My Friend Bonito* about a Mexican boy who raises a calf and struggles to save it from the bullring. Based on the true story of a bull freed by audience acclamation in Mexico City's Plaza El Toreo in 1908, the film had already started production, and some scenes had already been filmed in pueblos that looked little changed from the turn of the century. Instead of a feature film, "My Friend Bonito" could be a segment of the Pan-American opus, he thought.

In the December 21, 1941, issue of *Time* magazine, Welles found inspiration for another segment. Four impoverished fishermen had just made an epic voyage from Fortaleza, on the hump of Brazil, to Rio, sailing for sixty-one days on an open raft called a *jangada*, navigating only by their own experience of sky and sea. With the raft captain Manoel Olimpio Meira, called "Jacaré" after his native village, a natural leader who learned to read at night school, the crew represented thousands of hardworking but indigent *jangada* fishermen without healthcare, schools, or death benefits, laboring for middlemen who took half the catch for themselves. The fishermen presented their plight to President Vargas, and in the face of headlines about the sixteen-hundred-mile voyage, he quickly signed a law allowing *jangada* fishermen to join the Seamen's Union, with benefits. Whether Vargas acted to boost his populist image or because he wanted to correct an injustice didn't matter to Welles, to whom the raft captain Manoel Jacaré was a heroic figure. The extraordinary episode would anchor a segment Welles called "Jangadeiros."

Welles decided the opus would begin with "My Friend Bonito" and "Jangadeiros" in evocative black and white, and burst into color with the capstone of the film, the desired grand "Carnaval." Alongside his Goodwill Ambassador duties, Welles started the Rio extravaganza segment as soon as he arrived. From the beginning, however, nothing was easy about filming in Brazil.

On February 8, 1942, when the Pan Am Clipper and a U.S. Army bomber landed Welles and his crew of forty at Rio, the Mardi Gras festivities were already under way. Carnaval is like a tidal wave—it doesn't stop for anyone—and there was no time to scout locations or even to get oriented to the new place. Lighting equipment hadn't arrived, so the crew borrowed airplane landing lights from the Brazilian army to illuminate the nights, when much of the action took place. "Carnaval"—the Portuguese spelling—would be the first Technicolor film shot on location outside the United States, with the vibrant colors seen in *Gone with the Wind* and the *Wizard of Oz* given a new dimension in the streets and glittering dance clubs of Rio. But Technicolor cameras were a burden, too; Hollywood crews were unaccustomed to working abroad with any kind of equipment, let alone the heavy thirty-five-millimeter cameras required by the new process. One crew member griped in a letter to RKO headquarters of "the hot weather, the bad food and the impossibility of operating in an efficient Hollywood manner."

As Welles and his crew tried to cope with disorienting new ways, a terrible human tragedy occurred. In May 1942, Manoel Jacaré willingly accepted Welles's invitation to fly to Rio with his men from the *jangada* to reenact their December arrival on the raft. On a calm day when a small number of the crew was filming, the *jangada* inexplicably turned over. Three of the men survived, but Jacaré, the captain and charismatic activist, drowned. Welles was devastated. He made sure money reached Jacaré's widow and ten children. But nothing, it seemed, could assuage his feelings of guilt. Voices in the press blamed him for the death of the man who had become a national hero.

And trouble kept coming from RKO, and from certain Brazilians. They were alarmed about the places Welles frequented and friends he made, like the composer Herivelto Martins, whose "Golden Trio" included the prominent black singer Nilo Chagas, and Otelo Grande, who also was black. The RKO representative on the trip complained to the home office in a letter that Welles "ordered day and night shots in some very dirty and disreputable nigger neighborhoods throughout the city." A few days later, the representative reported, "We had a very full week as far as shooting goes. However, the stuff itself is just carnival nigger singing and dancing, of which we already have piles."

By day, Welles visited the favelas of Rio to film with Martins and Grande, and he drank with them long into the night. At a party at the Urca Casino, he asked for his friends and was told they were not allowed inside the casino for the social event. Welles searched nearby bars until he found Martins and Otelo Grande. "We drank until three o'clock in the morning," Grande told a Welles biographer. He said Welles told them, "Tonight we drink black beer."

•   •   •

The longer he spent in Rio, the more Orson Welles believed that the music that inspired, inflamed, and lifted Carnaval was born from the favela experience, resonating with African rhythms, just as jazz had been born in the black neighborhoods of New Orleans. Lourival Fontes and his Department of Press and Propaganda and the U.S. Embassy looked askance at Welles spending so much time in the shantytowns.

"The carnival for him was essentially a black story—a story of Brazilian music started in black communities in the slums," said Richard Wilson, Welles's assistant director, in a 1993 documentary about the abortive making of *It's All True*. But the black face of Brazil was the last thing that official Brazil, and the glamorous women and men who had been consorting with Welles, wanted to see representing their country before the world, and they made their displeasure known to U.S. diplomats.

By April 1942, Grande Otelo and others were filming on newly built soundstages in Rio, re-creating pieces of the music and life of the carnival for splicing into the documentary-style footage crews had captured on arrival. Every week, Welles sent the reels of raw footage to the studio. He was enthusiastic about "micro-sequences" that opened windows on "carnival's myriad forms of human interplay," showing how the spirit of the celebration brought people of different colors and different economic classes together, a metaphor for Pan-Americanism.

Away from the filmmaking, fears crested that Welles had gone dangerously off track. His movie was lionizing Latin Americans who were working class, the *jangadeiros*, and the Afro-Brazilians of the favelas. "The Brazilian establishment started to boycott the film and influenced RKO to do the same," said Wilson. The studio cut funds and stopped sending raw stock.

It is difficult to believe that Nelson Rockefeller and Jock Whitney, or RKO, did not know what they were getting when they recruited Orson Welles to make a film in Brazil. From the beginning of his career, black culture and labor rights had figured in his work. At age twenty, Welles directed the "Voodoo *Macbeth*" as it is commonly called, a version of Shakespeare's play with an entirely African American cast, the locus changed from Scotland to the Caribbean, with Haitian *vodou* replacing Scottish witchcraft. "Voodoo *Macbeth*" threw a spotlight on African

American theater and marked its director as an unpredictable genius. He produced a stage adaptation of *Native Son*, Richard Wright's coming-of-age novel about a poor black youth growing up in Chicago. He directed *The Cradle Will Rock*, the Brechtian opera by Marc Blitzstein about union organizing, religious hypocrisy, and corporate greed in "Steeltown, USA." The *New York Times* called it "the best thing militant labor has put into the theatre yet."

At the same time, Orson Welles might have been forewarned about Rockefeller had he considered the millionaire's behavior toward another idiosyncratic artist, the muralist Diego Rivera. In 1932, Rockefeller persuaded Rivera, one of Mexico's best-known painters and a favorite of Rockefeller's mother, Abby, to create a huge mural in the lobby of Rockefeller Center on the theme "Man at the Crossroads." The work was meant to spark thinking, to look ahead at the scientific, industrial, and social potentials of the unfolding twentieth century, and Rivera worked on it for months. Rockefeller was uncomfortable when he saw that Rivera pictured Vladimir Lenin leading a workers' May Day parade, and suggested he replace the revolutionary communist leader's face with that of an ordinary laborer. Rivera declined, offering to add Abraham Lincoln elsewhere in the composition, but that was not enough for Rockefeller, who called the Mexican artist down from the scaffold. In 1934 Rockefeller ordered the work demolished.

RKO fired Welles. As Welles saw the calamity in Rio, a cowardly Rockefeller had allowed the Brazilians and the RKO executives to scuttle *It's All True* even before its reels had been edited into a proper picture. Rockefeller knew how the director felt about him, describing Welles later as "a brilliant, austere, somewhat pompous but greatly respected man who really hated my guts." Welles expressed his opinion of Rockefeller in the 1947 noir thriller *The Lady from Shanghai*. He created the slimy, despicable George Grisby character as a rendition of the CIAA chief, complete with Rockefeller's telltale faux-casual mannerism of calling everybody "fellah."

Tantalizing bits of *It's All True* remain. From "My Friend Bonito," there are stark desert landscapes around the Mexican village where the boy raises his bull, footage of a timeless church and village, a remarkable sequence of the traditional rite of the blessing of the animals. The "Jangadeiros" segment, in a forty-minute version called *Four Men and a Raft*, shows the fishermen crafting their open vessel from tree to timber with handmade tools; they ride the waves in shots so layered and deep they look painted, not filmed. Almost all the "Carnaval" segment footage disappeared after being sent to RKO—Hollywood legend has it the studio dumped it into the Pacific. But Welles's synopsis and notes, held at Indiana University, and descriptions in documentaries by crew and cast such as Richard Wilson and Grande Otelo, depict a tour de force that captured the grandest displays and smallest gestures of dancers, singers, and costumed celebrants, from shantytown pathways to luxurious dance palaces, all united and woven through with the music of samba, alive and unending. *It's All True* may be one of the richest and most beautiful films never made.

Twenty years before the civil rights movement in the United States, Disney's sleek features ignored the presence of black and mixed-race Latin Americans. (His less-seen 1944 travel documentary, *The Amazon Awakens*, did show them.) For Welles, the black experience was the key to the Brazilian culture he wished to share.

In a 1993 television documentary, an aging Grande Otelo said that his old friend Welles "showed Brazil as it really was. He came to love not only Brazil but all of humanity through the mixture of races he saw here." Disney's beauty shots and cartoon characters do not leave the audience with an impression of Latin cultural depth. But they were very entertaining, and made the people of Latin America look friendly.

Millions saw the Disney version of the continent. For Rockefeller, that was good propaganda, and that was success.

9.

SPIES, MASTERS OF SPIES

The espionage war in Latin America was a duel between two spymasters who could not have been more different. The enigmatic Admiral Wilhelm Canaris of the Reich's intelligence agency, the *Abwehr,* was a cosmopolitan, skillful and daring. The FBI's methodical J. Edgar Hoover, the stern face of U.S. crime-fighting, never traveled abroad but laid down an ultimately effective system of international G-men. Each managed hundreds of agents. For much of the war, the Germans held the strongest hand.

In 1939 when Hitler annexed Czechoslovakia and invaded Poland, President Franklin Roosevelt's greatest fear was that Nazi subversion in Latin America would threaten the security of the United States. However, no proper spy network existed to track Nazi activities in the region. William "Intrepid" Stephenson's British Security Coordination (BSC), with its mission to convince Washington to join the war, to spread propaganda, and to gather intelligence in the Americas, was not established in its Rockefeller Center offices until May 1940.

And the United States lagged behind in foreign espionage thanks partly to old-fashioned politesse. In 1929, U.S. secretary of state Henry L. Stimson shut down the U.S. Cipher Bureau, known as the Black Chamber. Forerunner of the National Security Agency, the Black Chamber had been in charge of breaking the diplomatic codes of other countries. "Gentlemen do not read each other's mail," Stimson declared.

Hitler's spies had no such compunctions.

Canaris's *Abwehr* agents met with their Japanese counterparts in Mexico in 1936. Three years later the Reich's Latin American spy network was functioning on the ground.

Imagine a Mexico City salon on any given evening in the years before Pearl Harbor; well-dressed men and women speak a mix of Spanish, German, and English, drinking, laughing, occasionally whispering. Look around the room and you'd be unlikely to see American or British intelligence agents prying information from Mexican notables or foreign diplomats.

But you would see others working on behalf of Canaris's *Abwehr*, such as the vivacious blonde movie actress Hilda Kruger. In Germany, Kruger had been an intimate of Joseph Goebbels, Reich minister of propaganda. She headed for the New World after reportedly being pushed out of the picture by Goebbels's formidable wife, Magda.

Kruger stopped in San Francisco long enough to have an affair with an heir to a beer fortune and turn down his marriage proposal before continuing south to Hollywood, where she hoped to make a name for herself in American movies. Her poor English kept her from getting good roles, but in Hollywood she met billionaire oilman John Paul Getty, who became a frequent escort. They traveled together to Mexico City, where the glamorous German became the toast of the town. She also became the lover of more than one cabinet minister, including Miguel Aleman, who would be elected president in 1944. Pillow talk became reportable intelligence.

Kruger's fellow Reich spies were equally colorful. The *Abwehr* Mexico chief was tall, blonde Georg Nicolaus, code name "Max." A son of the director of Deutsche Bank in Berlin, "Max" had worked in banking in Colombia and as an engineer in Ecuador, and spoke perfect Spanish. In Germany he trained in telegraph communication and chemical formulas to make explosives. In Mexico, however, Georg Nicolaus was not likely to receive orders to explode anything, as both Admiral Canaris and the

German Foreign Office frowned upon violent covert actions that might undermine the neutrality of Latin nations. But his telegraph skills were well used.

"Max" reached out deftly from Mexico City to connect with German spies throughout Central and South America. He also controlled two *Abwehr* agents in the United States, who culled openly available publications, translated and collated the information, and sent it to him for dispatch to Germany. Four additional contacts "north of the border," "Max" told Berlin, provided him with a stream of classified materials on U.S. bombers and fighter planes, on production levels of oil, aluminum, and steel.

Friedrich Karl von Schlebrügge, code name "Morris" and second to Nicolaus, was a Prussian baron who had lived in Mexico for a year in 1938 pretending to sell sewing machines. In fact, the baron's specialty was selling Swedish armored cars and tanks as well as communications wares for the Mexican military.

"Morris" cut an aristocratic figure, with a monocle and a facial scar that looked like it came from a sword fight. He got to know Mexican officers well. He led a dive-bomber squadron for the Luftwaffe in 1939 during Hitler's invasion of Poland, but given the need for spies with experience in the Western Hemisphere, Schlebrügge was quickly trained in communications and secret inks and sent back to Mexico. There he recruited two more agents who became important in gathering and sending intelligence: Walter Baker, a shipping company employee who provided itineraries of merchant ships, oil tankers, and warships at Gulf ports, and Carlos Retelsdorf, code name "Glenn," a businessman with a powerful radio transmitter on his coffee farm in Veracruz that the spy network used to communicate with Germany.

Edgard S. Weisblat, an elegant gentleman of Polish origin, was also in Mexico. He worked not for the *Abwehr* but for the Gestapo, the Reich's feared secret police, one of its most capable agents. He posed as an entrepreneur who offered to build fast boats for Mexican national defense, a subterfuge that gave him cover to solicit photos and designs of marine equipment from U.S. and British companies.

Hilda Kruger, "Max," the baron, Weisblat, and dozens more agents in the network did their spying covertly, careful to avoid offending Mexican neutrality. Even Berlin's ambassador Rüdt von Collenberg, although a public figure, was exceedingly discreet as he constructed a network of informants among businessmen, bank employees, and government functionaries, not all Germans but all sympathetic to Hitler's Germany. Often, the same companies that financed the Reich's war provided cover for agents in their Mexican branches: IG Farben, Bayer, BASF, Agfa, Hoechst.

Before the attack on Pearl Harbor, when most—but not all—Latin countries felt compelled to join the Allies, nations considered neutrality a hallowed status. It allowed them to maintain relations with a wide range of players. Washington was not necessarily a natural ally, not an automatic partner—many feared or resented the big northern neighbor, not least because of its history of gunboat diplomacy. Latins often looked more comfortably to Europe, and not only to Spain and Portugal as "mother" countries. They traded heartily with European countries, and they admired Germany for its industrial accomplishments and military professionalism, and France and Italy for their culture and art. England was a source of finance, of investments in infrastructure. Families who could afford to send their children abroad often preferred European countries, not America, for the higher education and experience that would serve them as future leaders at home.

And why align with any of the contending powers? To protect commerce and diplomatic relations it was better to stay neutral. Besides, to some Latin Americans the European war was a conflict among empires, which Latin countries might wait out, far from the battlefields.

Meanwhile, presence in "neutral" countries was vital for Axis spies. Admiral Canaris chose the Aztec capital for his agents' Latin American headquarters because Germany wanted to keep close watch on the supply of oil and other primary materials for war industries Mexico could provide: mercury for explosives, manganese, sulfur, aluminum for airplane fuselages, iron, tungsten. And Mexico shared a porous border with the United States. As Washington weighed whether to join the war, Germany and Japan felt it was urgent to track the U.S. level of preparedness, its new technologies, the movement of its fleets.

The Reich's agents worked without much concern about arrest in the early Mexican years. Fascism ran against the purported values of the revolutionary government of President Lázaro Cárdenas, but neither Cárdenas nor members of his cabinet took a formal stand against it. There was no intensive effort to hunt down spies. When eyebrows were raised, police and authorities could easily be bribed. Besides, thanks to the boycott by U.S., British, and Dutch petroleum companies, the best customers for Mexican oil were Germany, Italy, and Japan, whose payments supported government programs. There was no reason to offend them unnecessarily.

And Nazi spies could watch a theater of support in the streets. The Gold Shirts, a nationalist, anti-Semitic, anticommunist paramilitary group (*Acción Revolucionaria Mexicana*), demonstrated openly, sometimes violently, strutting with arms held in the fascist salute. Not to be outdone, the Italian community organized parades with goose-stepping teenagers in support of the Axis. Militants of the rightist National Union of Synarchists, a huge Catholic peasant movement against Cárdenas reforms such as secular education, maintained connections to Nazis and the Japanese. They marched with the same strong-arm salute. The Hitler Youth had branches at German schools and the German Center, which was also Nazi party headquarters. In the north where residents were sympathetic to Hitler, the swastika became a kind of design statement found on floors of houses, even on the floor of the nave of the cathedral of Tampico.

A few of the Reich's spies drove flashy cars, but otherwise they operated in the shadows. The high-profile exception: Hilda Kruger. The sweet-faced Hilda appeared in Mexican films with titles such as *Adultery* and *He Who Died for Love*. She showed up at fêtes and dinners on the arms of government officials and members of high society. One period photograph shows her singing informally but with apparent delight alongside Mario Moreno, the picaresque Mexican icon better known as Cantinflas.

At a time when foreigners were obligated to report their movements outside the capital to the Ministry of the Interior, Hilda Kruger appeared to travel wherever she wished without red tape, her excursions approved by Aleman, the head of the ministry. At the U.S. Embassy, agents of the Office of Naval Intelligence (ONI) were convinced that Hilda's travels, facilitated by the "unscrupulous" Aleman, were related to the contraband of mercury and other precious war materials. So great was Hilda's influence over the future president that, in a 1941 report on penetration of foreign spies in Mexico, the ONI considered kidnapping her and bringing her to the United States under custody.

The German spies were well connected, but sending their information safely to Berlin was a challenge. Ambassador von Collenberg sometimes enclosed dispatches to Germany securely in a diplomatic pouch. Radio transmissions were generally sent to *Abwehr* agents in Brazil, who bounced them to Europe. Agents crafted written messages with invisible ink, jotted into the corners or along the margins of seemingly innocuous letters, then mailed to a fictitious name at a designated drop in São Paulo, or in Lisbon, or a dozen other European cities.

The ideal secret ink was made from something an agent might have around the house or in a suitcase. It should be readable with a simple developer and leave no odor or traces such as crystals that might be detected when a piece of paper was held up to the light. Typically in Latin America a German V-man made secret ink from Pyramidon tablets, a preparation of aminopyrine, a pain reliever like aspirin sold over the counter. Dissolved in alcohol, the tablets become a writing liquid whose messages emerge when the paper is treated with a solution including ferrous oxide—rust—and ordinary table salt. Another method included typing on paper covered with a thin film of wax. But with this method the agent had to be careful not to use periods or other punctuation marks that left a heavier imprint than letters, and could be more easily detected.

In 1941, a revolutionary new way of sending written messages was developed by the *Abwehr* in Germany. By his own account, a dashing young agent named Duŝko Popov was the first to handle a secret message created by the new method. The claim is easy to believe because Popov, a wealthy Yugoslav business lawyer and bon vivant, was not quite like any other *Abwehr* spy.

Blonde and athletic, with a winning smile, Popov was unapologetic about his high living, his taste for fine wines. If any spy were a model for James Bond, it was the debonair Duŝko Popov.

With cover as a businessman in the import-export trade, Popov spied in London and traveled regularly to Lisbon, the neutral capital where every intelligence service had at least some agents and controllers. In 1941, at a villa on the Portuguese Riviera west of the capital, Popov's *Abwehr* controller told him he was being assigned to the United States. He led him into a study where Popov saw an antique table, oiled black with age, on which a microscope gleamed in the afternoon light. "Have a look," the controller said, slipping a glass slide from under the lens. "It's the *micropunkt*."

It looked like a speck of dirt. It was really a small piece of film, the handler said, "and with a tiny drop of collodion"—a syrupy cellulose solution—"you stick it on anything you want. Any old scrap of paper, your luggage, on your skin if you want." Then he called for champagne.

Popov learned that an entire page of text could be reduced through a new microphotography technique to the size of the dot on a printed "i." He could carry a volume the size of a Bible or a technical manual without detection. The dot could be read with any two-hundred-power microscope. Peering again as he sipped the champagne, Popov examined a long list of questions that he was supposed to answer for the *Abwehr* in America. They were all contained in the dot. Popov left the villa with a supply of secret ink and the *micropunkt* stuck to a personal letter, but he was not given the contraption to shrink pages into dots.

A few months later, Popov made one of his frequent visits to the chief German spy in São Paulo, an electrical company executive named Albrecht Engels, code name "Alfredo." Popov agreed to carry a seven-page questionnaire back to Engels's subagent in the States. The document listed queries about U.S. firms that had been looking at South American uranium mines: how was the ore processed, how much did U.S. firms have in stock? At the time Popov had no idea about the race for the atomic bomb, so he had no idea why the questions were of interest.

Popov did notice, however, that "Alfredo" had the microphotography apparatus, with which he reduced the sheaf of questions to the size of a few freckles. When Popov expressed envy, Engels volunteered to get him a machine from Berlin headquarters.

The route of the promised machine gives an idea of the facility with which objects could move surreptitiously around the region. From Europe to South America was easy. In Brazil, "Alfredo" would have the machine hidden in a cotton bale for its journey to North America. The cotton exporter was in his pay, as were the Portuguese captain of a tramp steamer and a Canadian shipping agent. When Popov received a coded message, he was to travel to Quebec, check into a certain hotel and feign illness, and he would receive a visit from a bald-headed doctor. The doctor's prescription would have instructions about where to pick up the machine. Carrying suitcases into the United States from Canada was not a problem.

What "Alfredo" did not know was that Popov reported everything he found out to the FBI man in Rio. The raffish Duŝko Popov was a double agent who worked for the British MI5, a clandestine member of its "Double-Cross System." The system handled men and women employed by the German secret services but who, taking great risk, delivered information to British Intelligence. "Double-Cross" agents also funneled disinformation back to the German services. Popov's British controller had instructed him to work with FBI chief J. Edgar Hoover when he was on assignment for the *Abwehr* in the United States.

Popov shared the secret of the microdot with the FBI. After the war Hoover described the microdot's "discovery" in self-serving style in *Reader's Digest*, as if it had been captured by his agents. Hoover said they found the dot hidden on a "playboy" German agent, son of a millionaire businessman. He gave no credit to Popov, who was engaged in a dangerous game that could be fatal had the Germans uncovered it.

Bold but suave, with the capacity to lie through his teeth, Duŝko Popov provided invaluable intelligence to the Americans and the British while keeping his *Abwehr* masters in the dark about his allegiance to the Allies. He was also a rake whose British code name—"Tricycle"—reportedly came from his proclivity for bedding two women at the same time. The straightlaced Hoover couldn't stand him. He had "Tricycle" watched as closely as if he were the enemy.

"If I bend over to smell a bowl of flowers, I scratch my nose on a microphone," Popov complained to a British agent. Once when Popov took a lady friend to Florida, the Bureau threatened him with jail for violating the Mann Act, which forbids transporting a woman over state lines "for immoral purposes."

· Whether Hoover's judgment was clouded by his prejudice against Popov or whether other forces were at work, the Bureau chief appeared to ignore information from him that ought to have raised a red flag about Pearl Harbor. Popov's German handlers had instructed him to go to Hawaii with the detailed questionnaire he carried on the first microdot he shared with the FBI. A third of the requests were "highest priority" items about Pearl Harbor on behest of the Japanese: sketches of airfields, water depths, condition of dry docks, positions of oil repositories, the status of dredging at the harbor, of new British and U.S. torpedo nets. Were they installed? Was Punchbowl—the crater of an extinct volcano in Honolulu—being used as an ammunition dump?

Popov also shared that, on behalf of the Japanese, an *Abwehr* colleague had traveled to Taranto, Italy, site of one of the war's most successful air raids. The Japanese wanted to know how the British destroyed almost all the Italian fleet in November 1940, using torpedo planes launched from a carrier. The Japanese interest in Hawaii and Taranto hinted, at least, at a possible attack at Pearl Harbor, headquarters of the U.S. Pacific fleet.

The FBI chief, however, seemed more taken by the new technology— the microdot—than the implications of the questions it carried. Popov suggests that the information was "undervalued."

The British, who knew about the questions on the microdot, did not push Hoover. After the war, Sir John Masterman, the British chairman of the committee that ran the Double-Cross System, confirmed that "Tricycle's questionnaire . . . contained a somber but unregarded warning of the subsequent attack on Pearl Harbor." It had been up to the Americans, he said, "to make their appreciation and to draw their deductions from the questionnaire rather than for us to do so."

Did the British hold back because they wanted the Americans to enter the war with them? Or was distrust on Hoover's part at the bottom of the missed signal? The British and U.S. intelligence communities were still cautious of each other, far from the close collaborators they became after the war. And Hoover, despite assurances from the British, deeply mistrusted the messenger, Popov. He called the Yugoslavian Serb a "Balkan playboy."

Unable to work successfully with the FBI, Popov pleaded with his MI5 handlers to allow him to return to Europe. He convinced the *Abwehr* that their U.S. mission for him had been ill-conceived. The Germans sent him back to London, unaware until the war's end that he was a double agent for the British.

European agents in Latin America for both sides worried about their families and friends close to the battle lines. In Europe Popov discovered that his parents had escaped from Dubrovnik by boat as the Croatian Ustashi movement, newly installed as a Nazi puppet government, launched a reign of terror against nationalists and Serbs. Popov's uncle and two cousins were not as lucky. They were hanged from a tree in the courtyard of their house.

Roosevelt wanted to openly help beleaguered Great Britain, but the public was not with him. The powerful "America First" movement and others militated against declaring war; some were pro-Nazi, others isolationist or with other reasons to stay above the fray. They included some of the wealthiest and most influential figures in the country, such as aviation hero Charles Lindbergh. Some polls said as much as 80 percent of the population was against the war. Formally joining the Allies would be Roosevelt's political suicide. Nevertheless, Americans remained suspicious about German designs on Latin countries.

On October 27, 1941, Navy Day, the president came up with a trump card to change all but the hardest minds about declaring war. "I have in my possession a secret map, made in Germany by Hitler's government by the planners of the New World Order," he told a national radio audience.

The map showed the South American continent and part of Central America carved into four large vassal states to be administered by Germany at some undetermined date. "That map, my friends, makes clear the Nazi design not only against South America but against the United States as well," said the president.

The secret map was supposed to have been snagged from a German courier in Argentina by a British intelligence operative. At the BSC office in New York, "Intrepid" gave it to his friend Bill Donovan, a White House advisor who would found the Office of Strategic Services (OSS), and Donovan shared it with the president. Roosevelt refused to display the document to the press, insisting only that it came from "a source which is undoubtedly reliable."

Later the map did become available. The fiefdoms even had names: *Brasilien*, *Argentinien*, *Neuspanien*, and *Chile*. In the margins were handwritten questions in German about fuel supplies for air routes, about airlines that went to Panama and Mexico.

Over the years researchers suggested that the "secret map" was a fabrication by the British Security Co-ordination to help Roosevelt achieve a mandate to enter the war. Neither Roosevelt, Stephenson, nor Donovan ever admitted deception. At any rate, a month later the chilling document was forgotten with the attack on Pearl Harbor. The decision to join the Allies was made for the United States not by Hitler or Churchill, but by Japan.

Hardly had the smoke cleared over Pearl Harbor than the Mexico-based chief *Abwehr* agent Georg Nicolaus was sending information to Berlin that was startling in its accuracy. A local Japanese intelligence agent working with a U.S. informer, who has never been named, needed help from Nicolaus to send out intelligence—the Japanese agent was being watched too closely after the attack to send it himself. Thus Nicolaus was able to send two letters to Berlin carrying microdots that reported nothing less than the shape of the upcoming U.S. Navy offensive in the South Pacific and northern Japan, "lightning-like" aircraft carrier raids. He reported the U.S. losses on December 7 and the number of aircraft available to U.S. volunteer pilots in Burma and China. He reported the names of a carrier and certain battleships then transiting the Panama Canal and headed for the Pacific.

THE SPYMASTERS

With the United States' entry into the war, the contest between Hoover and Canaris became more acute. They brought vastly different life experiences to the fight. Each was a second son born on a New Year's Day, Hoover in 1895, Canaris in 1887, but there the resemblance ended.

J. Edgar Hoover looked hefty, always dressed nattily, and lived with his mother in the house where he was born until she passed away when he was forty-three. Wilhelm Canaris was short and rather plain, had a wife and family, and is reputed to have counted among his lovers the spy and courtesan Mata Hari. Canaris was Catholic, Hoover a Presbyterian who "liked to find a few minutes each day . . . to meditate and pray."

The contrast extended to the way they worked. Hoover was a desk man who didn't travel, while Canaris knew the world, as experienced in the field as any of his spies. Hoover kept to his routine like clockwork, walking to work in the morning, lunching daily with FBI associate director Clyde Tolson, his lifelong friend. Canaris had a reputation in his early years of disappearing for spy assignments and being good at disguises.

Despite their differences, Hoover and Canaris had a compelling attribute in common. They were both deeply patriotic.

By far, it was the enigmatic Wilhelm Canaris who knew the Latin continent the best. The son of a well-off industrialist, bred to move into the manufacturing elite of the Ruhr Valley's new steel industry—makers of ships, weapons, steam engines, and trains—young Wilhelm overcame his father's protests to fulfill a desire he had nurtured since boyhood: to go to sea. In 1907, at age twenty, fresh out of the strict officers' training academy of the German Imperial Navy on the Baltic Sea, Canaris set off on his first voyage as adjutant to the captain of the light cruiser *Bremen*, bound for Central America.

Always good at languages, Canaris immersed himself in Spanish and used it with locals he met amid the white-painted wooden buildings and lush palms of the Gulf ports of Mexico and lands to its south. In South America, the captain took young Canaris along on visits inland, where he met New World Germans and Germanophiles, ranchers, and businessmen. Canaris's shipboard title also included the term "intelligence officer," a duty that then meant little more than noting what other ships were present in harbors. But Canaris did more than the minimum. By absorbing a wide sweep of information useful for military intelligence, seeing firsthand the lay of the land, and making contacts, he began to construct what would become the Latin American espionage network.

And he made an important visit to the United States, serving on the cruiser *Dresden*.

In September 1909, the *Dresden* was among hundreds of ships gathered on the Hudson River to commemorate the three hundredth anniversary of the founding of New York and centenary of Robert Fulton's first steamboat. Canaris, in the dress whites of an Imperial German Navy officer, watched closely from on deck. Before him, U.S. naval might was purposefully on display.

More than thirty countries sent warships to the celebration; small Latin nations such as Cuba and Guatemala sent their entire tiny navies. At a time when most houses were not yet wired for electricity, nights turned magical with maneuvers on the river, ships' masts illuminated amid a display of fireworks. Wilbur Wright soared up and down the river and looped around the Statue of Liberty as hundreds of thousands of New Yorkers watched their first airplane flight. The regatta, parades, and exhibitions were staged to promote New York as a world-class city, but Canaris was also witnessing something else.

Germany possessed a fleet that reached to the Eastern Pacific, and Great Britain called itself the ruler of the seas, but the U.S. Navy was announcing its hegemony in the Americas, the capacity to control regional seas and back up decisions made in Washington. And the capacity to support its allies, should the need arise.

Five years later, Canaris performed feats of quick thinking and endurance in South America that would give him a near-mythical fame for survival. Early in World War I, the *Dresden*, sailing in the German East Asia Squadron under command of the legendary Admiral Graf Maximilian von Spee, was the only ship to escape the German defeat at the Battle of the Falklands.

English battleships chased the *Dresden* for a hundred days until they cornered it in the bay of an island called Más a Tierra and set the ship aflame. The German captain, stalling for time to transfer his dead and wounded ashore and scuttle the ship, sent Canaris in a rowboat under fire to treat with the British captain. In perfect English the junior officer discussed points of maritime law about his hors de combat ship with the British commander until the German crew were evacuated, explosions set, and the *Dresden* sank, denied to the enemy. The English crew treated Canaris with extreme politeness, he later recalled, despite his relatively low rank, leaving him with a lasting positive impression of His Majesty's Navy.

The crew of the *Dresden* was held on Más a Tierra, a speck in the sea so isolated that the English author Daniel Defoe once used it as a symbol of the end of the earth, where Robinson Crusoe washed ashore. But Canaris soon escaped to the mainland.

On foot and horseback, disguised as a peasant, he trekked across the Andes through icy wind, growing gaunt with bouts of malaria until he reached Argentine Patagonia. Changing disguises, posing as a young widower bound for Europe, Canaris took a train a thousand miles north to Buenos Aires and booked passage to neutral Holland. The British forced his Dutch liner into Plymouth to remove suspected Germans, but "Mr. Reed Rojas"—Canaris—who spoke fine English, remained aboard, landing safely in Rotterdam. He reported for duty at Imperial Navy headquarters at Kiel, on the Baltic. Honored with an Iron Cross and promoted to commandant, he was given a say in his subsequent assignment. He chose intelligence.

The Allied spymaster J. Edgar Hoover had a trajectory that appeared as plodding as Canaris's was exciting. Yet Hoover, too, in his early years lived in an atmosphere of war that inspired him for the rest of his life.

On July 30, 1916, when Hoover was twenty-two, a notable act of World War I sabotage occurred in New York Harbor. The Black Tom explosion, named for the island where it occurred, has been called the first terrorist attack on U.S. soil. German saboteurs planted dynamite and delayed-release pencil bombs—ingenious devices no bigger than a cigar—at a munitions depot on the island where arms headed for the Allies were stored. The explosion sent pillars of fire into the sky, killed seven and injured hundreds, leveled blocks in downtown Manhattan, and damaged the Statue of Liberty, leaving Americans in shock. The German saboteurs who blew up Black Tom were based in Mexico. With this horrific sabotage fresh in his mind, J. Edgar Hoover began work a few months later at what would be a lifetime at the Justice Department.

As Hoover settled into the first steps of his career, another World War I event, the Zimmerman Telegram, warned Americans that German activities in the Western Hemisphere must be closely watched. In January 1917, the Kaiser's foreign secretary, Arthur Zimmerman, advised his ambassador in Mexico City that unrestricted submarine warfare in the Atlantic against the British was about to begin. If the United States joined the war as a result, Berlin's ambassador should offer the Mexican president a deal: join Germany and Japan against the United States, and Mexico would receive financial aid and the return of territory lost to the Americans a few decades before in Arizona, Texas, and New Mexico. The Zimmerman Telegram was intercepted and decrypted by the British and shared with the Americans, helping to trigger U.S. entry into the European war.

A third-generation civil servant, unobtrusive in behavior, young Hoover often was the last to leave the office. Sometimes his superiors at the U.S. Justice Department War Emergency Division, whom he was always anxious to please, discovered he had come in to work weekends, too. Hoover labored unflaggingly, writing notes and filling boxes, file cabinets, and entire rooms with confidential data to keep his country safe, sometimes including dirt on political officeholders or their families, a habit he would continue. He rose quickly, becoming head of the Alien Enemy Bureau with authority to jail without trial foreigners deemed disloyal. In 1924, President Calvin Coolidge named Hoover director of the Justice Department's General Intelligence Division, forerunner of the FBI, to track domestic radicals. He was twenty-nine years old.

SPECIAL INVESTIGATION SERVICE—THE ROUGH START OF THE SIS

The brief of the FBI was domestic, but as the next war drew nearer, Hoover inserted himself into meetings among military intelligence agency chiefs about who would take the lead in foreign espionage. The FBI already was tracking suspected spies in the United States. "The best way to control Nazi espionage in the United States is to wipe out spy nests in Latin America," he would say. Hoover argued with the military chiefs,

made private approaches for the FBI to Roosevelt, lobbied Assistant Secretary of State for Latin American Affairs Adolf A. Berle. Finally Roosevelt, frustrated at the infighting, made the FBI the sole agency responsible
for foreign intelligence in the Western Hemisphere. Hoover christened
the new spy unit the Special Intelligence Service (SIS).

To hide its real purposes, the SIS opened a fictitious firm in the
summer of 1940 called "Importers and Exporters Service Company" in
the same Rockefeller Center building that housed the BSC, which was
far smoother in its operations. Within a month, SIS agents took the phony
sign off their door to fend off a stream of salesmen and ad men who were
coming to solicit business. They also realized they were unprepared for
the new mission. "The Bureau discovered upon undertaking the program
that there was a complete absence of any accurate data or details concerning the true extent or nature of subversive activities, current or potential, in Latin America," said an internal report written in 1962. And there
was the issue of language. Agents took crash courses at Berlitz or brief
language studies through their cover companies such as General Motors,
Firestone, or Pan American, but most headed for the field woefully lacking in Spanish or Portuguese.

Masquerading as businessmen or as journalists, the would-be sleuths
relied on written, encrypted messages to send their information. British
security censors who maintained a facility in Bermuda to quick-check
all correspondence leaving Latin America became suspicious of mis-
sives written by the agents; urgent messages were delayed while bona
fides were checked. At FBI headquarters, proper reagents that might reveal what was written by agents in secret ink were still at "an experi-
mental stage."

And in the field the appearance of the SIS "businessmen" gave them
away. They were uniformly young, unmarried, fit-looking, and suspi-
ciously not in the U.S. military at a time of national conscription. As their
number grew, Hoover managed to get many agents attached to U.S. embassies and consulates as "civil attachés" or "legal attachés," to the dis-
gust of some in the State Department, who were unhappy with intelligence
activities they could not control. Before World War II, "legal attachés" did
not exist at U.S. embassies, but they have been there ever since, spreading

from Latin America to around the world, giving the FBI a permanent presence abroad.

Between the talents of the famous Canaris and the shortcomings of his own SIS, Hoover had plenty to worry about. But his Latin America turf was also being challenged by an old rival, William Donovan, founder of the OSS, which would someday be the CIA.

OSS: THE MEXICAN EXCEPTION

Standard operating procedures were almost taboo in OSS. Effective action was the sole objective.

—R. HARRIS SMITH, *OSS: The Secret History of America's First Central Intelligence Agency*

In the 1930s, the joint Army-Navy MAGIC cryptography project to decode Japanese secret communications revealed that the Japanese had extensive surveillance networks in Latin America. In case of war with the United States, MAGIC revealed, Mexico would become the center of regional spying. The navy, which had maintained an attaché at the U.S. Embassy in Mexico City since 1937, was concerned about Mexico's West Coast. Despite his jealousy over control of Latin American espionage, Hoover did not object to early ONI surveys and information collecting in Baja California beginning in April 1941.

The rugged Baja peninsula, and the sleepy Mexican ports that we know today as glamorous resorts such as Acapulco and Manzanillo, held potential for Japanese infiltration because of their strategic location on the Pacific. Navy spies discovered such a Japanese presence among a plethora of suspicious fishing companies.

On July 11, 1941, Roosevelt appointed Colonel William Donovan to head an intelligence office called "Coordinator of Information," COI. Donovan chafed when he realized Hoover's hegemony over Latin America left his COI agents no room to operate in Mexico or Central or South America. The limitation violated Donovan's principle that "in modern war, all phases of the military activity of a belligerent must be world-wide in scope." Even when the COI became the OSS in 1942, charged with collecting and analyzing information required by the Joint Chiefs of Staff and conducting special operations, Latin countries were forbidden to Donovan. His new global intelligence service would be absurdly truncated without covering an entire continent, he pointed out—one connected to the United States at that. He argued in vain.

Competition over Latin America between Hoover and Donovan beginning with Mexico contained the seeds of jurisdictional arguments between the FBI and the CIA that continue to this day.

The chief of the OSS brought a colorful personal history to the argument, and a strong character. Canaris once remarked that of all the Allied leaders, he most would have liked to know William J. Donovan. Adolf Hitler, who once met Donovan, made it understood that he always feared and hated him more than any other American.

As a dashing twenty-nine-year-old lawyer from Buffalo, Donovan formed a cavalry unit in the New York National Guard that fought in the ranks of General John J. Pershing against Pancho Villa on the Mexican border. During World War I, he led assaults and rescues as an infantry officer in France that earned him the Medal of Honor, celebrity at home, and confirmed a nickname that stayed with him all his life—"Wild Bill."

Dissention between Hoover and Donovan began between the wars when Wild Bill was briefly Hoover's boss at the Justice Department. Their characters were impossible to reconcile. When Franklin Roosevelt became president, he exchanged information with Donovan and depended on his assessments of tensions in Europe. Hoover, jowly and officious, often used the press to blow his own horn, deliberately pushing his role in FBI successes. He probably winced to see how effortlessly Donovan, silver-haired, square-jawed, gallant, and physically magnetic, became a public celebrity when his World War I heroics were splashed across the silver screen in a 1940 Warner Bros. hit, *The Fighting 69th*.

The fundamental difference between Donovan and Hoover, however, was over what an intelligence agency should be about, and how it should be run. Bill Donovan believed in strategic intelligence, analysis, covert action, tradecraft, and sabotage, which gave the OSS an advantage abroad over the more dogged, policeman-like methods of the FBI. Wild Bill was against bureaucracy, against hierarchy. Any way an OSS agent could get the job done was acceptable. In contrast, Hoover believed most in fact-finding and exposure of targets, like composing the blacklists of "enemy aliens." Hoover, however, the ultimate bureaucrat, was able to strengthen his political base at home to Donovan's disadvantage precisely because he knew how to manage the Washington bureaucracy. Each man began keeping a dossier on the other.

Unwilling to keep to Hoover's rules, Donovan sneaked his operation into Mexico with the aid of a civilian with a rich life history, Wallace Phillips, who was running a local operation for the Office of Naval Intelligence. Phillips graduated from West Point, studied at the Sorbonne and served in World War I, and—unlike many American spies at the time—had experience in espionage. He was a rubber-company executive, but he also ran his own independent industrial intelligence organization whose clients paid him for information on business competitors. Phillips's secret agents—"including seven ex-Prime ministers," as he liked to boast—reported from the Soviet Union to the Balkans to Mexico. In Mexico, Phillips wrangled a lucrative private arrangement with President Ávila Camacho to find employees for the leader's small special service to track subversive activities. In late 1941, Phillips decided to pass his private agency, called "K Organization," as a single package over to Donovan's OSS, with the blessing of the ONI. Phillips became Donovan's director of espionage. All—Phillips, Donovan, and the navy—kept the maneuver secret.

Immediately after Pearl Harbor, Hoover dispatched seven agents to Mexico to cover "Baja California and other danger points from the standpoint of possible enemy landing or subversive activities." By February 1942, more than two dozen agents were working secretly under Donovan in Mexico. His analysts reported valuable information: wealthy and influential Mexicans, they said, anti-Yankee and very Catholic, tilted totalitarian, not democratic. The only Mexican sectors with potential as allies for Washington were the organized labor movement and the Communist Party.

•   •   •

Sometimes the tug-of-war between Donovan and Hoover undermined operations that might have served the Allied cause. In 1943, the OSS wanted to place operatives from its ultrasecret Insurance Intelligence Unit in Buenos Aires and Santiago. The OSS unit not only aimed to discover the structure of Nazi war finances but also mined German insurance companies' records wherever they could find them for strategic data such as tide tables or weapons plant blueprints, important for Allied planners to attack industries and enemy cities. German insurance firms, heavy financers of the war, managed almost half of the world's policies from Berlin to Bangkok. The Nazi business was handled in Switzerland, but much of the money was laundered in Latin America, especially Argentina. The FBI turned down Donovan's request.

Just because the maverick Donovan did not have permission did not mean he refrained from sending secret agents not only to Mexico but to the rest of Latin America as well. In 1954, when the CIA orchestrated a right-wing coup against a democratically elected leftist president in Guatemala, one of the perpetrators, an agent named Joseph Rendon, proudly told reporters he had first warned against communist infiltration there a decade before, during the war, when he was on an OSS mission in the country.

Donovan's spies were officially forbidden to operate in the field in Latin America, but his OSS division called R&A (Research and Analysis) studied the world from its Washington headquarters and maintained an active Latin America desk. For R&A work, the OSS begged, borrowed, or stole experts from America's finest universities, museums, and research laboratories, bringing their expertise to information gathered from other government agencies and from spies abroad. R&A reports went to the president with recommended actions.

The R&A Latin America desk under historian Dr. Maurice Halperin was one of the agency's most productive. Halperin produced a damning report about U.S. diplomacy in Mexico. Combined with the rivalry between the OSS and the FBI, the report earned him the everlasting ire of J. Edgar Hoover, who charged Halperin after the war with being an agent for the Soviet Union.

Using the R&A desk, Wild Bill created another way into Mexico. Donovan always saw film as a tool to stir patriotism, intimidate the enemy, and promote his OSS. If his spies could not have free rein, Donovan could at least shoot a film or two in Mexico as research for R&A and snoop at the same time. When the navy suggested a need for photographic surveys and a propaganda film in Mexico, Donovan was ready.

Ford professed not to give a good damn about his Academy Awards. But if you mentioned that he won four Oscars, forgetting the two he won for Navy documentaries, he would snap: "Six."

—JOSEPH MCBRIDE AND MICHAEL WILMINGTON, *John Ford*

Donovan's partner in the film operations was John Ford, the Hollywood director who won six Oscars and became famous for iconic dramas that explored the roles of war and history in the lives of unforgettable individuals—*The Grapes of Wrath, How Green Was My Valley, The Searchers, Stagecoach, They Were Expendable*. Donovan didn't drink and Ford did, but otherwise they were kindred spirits, friends before the war. They shared a special, mystical bond of Irish Catholicism, and both were unquestionably brave—on assignment for Donovan, Ford shot with a handheld camera under Japanese attack at Midway, at the invasion of Sicily, and at Normandy.

Both Donovan and Ford were independent thinkers who respected a chain of command but liked to keep it simple. Ford had created a wartime Field Photographic Unit with top-notch professionals, newly inducted in the services, and he was glad to incorporate the unit into Donovan's OSS operation because the chain could not have been simpler: Ford to Donovan to Roosevelt.

Since the time he was commissioned as a lieutenant commander in the U.S. Navy Reserve in the mid-1930s, Ford had sailed along the Mexican and Central American Pacific coast on his beloved 110-foot ketch *Araner*, named for the Irish Aran Islands, his mother's home. Ford explored as far south as Panama. U.S. officers knew that Japan, starved of resources for its militarism in Asia by a Western embargo, was likely to be planning war to ensure access to what it needed. An invasion of North America was possible, and Ford's commander in the Reserve encouraged his reports.

While an onlooker might see only a wealthy yachtsman at leisure, the Hollywood director surreptitiously gathered intelligence and mapped waters. He said a certain lagoon was "close enough to shipping lanes to serve as an ideal place to either stockpile supplies or to serve as a rendezvous point for submarines and sub-tenders." He recorded photography conditions and camouflage issues at La Paz, Mazatlan, the Tres Marias Islands, and Panama. He brought his knowledge to Donovan's outfit.

John Ford's spy journeys were made at his own expense, and in Baja sometimes under cover of a glamorous boys' lark of Hollywood stars. While John Wayne, Ward Bond, and Henry Fonda recovered aboard the luxurious *Araner* from wild booze fests in coastal bars, Ford compiled copious, detailed notes about what he had seen on shore. He wrote about Japanese "tourists" with Leica cameras fitted with telephoto lenses, shooting excessive numbers of pictures of bridges and oil storage tanks. Men supposedly on liberty from Japanese shrimp boats were too sharply dressed to be fishermen, "in well tailored flannels, worsted and tweed . . . black service shoes smartly polished."

"It is plausible that these men know every Bay, Cove and Inlet in the Gulf of California, a Bay which is so full of islands, and so close to our Arizona borderline they constitute a real menace," Ford reported.

In a psychological operation to stir regional pride and impress reluctant potential allies, Ford made a five-reel picture showing Mexico on a war footing and shorter films aimed at Latin American audiences. "Be sure the Mexican flag is carried at full gallop," he wrote in instructions to the crew. "Show their air fields carefully. Line up their planes to look smart, efficient and in great number."

After the United States entered the war, the German espionage advantage slipped, not so much due to the expertise of the SIS—although the FBI agents got better at the job every day—but due to the Germans' own mistakes, and some bad luck.

Getting money from Berlin to its Latin American spies was never easy, a handicap that would plague the German networks until the end of the war. One attempt to fund Georg Nicolaus and his *Abwehr* circle through Mussolini failed in part thanks to an early example of cooperation between J. Edgar Hoover and the BSC's William Stephenson. Unable to send funds directly to Mexico and Brazil, Canaris asked his ally Il Duce to remove US$3.85 million in small bills from the Italian Embassy bank account in Washington and send it south with couriers. In October 1940, two consuls and an Italian Embassy secretary carried the money in diplomatic pouches as far as Brownsville. From there two of the Italians traveled to New Orleans to take a boat for Pernambuco, Brazil, while the other headed by train for Mexico City. Hoover's men, who got wind of the transfer and contacted the BSC, kept the Italians under surveillance until they reached the border, while Stephenson's men made elaborate provisions to cover the arrival points.

Unfortunately for the Allies, the Italians' ship bypassed Pernambuco where the British spies had been waiting and steamed on to Rio, where Brazilian president Getúlio Vargas promised the Italian ambassador he would protect the delivery. At the Mexico City train station, however, the hugely surprised Italian courier had his belongings searched. This of course violated the basic tenets of diplomatic privilege, and in the face of the Italian ambassador's righteous umbrage, the Mexican government politely apologized for the stupid and unfortunate act of "a new and inexperienced clerk." But the money, US$1.4 million, went into a blocked account so the Germans couldn't touch it.

The toughest blow to the *Abwehr* in Mexico came from inside when local spy chief Georg Nicolaus metaphorically shot himself in the foot, bringing down much of the network with him. Nicolaus had taken a lover, who was also the caretaker of the swank apartment house where he lived. Early in 1942, news arrived that Nicolaus's wife was coming from Germany, and his mistress would have to take a backseat, at least for a while. His lover wasn't having it, and became angry. She took the information she had on him to the Mexican police, who arrested Nicolaus. Most of his agents were discovered.

When U-boats torpedoed two Mexican tankers in May 1942, Mexico declared war and German agents became the enemy. By this time

Mexico had stopped selling oil to the Axis; the FBI had been advising Mexican police about the spies it had been tracking, and now local detectives began arrests of men like Baron von Schlebrügge and Weisblat, the elegant spy with Polish roots who posed as a shipbuilder. Georg Nicolaus was delivered to U.S authorities and taken to a prisoner-of-war camp in Bismarck, North Dakota. Mexico repatriated other agents on the SIS spy list to Germany. Except for one.

Hilda Kruger had precipitously married a grandson of former president Porfirio Díaz, a union reportedly arranged by Aleman. She offered gala fiestas at her new husband's hacienda outside the capital, protected as she was from repatriation and from delivery to the United States. Mexican investigators could not or would not prove espionage charges against her. Unpredictably, Kruger became involved with intellectuals at the National University of Mexico, where she studied Mexican culture and wrote a biography of La Malinche, the intelligent and beautiful indigenous translator who was also the lover of the Spanish conqueror of the Aztecs, Hernán Cortés. Kruger married twice more, first a wealthy Venezuelan sugar king, then a Russian industrialist. She lived her last years in a luxury apartment in New York City, facing Central Park.

Hoover may have won the duel in Mexico, but Canaris was far from fatally wounded. As the war progressed and the Battle of the Atlantic began, German spy activity shifted from political and industry espionage to include the much more deadly intelligence gathering on the movement of ships in the Caribbean and South America. Canaris was there with a strong network in place, ready for action.

10.

OPERATION BOLÍVAR, GERMAN ESPIONAGE IN SOUTH AMERICA

Every politician seeking legitimacy and authority in South America tries to link himself in the public mind with Simón Bolívar, the early nineteenth-century hero regarded as a unifier who once ruled from Argentina to the Caribbean. Bolívar aspired to defend the hemisphere's newly independent countries from the old colonial power, Spain, but also from the emerging continental power, the United States. In World War II, a hydra-like Nazi system of intelligence and communications operated five thousand miles south of Mexico in Brazil, Argentina, Chile, Paraguay, and Uruguay. Its name: Operation Bolívar.

The heart of the operation was radio, the same technology that was permeating the continent.

In 1935, when the Argentine tango idol Carlos Gardel was killed in a plane crash near Medellín, Colombia, at the height of his fame, the same medium that had made the singer famous across the continent—radio—brought news of his death from the crash site. One of the first live broadcasts in Latin America, the transmission engendered a shared period of intense mourning across the lands.

By the 1930s, radio carried human voices into every home where someone could make or buy a receiver. The voice of President Roosevelt brought comfort and information to Americans with his "fireside chats" during the crises of the Depression and war. Latin leaders, too, saw the advantage of using radio with its capacity to convey the illusion that the speaker was talking directly to each listener. In 1938, when President Lázaro Cárdenas made the defiant decision to nationalize the oil of Mexico, he announced it first to the radio public and two hours later to his cabinet.

For the nuts and bolts of espionage, the Reich's spies used radio transmitters and receivers large and small in dozens of locations. Atmospheric conditions in the southernmost part of the continent were better than in the north for transmitting to Europe, so Operation Bolívar received messages from agents in the United States, Mexico, and other points throughout the Americas and bounced them across the Atlantic to receivers in Berlin, Cologne, and Hamburg. Some Operation Bolívar cells also forwarded dozens of microdot letters to Berlin and to drops in Spain and Portugal.

Captain Dietrich Niebuhr embodied the qualities of the best local spy chiefs in the network: loyalty to the Reich, command capacity, a web of contacts from members of the upper crust to shady forgers. When Niebuhr arrived in Buenos Aires in 1936, he eased into his cover as naval attaché. Armed with introductions from a cousin who owned eighteen large firms in Germany, the tall, blonde, suave officer quickly developed valuable relationships among political and business elites throughout the Southern Cone.

One of the smartest early moves Niebuhr made was to argue successfully with his chiefs in Germany against a new, ultrasecret *Abwehr* sabotage unit for South America, called Operation South Pole. Violence against British targets, such as sabotaging ships in port, was an abuse of a host nation's neutrality and could undermine his nascent operation. (Later, Operation Bolívar provided information to U-boats that sank Allied ships anyway, on the open seas.)

In 1939, when the German pocket battleship *Admiral Graf Spee* sank on the River Plate, Niebuhr arranged for "internment" of its thousand-man crew in relatively pleasant conditions in Argentina, where many formed families. Niebuhr also arranged for the escape of more than two hundred of the men, those who were most skilled and valuable to the Reich. He hid them as stowaways with help from crew on Spanish and Portuguese ships or sent them with guides across the Andes to Chile. From there they took a Eurasian route favored by German spies during the war: via Japanese freighter across the Pacific to Vladivostok, overland by train to Western Europe. Some who escaped under Niebuhr became U-boat aces and continued to contribute to Allied losses at sea.

At the embassy in Buenos Aires, Niebuhr had one of the fabled Enigma Machines, the top-secret, exceedingly complex Nazi encrypting apparatus—its possible combinations were in the range of a hundred and fifty million million million. During the war, Enigma Machines were located in at least half a dozen other places in Latin America and the Caribbean, as well as aboard U-boats that plied their coasts.

The Enigma Code was broken in July 1941 without the Germans knowing it. Eventually cryptanalysts at the top-secret Bletchley Park facility outside London were reading three thousand messages a day, although the pieces of information generally could not be acted upon individually without revealing the fact that the code had been broken. Nevertheless, an enormous amount of intelligence was garnered to help the Allied cause, including from Latin America.

A document from one section at Bletchley Park (Hut 18, ISOS [Intelligence Section Oliver Strachey]) contains records of messages exchanged to and from transmitters in Berlin, Brussels, Prague, and Rio de Janeiro, and unspecified locations in Germany, Brazil, Argentina, and "South America." Of the dates that are visible, the document shows the messages were recorded from August 7, 1941, almost immediately after the Enigma Code was broken, until August 1944.

For all the importance of the Enigma Machines, the workhorse of Operation Bolívar was its system of radio communication for transmitting encoded messages—it was widespread and used directly by agents on the ground. In Argentina alone, operatives established eleven stations along the coast, from Patagonia in the south to Santa Fe province northwest of Buenos Aires. One large transmitter was buried on a working farm in a pit under a chicken coop, its antenna hidden in a grove of trees. In Brazil, agents who had not brought their own portable transmitter and receiver outfits with them from the *Abwehr* spy school in Hamburg had miniature systems built for about US$1,000. They fit into a suitcase and were employed at certain hours when transmission conditions were best, in residential neighborhood houses or rented offices.

The *Abwehr* was not alone in spying for Germany and managing transmissions. SS captain Johannes Siegfried Becker, code name "Sargo," was chief of all fifty intelligence agents in the region who worked for the *Abwehr*'s rival intelligence agency, the *Sicherheitsdienst* (SD). Considered among the most dangerous German spies for his technical skill and ability to organize agents reporting on Allied convoys, ore shipments, and the like, Becker had come to Buenos Aires on a sabotage mission, but was soon switched to espionage when the German Embassy objected to operations that might abuse Argentina's neutrality. Among other places he traveled to was Brazil. There, in an unusual example of cooperation between the SD and the *Abwehr*, he boosted the quality and capacity of the network operated by the São Paulo businessman Albrecht Engels—the "Alfredo" often visited by the double agent Duŝko Popov. About half of Engels's transmissions dealt with British and U.S. maritime activity, including descriptions of cargo and destinations. The information was not difficult to obtain—"Alfredo's" informants included employees of a major shipping company.

Albrecht Engels was a fine example of an Operation Bolívar spy, because he didn't always wait for orders but did things on his own initiative. In 1939, the Germans staged two cargo vessels in Rio to provide tactical support for sea raiders set to be loosed upon English shipping. When one of them was about to depart, Engels took to the sky with a Brazilian Air Force pilot and spotted two British warships; he got word back to the port and saved the cargo ship from certain attack. In 1942, J. Edgar Hoover reported to Roosevelt that Engels's post "appears to be the most important station in the chain of clandestine German radios in South America."

Despite the efficient and sometimes imaginative work of agents like Engels, some V-men fumbled in laughable ways. Dr. Emil Wolff, who worked for IG Farben, became nervous when he suspected the FBI was tailing him and threw his briefcase—with a codebook inside—overboard from a boat in the Panama Canal. (The FBI recovered it.) A subagent in Brazil, flummoxed on his first assignment, asked a German dentist who owned a microscope to read a microdot for him. (The dentist reported the event to local Nazi authorities.) When Engels and the German naval attaché in Rio became fed up with a newly arrived agent who insisted on superiority over "Alfredo," they sent the man a fake telegram that said his presence in Germany was required immediately. Two weeks later, having sailed across the Atlantic to Europe and breathlessly arriving at a supervisor's office, the irksome agent discovered he had been fooled. (He didn't return.)

FBI estimates put the number of agents in Latin America who answered to Berlin over the course of the war, mostly to the *Abwehr*, at up to eight hundred. Canaris believed in using many operatives, including locals, in a kind of big-net theory: the wider the net, the more likely to catch useful information. Also, Hitler harbored a deep fear of the British foreign secret service—MI6—and wanted a vast network of intelligence agents to counteract it.

With such large numbers in a region where people of many ethnicities lived, Nazi preoccupation with "racial purity" went out the window, especially after it became clear that the war would not end quickly. Miscegenation was overlooked. V-men and informants were not necessarily Nazis, but they were loyal to Germany, and some went unpaid—Canaris believed espionage was something one did out of allegiance to the fatherland. The spy rings' paymasters, usually diplomats, could not always disburse enough funds at the right times to keep things running. Illicit methods were used to generate cash, such as trading in pharmaceuticals and contraband gems like emeralds and industrial diamonds. The black market goods, easy to hide, sailed to Europe with accomplices called "wolves," who traveled as crewmen on Spanish and Portuguese ships.

The bitter, dangerous rivalry that grew in Germany between the *Abwehr* and the fearsome SD with its Gestapo agents did not affect espionage operators in the New World the way it did in the Old. In Berlin, the SD, the intelligence agency of the SS and the Nazi party, kept card files on citizens, using extortion, blackmail, and torture to get information and preserve loyalty. Its operatives tapped the files of the *Abwehr* in a fight for turf, but also over ideological purity. Canaris, the *Abwehr* director, had never joined the Nazi party.

Canaris thought he could protect the *Abwehr* from the SD's director, Reinhard Heydrich, who once served as a junior officer to Canaris in the Imperial Navy, and who was dismissed in 1931 for "conduct unbecoming to an officer and gentleman." Heydrich and Canaris not only knew each other, they became neighbors in Berlin. Despite the silent struggle between their services, the men and their wives sometimes met at each other's houses in evenings to dine—Canaris often cooked—and to play chamber music together. Some reports speculate that Canaris knew a secret about Heydrich: that he had Jewish forbears.

Canaris determined to work around the SD, to insulate the *Abwehr* from the most savage Nazi methods. He wanted his agency to expand, to be an instrument that maintained independent thought and action, a strong part of the future Germany. In Latin America as elsewhere, he instructed his men to evade orders from outside that involved brutality.

PATROLLING THE ETHER

Operation Bolívar in Brazil was finally crippled by the covert work of a largely unsung band of civilian specialists and aficionados led by an unassuming middle-aged man who had lived and breathed radio since his adolescence. On an island in Maine in 1908, when he was just fourteen, George Sterling became enamored with wireless radio. He served under General Pershing on the Mexican border, and in World War I in France, again under Pershing, Sterling organized and operated the first radio intelligence section of the Signal Corps. He located enemy transmitters and captured their messages. In civilian life again, Sterling worked for the government on the edge of the underworld. He located racetrack touts who wore small hidden transmitters and tried to beat bookies by placing bets just as winners came in.

During Prohibition, Sterling later wrote, he accumulated what he called "good target practice" for ferreting out Nazi spies. He helped find bootleggers who employed clandestine stations to communicate with boats inbound with contraband booze.

In 1940, with war coming, Sterling created the FCC's Radio Intelligence Division (RID), marshaling expert radiomen and ham operators for the cause. Sterling agreed to a liaison and exchange of information with the RID's British counterpart, the Radio Security Service. For Sterling, the RID's "most active and critical theater of espionage" was Latin America.

By 1942, the RID had sent teams to a dozen countries, although the level of cooperation its operatives received from local governments varied widely, from ready help in Brazil to folded arms in Chile. Nevertheless, primary RID stations were well equipped with receiving and recording equipment and large direction finders, special rotating antennae sensitive to the direction of shortwave signals bouncing off the ionosphere. Mobile units, disguised as delivery vans, could crawl around neighborhoods or travel into the countryside, equipped with a simple loop antenna capable of picking up the ground-wave component of a signal within a few miles. For homing in on transmitters in very close quarters, a risk that operatives sometimes took, they developed what they called a "snifter," a signal-strength meter that a man could carry in the palm of his hand while inspecting a building to determine which room a signal came from. Listening around the clock, the RID men came to distinguish the distinctive "fists" of various spies sending messages—experts will tell you no two operators transmit Morse code with exactly the same touch and rhythm.

In March 1942, RID agents detected a station in Rio encoding its message based on a book—a commonly used technique—whose title they discovered from an accidentally undisguised transmission: *The Story of San Michele* by Axel Munthe. Cryptanalysts determined—without computers—the indicated pages, lines, and letter substitutions being used to make out a chilling message:

QUEEN MARY REPORTED OFF RECIFE BY STEAMSHIP CAMPEIRO ON
ELEVENTH AT EIGHTEEN O'CLOCK MIDDLE EUROPEAN TIME.

The legendary liner had been repurposed as a troop carrier and was carrying ten thousand American and Canadian men. Other Operation Bolívar transmitters were full of the news, and the radiomen tracked down their locations. The liner was diverted, and the biggest spy sweep of the war in Latin America netted two hundred operatives and informants, arrested by Brazilian police.

Even after the war when RID's activities became public, J. Edgar Hoover gave the radio counterespionage agents no credit for arrests like these and more, which he attributed only to the FBI. Hoover held a grudge against FCC chairman James Lawrence Fly, who long blocked the FBI's wiretap power, and anyway, sharing credit was not the FBI chief's style.

More British and U.S. covert operatives arrived in countries that joined the Allies. They mixed unknowingly with the Reich's agents, and with local informants who often saw little reason to abandon their allegiance to old contacts and networks, and continued to collect information for Germany. In Brazil, Allied and Axis spies and counterspies might pass as enemies unrecognized amid the dark buildings of the capital's historic center or stroll the same breezy seafront from Ipanema to Copacabana.

THE "MASTER SPY" OF THE AMERICAS

Ironically, for all the damage done by agents who helped U-boats and other Axis vessels target Allied ships, the only German operative ever executed for spying in Latin America could never get his radio to work properly. Agent A-3779, Heinz August Lüning, had been trained in the Hamburg *Abwehr* spy school to make invisible inks, but once in the field he often couldn't get the formulas right, whether using lemon juice, urine, or headache tablets. He had thought he was escaping the worst—being drafted into Hitler's army—by becoming a spy and going to Cuba. He went in the guise of a Jewish refugee, traveling on a Honduran passport.

Lüning's time in Havana coincided with the Battle of the Caribbean, a spectacular serial disaster for Allied shipping. In just ten months, from February to November 1942, German submarines from the South Atlantic to the Caribbean sank 609 Allied vessels—about two a day, or 17.5 percent of Allied merchant tonnage lost between 1939 and 1945 on all seas to all forms of attack (German losses: 22 subs).

In the Caribbean and the Atlantic, north and south, the sixteen-hundred-ton German *Milchkühe*, the Nazi "milk cow" submarines, seemed to be everywhere. The refueling and reprovisioning subs allowed the combat subs to stay constantly on the hunt without returning to European bases. U.S. defenses—trained personnel, appropriate planes and vessels, effective detection equipment—were not yet up to speed.

In the fall of 1942, things looked bad all around for the Allies. Nazi forces controlled most of North Africa and were pummeling Stalingrad; the Japanese were fighting for control of the South Pacific at Guadalcanal, Port Moresby, Northern Australia. U-boats virtually controlled the Caribbean; half the ships they sunk were oil tankers. If sea lanes could not be protected, the United States and Great Britain could not count on the flow of fuel, or of other raw materials like bauxite (aluminum ore), or meat, or provisions essential to soldiers' rations like sugar and coffee.

Cuba's size and location made the island ground zero in the fight against the U-boats. Both the British and Americans had plenty of spies in place. Even Ernest Hemingway supervised, blunderingly, a private counterintelligence network of Spanish Republican refugees. But losses in nearby seas were deemed to be proof of the effectiveness of Nazi spies in Cuba. Unfortunately for the inept Lüning, he was the spy who was caught.

Lüning, code name "Lumann," was tagged by a compromising letter spotted at the British Imperial Censorship station in Bermuda, where twelve hundred trained staff scrutinized sea and air mail between Europe and Latin America. Some of the Reich's most deft espionage agents were discovered by the sharp women at the Bermuda station. The spies often never realized it, or only figured it out later when their operations, tracked by the British or the Americans, went wildly awry.

Heinz Lüning, however, was by all accounts an incompetent spy. The author Graham Greene, working for MI6 on the Portugal desk that kept tabs on the *Abwehr* in the Western Hemisphere, shared supervision of Lüning's case. Greene was said to have used "Lumann" as a model for the character of James Wormald, the vacuum-cleaner salesman and notional espionage agent in *Our Man in Havana*.

There was nothing funny about Lüning's fate, however. At his trial, his radio was shown to be inoperable, and there was no proof he had ever sent out an important piece of intelligence. His story made the pages of *True Detective* magazine, which ran photos of Hoover in Washington,

D.C., looking at a map alongside the Cuban chief of police, Manuel Benitez, the vain, self-serving former immigration official who had sold thousands of invalid landing permits to Jews. Other photos showed Lüning at an open jail cell door with his arm at his waist like a clothing model, as if trying to look his best. Benitez invented "subagents" supposedly controlled by Lüning throughout the Americas. U.S. agents called him a "master spy."

All this was fine with the *Abwehr*, because Lüning's arrest diverted attention from more capable agents in the German network. The capture cast a favorable glow on Cuba's dictator, Fulgencio Batista, and his lackey Benitez, who were invited to Washington together. There in front of photographers' flashing bulbs, J. Edgar Hoover shared the glory of capturing the "master spy" of the Americas. Lüning wrote a letter to his wife, son, parents, and an aunt and an uncle saying that the Cubans treated him well in jail, that "I never liked this job," and condemning the *Abwehr* for "bad preparation and a very bad organization." He sent kisses and an admonition to "hold your head high." On the morning of November 25, 1942, Heinz Lüning refused a blindfold and was shot to death by a Cuban firing squad. Lüning's demise did nothing to end the attacks on Allied ships, which continued until early 1944 when improved antisubmarine warfare drove the U-boats and Italian subs from the Caribbean.

ENDGAME

SIS agents, numbering some seven hundred open and covert G-men over the course of the war, continued to investigate leads about suspicious businessmen and community leaders, arranging with local police for their deportation to Europe and Japan or to the concentration camps for captured "aliens" in the United States. During the war, diplomats in Latin countries often took an open attitude toward the peaceful movements of labor, student, and other civil society movements that were organizing for more democracy, but Hoover was suspicious of them. Viscerally anticommunist, he ordered surveillance of the groups and infiltrated their meetings, especially after 1943 when the Nazi espionage "threat" seemed contained. The FBI agents trained secret police. They established relationships with police and investigative agencies that would be continued decades hence by U.S. diplomats and covert operators to uproot undesirable Latin governments and leftist forces. The OSS, soon to become the CIA, continued to build up intelligence on the region.

Despite blows, Operation Bolívar persisted beyond 1942, vindicating the approach Canaris had insisted upon from the beginning: cast a wide net of many agents in many cells, operating independently of each other, so that the entire weave is less likely to come undone when a string or two is pulled out. The Reich's agents remaining in Brazil kept their heads down. They no longer met casually over *cortados* at the Sympathy Café in Rio and could not recur for funds to the German Embassy, closed after Brazil declared war against the Axis in June 1942.

But information continued to flow by way of Buenos Aires. SS captain Johannes Siegfried Becker, the genius SD spy who had expanded "Alfredo's" operation into a first-class espionage station, was in Europe when the Brazil crackdown occurred; now he returned to Argentina where the German Embassy remained open. Antifascist Argentines reported suspicious activity to authorities, but their efforts were to little avail.

"All our family and friends sympathized whole-heartedly with the Allies and with Russia, desiring the defeat of the Axis, and we cheered the victories of the Red Army," Ernesto Guevara Lynch wrote in a memoir. In the early 1940s, Guevara Lynch had owned a plantation for growing yerba mate for the ubiquitous hot Argentine drink and made common cause with other antifascist young men. They spied on *Graf Spee* crewmen settled by the government in Cordoba, four hundred miles north of Buenos Aires. They saw the crew holding military exercises with dummy rifles.

They submitted a report about the Germans and other suspicious sightings—a truck loaded with arms, a hotel with a radio transmitter—to *Acción Argentina*, a nationwide organization that promoted entry into the war on the Allied side. But the organization was proscribed in 1943, and such citizen spy reports came to naught. Ernesto Guevara Lynch did become a part of history as the father of guerrilla leader Ernesto "Che" Guevara. When Che was a boy, wrote his father, the future revolutionary icon "was always asking me to let him help" with the spy operations.

Anti-Nazi Argentine congressmen, too, tried to weed out spies with reports, and their efforts resulted in some arrests. But much of the old network stayed in place. The government, Guevara Lynch said, "did not hide its sympathies for Hitler and Mussolini."

After the war, J. Edgar Hoover went on to fight "the enemy within": communists, civil rights advocates, and antiwar protesters in the United States. In 1947, Donovan's OSS became the CIA, the intelligence agency assigned to cover the rest of the world, now including Latin America.

William Donovan won the larger fight with Hoover over international espionage, but he lost a personal battle to head the postwar agency. What Wild Bill did not understand, but Hoover did, was how to manipulate Washington and the public. "Donovan knows everything we know except what we know about Donovan," an unnamed FBI source told a columnist for *Colliers* magazine in late 1941. Donovan's appeal to Roosevelt didn't help. "No President dare touch John Edgar Hoover," Donovan told an OSS colleague. "Let alone congressmen. They are all scared pink of him."

In late 1944, Donovan's "Top Secret" plan for the new global intelligence agency was leaked to a reporter who was a close friend of J. Edgar Hoover. Subsequent headlines warned of a "SUPER GESTAPO AGENCY," and the plan was shelved. Allen Dulles, Donovan's former OSS chief in Berne, became head of the CIA. J. Edgar Hoover led the FBI until his death at age seventy-seven in 1972.

Wilhelm Canaris, the Reich's legendary spymaster, did not survive the war. Like Hoover, Canaris was anticommunist to the core, ever since he had witnessed the mayhem of a Marxist-inspired revolt among shipmen of his beloved Imperial Navy at the end of World War I. And he had long held the trust of Hitler, holding seventeen private meetings with him, for instance, in 1934 and 1935. Canaris effectively performed secret intelligence missions on his own—even the British Admiralty lost track of him between 1935 and 1939. In Spain, where he operated in disguise, he barely escaped with his life. In Japan he overrode Versailles prohibitions by setting up a secret program in Osaka to build submarines for Germany. His loyalty to the fatherland was beyond doubt.

Canaris had been aghast, however, to hear that the Waffen-SS, the

armed wing of the party, was torching villages without military justification during the German invasion of Poland in 1939, killing intellectuals,
Jews, priests, members of the aristocracy, and political leaders. He went
to the front to see for himself, demanding on his return the carnage stop,
but General Wilhelm Keitel, chief of the General Staff, effectively told him
to return to the *Abwehr*. "A day will come when the world will find the
Wehrmacht responsible for these methods," Canaris warned.

Wilhelm Canaris was a well-traveled, well-read man of the world
who could coolly assess the strengths of various belligerents, even when
the *Wehrmacht* seemed unstoppable. He believed it was a mistake to go to
war against Britain. Perhaps recalling his early experience on the decks
of the *Dresden* where he watched the young U.S. fleet show its colors and
energy in New York Harbor, he intuited that it was also a mistake to go
to war against America. Canaris wanted his homeland and its opponents
intact when the fighting ended. He secretly, and vainly, approached the
British in various ways to make a diplomatic bridge that might serve both
sides and save his country from ruin.

When Roosevelt and Churchill met at Casablanca in 1943 and declared they would accept only "unconditional surrender" of the Axis,
Canaris lost hope in negotiations. "I believe the other side have now
disarmed us of the last weapon with which we could have ended the
war," he told a friend. No German general would accept "unconditional"
defeat. Goebbels riled up the population in the press and over the airwaves after Casablanca, describing horrifying conditions that would
come with total surrender.

"The students of history will not need to trouble their heads after
this war as they did after the last to determine who was guilty of starting
it," Canaris said. "The case is however different when we consider guilt
for prolonging the war."

Among some of the most patriotic German officers, including Canaris,
Hitler's terror tactics, mass murders of Jews, and patronage of a secret
police state eventually outweighed his role for them as a bastion against
Bolshevism. Canaris joined the conspiracy to assassinate the Fuehrer, a
desperate attempt to seize the armed forces from Nazi control and bring
forward a peace agreement with the Allies.

On July 20, 1944, in his Wolf's Lair, Hitler escaped the bomb meant to kill him. Canaris was arrested three days later in Berlin and brought to Flossenberg concentration camp in Bavaria. For months he underwent questioning, and when he did not provide answers or his answers were found to be elaborate ruses that implicated no one and arrived at dead ends, he was tortured.

On April 8, 1945, Canaris tapped a message in code to the former director of Danish intelligence, who was being held in the next cell: "Badly mishandled. Nose broken at last interrogation. My time is up. Was not a traitor. Did my duty as a German. If you survive, please tell my wife." With four other conspirators, including the theologian Dietrich Bonhoeffer, Canaris was stripped naked and hanged the next day. Two weeks later the camp was liberated by U.S. troops.

PART IV

The Warriors

11.

THE BATTLE OF THE ATLANTIC: SOUTHERN SEAS

Long, low, gray, and bristling with gun turrets and antennae, a *Panzer-schiff* lay off the coast of Brazil in September 1939, hidden by the vastness of the Atlantic, waiting for orders. One of three *Kriegsmarine Deutschland–*class cruisers, the *Panzerschiff* (armored ship) carried over a thousand men and weighed 10,600 tons, more than the weight limit imposed upon German military vessels by the Treaty of Versailles. When the British looked at plans for the "cruisers," they judged they were not cruisers at all, and gave the *Panzerschiffe* the nickname by which they became most widely known: pocket battleships.

The mighty new ships astonished war planners of other nations: their seams were welded, not sealed with rivets, and they were built with more aluminum than usual in order to be lighter. They were not powered by conventional steam turbines but by fifty-four-thousand-horsepower diesel engines that could cruise ten thousand miles without refueling.

Captain Hans Wilhelm Langsdorff knew he commanded a special vessel. To make up for the restrictions placed on the German Navy by the World War I treaty, each *Panzerschiff* had to serve the purpose of many ships. They could outspeed more powerful vessels and outgun most vessels at sea. At one time Langsdorff had considered becoming a priest, but he also wanted to go to sea so badly that, like Wilhelm Canaris, he defied his father's wishes and became an Imperial Navy cadet. At age forty-five, he was captain of one of the most valuable vessels in the *Kriegsmarine*, the navy of the Reich.

Langsdorff's assigned region of operation: south of the equator. His mission: Go after enemy commerce ships or ships with cargo that would serve the enemy, especially Britain, which was utterly dependent for survival on imports by sea. Strip the commercial vessels and take them as prizes, or destroy. Do not engage fighting ships of any flag. Hitler invaded Poland on the first of September. In the following weeks, Langsdorff received orders to begin his mission. The first victim of a pocket battleship in World War II was in South American waters, the British tramp steamer *Clement*.

"Ship on the port bow!" called the *Clement*'s lookout on the morning of September 30. A warship was the last thing on the mind of the *Clement*'s third officer while sailing off the northeast coast of Brazil, bound for Bahia. But he looked through the glass and there it was, a ship bearing straight at them at high speed, water jumping from the sides of its bow. He advised the ship's master below through the speaking tube. "Captain, there's a man-o'-war . . ."

When the officers couldn't identify the ship, they thought it must be His Majesty's light cruiser *Ajax*, known to be in southern waters, and the captain went back below to put on a jacket to receive visitors. As he came topside again a seaplane flew from the deck of the oncoming ship, soared overhead, and peppered the *Clement* with machine-gun fire. Someone saw markings on the wings. "My God, it's a Jerry!"

The *Clement*'s radio operator began transmitting "RRR," code for "I am being attacked by aircraft," but a signal went up on the attacking ship, in English: "Stop. No wireless transmitting." No sooner did the captain of the *Clement* stuff the ship's confidential papers into a weighted bag and drop them into the sea, giving lifeboats the order to launch, than a piquet boat arrived and ordered him to scuttle.

Except for strafing the *Clement*, the Germans acted graciously. Langsdorff placed the captain and chief officer on a passing Greek vessel and ordered a radio message broadcast asking other ships to "Please save" the other men, giving the position of their lifeboats. Within two days, all were safe. The *Clement*'s men reported to the Admiralty with a variety of descriptions of the ship that ended their voyage, but all agreed it had no markings. Yet some had noticed the name *Admiral Sheer* painted on the piquet boat. British admirals put out the word that pocket battleship *Admiral Sheer*, Hitler's secret weapon, now roamed the Atlantic coast of South America.

But Langsdorff had more than one trick up his sleeve. Not only did he surprise the *Clement* and have it scuttled in a model operation, without loss of life, he had also sown confusion among the British by faking the name of his ship, having the piquet boat painted with the name of his sister pocket battleship. Soon the British Admiralty and its allies would believe there were two of the dreaded *Panzerschiffe* on the seas, because when Langsdorff attacked his next prey less than a week later, on October 5, he showed his ship's true name, the *Admiral Graf Spee*.

When the *Graf Spee* came upon the British cargo ship *Newton Beech*, her captain had just managed to jettison the ship's documents and change out of his pajamas. He figured whatever came next would be better faced in uniform.

Langsdorff placed the *Newton Beech* under a prize crew and received the captives politely, then ordered them into clean quarters where they were fed from the same mess as his own crew. He interviewed the captain in his quarters. Langsdorff knew the rules of war mandated decent treatment of prisoners, and besides, by all accounts he was an affable and naturally gracious gentleman, about whom none of his prisoners would complain—and there would be many prisoners. Two days later another British ship, this one carrying sugar, was overcome by the *Graf Spee* so quickly that instead of dropping the ship's papers into the weighted bag, which the captain feared might be recovered, he ran below and threw them into the furnace. Langsdorff's ship was getting crowded.

Over the next six weeks the *Graf Spee* took six more ships, sometimes sailing under its own ensign, sometimes under a French flag that Langsdorff carried for the purpose of sneaking up on vessels friendly to the Allies. Once, he sailed around the Horn of Africa and attacked an oil tanker, the *Africa Shell*, south of Madagascar. An alarmed Whitehall believed the British Navy was facing another front in its struggle with

Panzerschiffe, not only the Atlantic but also the Indian Ocean. Twenty-five British and French warships in nine task forces were already on the hunt, the largest sea search in history until that time. The British drew forces away from places where they were needed in order to find the *Graf Spee* and, they believed, the *Admiral Scheer*.

The captain of the *Africa Shell* joined the other prisoners. Langsdorff saw to it that the rest of the crew was in boats rowing to shore, just two miles away. He had the tanker drained for its oil and destroyed, then doubled back to the Atlantic and picked off more vessels. He made good use of the speed of the *Panzerschiff*, remarkable for its size—up to twenty-seven knots, about thirty-two miles per hour. And he used its marvelous innovation: an early version of radar that allowed a captain to see over the horizon, to spot ships still invisible to human eyes even with binoculars of the finest glass.

Langsdorff took more than fifty thousand tons of shipping—nine vessels—in twelve weeks without loss of life among his crew or opponents. All of that changed on the fateful morning when the *Admiral Graf Spee* met three British battleships: the heavy cruiser HMS *Exeter* and the light cruisers HMNZS *Achilles*, manned chiefly by New Zealanders including some Maori, and the *Ajax*.

Commodore Henry Harwood, who commanded the British Navy's South America Division, was captain of the *Ajax* and led the three-ship force. He had been hunting the marauder for two months. Given new intelligence about the date, time, and position of a *Graf Spee* attack in the Atlantic, coupled with Harwood's knowledge of the South American sea lanes, the commodore brilliantly calculated the time and place when the German ship was next likely to appear: December 13, 1939, off the great estuary where the Plate River between Uruguay and Argentina empties into the South Atlantic.

"Attack on sight by day or by night," he ordered.

At 6:04 a.m. on the day Harwood had divined, a thunderous volley of explosions heralded the beginning of the first sea battle of World War II, the Battle of the River Plate. Why Langsdorff engaged the British force despite orders to avoid battle has never been explained—he would have spied them with his long-seeing radar before they saw him, with time to turn and flee. The *Achilles* and the flagship *Ajax* tailed the *Graff Spee* on one side, the heavy cruiser *Exeter* attacked on the other.

Langsdorff had more firepower. He lost time and favorable position when he made turns to shell the smaller cruisers, however, when he might have given everything he had to blow the *Exeter* out of the water and then address the other vessels. When he laid down a smokescreen, the *Achilles* and the *Ajax* used the obscurity to their advantage, gaining distance on the *Graf Spee*.

Soon after the first shots, a German officer looked down into the hold where the prisoners were being held. "Gentlemen, I am afraid I must leave you to your own devices today," he said, closing the hatch and bolting it from the outside. A gun turret shook with unbearable noise just above the prisoners' heads. For hours they suffered an emotional quandary, hoping for the Germans' defeat but fearing that one tremendous hit could send them to the bottom.

Sixty-one men were lost on the *Exeter*—more than on the other ships. When an exploding shell created a peephole for the prisoners on the *Graf Spee*, they looked out and saw disinfectant being poured over the dead bodies of German sailors stacked on deck.

Langsdorff was only slightly wounded in the face from flying wood splinters, but he saw dead crew members all around. His water desalination apparatus was destroyed, the onboard refinery that processed crude oil into the fuel that he needed to get back to Germany was badly damaged. The injured needed tending to save their lives. He made upriver for the neutral port of Montevideo.

Harwood sent out a call for other British ships to trap the pocket battleship at the river's mouth, but the closest ship that could help was a full two days away. The big *Exeter*, badly disabled, sailed to the Falklands for repairs. Only the *Achilles* and the *Ajax* stood watching in place lest the *Graf Spee* try to escape. There was no guarantee, however, that two light cruisers could block the *Graf Spee* if its captain was determined to break through again to the sea.

Now began the three days that truly determined the outcome of the Battle of the River Plate. Victory would go to the side that best handled the auxiliary armament of modern war: propaganda, political maneuvering, deliberately false information. The British put out the word that a force of numerous ships was bottling in the *Graf Spee*, waiting to attack the *Panzerschiff*. It wasn't true, but the BBC and U.S. reporters who flew in to cover the big event repeated the false "news" without confirmation. Langsdorff wanted to see for himself, but his ship's aircraft was out of commission and no one would rent him a plane—Uruguay was "neutral," but favored Britain. Captain Dietrich Niebuhr, the naval attaché at the German Embassy in Buenos Aires, flew in to arrange for aid and repairs because the good citizens of Montevideo did not want to help.

To make sure that the *Graf Spee* was stalled for as long as possible in port, the British minister to Uruguay, Eugen Millington-Drake, made clever use of an item of international law stipulating that no warship may leave a neutral port within twenty-four hours of the departure of a merchant vessel. Millington-Drake called an emergency meeting of British merchant captains in Montevideo and arranged for them to set sail one per day, effectively preventing Langsdorff from departing. By the third day, more than twenty thousand onlookers—the men in hats and ties, the women in fine dresses—were crowding the long quay at Montevideo, eager for the first shots to be fired. Across the globe, millions read about the standoff in newspapers, and millions more followed the drama on the radio, the first time a war event was broadcast live to the world. News came from London that the king had honored Commodore Harwood with a knighthood.

On shore in Montevideo, Hans Langsdorff led a procession of notables, officers, and men to bury the thirty-seven men of the German crew who had died. The British prisoners whom Langsdorff had carried were freed the first hour the *Graf Spee* landed, but they returned to accompany the cortege, in honor of the pocket battleship's captain. Langsdorff sprinkled a handful of earth on each casket.

In the late afternoon of December 18, Langsdorff ordered the *Graf Spee* moved to a side channel of the river, out of the shipping lanes. Accompanied by officers and two Argentine tugs, he supervised the placement of explosives that would destroy the vessel, and had them detonated at sunset. Langsdorff wanted to stay aboard and go down with the ship, but was dissuaded by his officers. The *Admiral Graf Spee*, one of the marvels of the German Navy, named for the hero who overcame the British at the Battle of Coronel during World War I, went up in a huge ball of flame and burned for two days.

The German crew, over a thousand men, went across the Plate River to Argentina, where they were interned. On December 20, having assured himself of arrangements for his men, Langsdorff climbed the stairs of the naval center on a downtown corner of Buenos Aires, an old building faced with white columns, a pure and elegant facade. In his quarters he spread the battle ensign of the *Graf Spee* neatly upon the floor—not a flag with a swastika but a banner that evoked the Imperial Navy. In full dress uniform, he lay upon the cloth and with a gray Mauser pistol shot himself in the head.

In the German cemetery on the edge of Buenos Aires, Hans Langsdorff is buried at the center of a row of graves with handsome but modest tombstones belonging to officers from the *Graf Spee*, the grounds around them kept neat and trim. When I was there on an afternoon in 2017, there were freshly cut flowers on a few of the graves, including Langsdorff's. Next door, under elms in the English cemetery, a long, black marble wall is incised with the names of 861 Anglo-Argentines who lost their lives in the First and Second World Wars. An archivist at the nearby Recoleta Cemetery told me she believed that at one time all the cemeteries on the long street were open, one to another, but that between the wars walls went up between them.

In 2011, when I visited the cemetery in Montevideo where the dead of the *Graf Spee* lay buried under simple metal crosses, I had found myself wondering what made Langsdorff destroy his ship and then take his own life. The Uruguayans, pressured by the British and protective of their neutral status, had finally ordered the *Graf Spee* to leave the port, and the German captain had no choice under international law.

Perhaps Langsdorff believed that a fleet indeed waited to attack the *Graf Spee* if he tried to plow through to the sea and that more lives would be lost. He could hardly have left the ship intact where it lay, or it would surely end in the hands of the British. In photos of the burial of the crew members, the German sailors, officers, even a priest extend their arms in the Nazi salute for the final farewell; only Langsdorff, in dress whites, does not, giving instead the naval salute. Could he not have imagined returning to the Reich? Was his honor so besmirched? Did he

fear punishment from the Fuehrer? Or was he shaken by the loss of so
many men? Around me in the graveyard I noticed the ages of those buried: seventeen, eighteen, nineteen.

The Battle of the River Plate began the Battle of the Atlantic, the longest
continuous military campaign of World War II, from 1939 to 1945. *Graf
Spee*, *Exeter*, and *Ajax* are names that echo in the memory of naval history. The encounter of two forgotten vessels, however, the Liberty ship
Richard Caswell and the German submarine *U-513*, is more like the clash
experienced by most men who plied the seas off South America during
those years. They were the kinds of vessels that ran along the coasts
regularly—ships carrying troops and trade items vital to the war, and the
attack submarines that pursued them. Each sailed from its home port for
weeks, their voyages typical for vessels of their kind, toward a deadly
meeting off the coast of Brazil.

In June 1943, the *Richard Caswell* headed out of the harbor in Wilmington, North Carolina, crewmen standing at ease on the aft deck with
hands behind backs under a hot sun. The ship sailed down the Cape Fear
River to the sea as the sound of screeching gulls overcame the brave
strains of "The Washington Post March." Boy Scouts stood at the edge of
the pier, hands at smooth foreheads in a salute they would not drop until
the *Richard Caswell* disappeared. Master Solomon Suggs, standing on the
bridge, probably marveled that towns still came out after a year and a half
of watching ships go to war.

Liberty ships like the *Richard Caswell*, named for a Revolutionary
War hero, were being produced fast, designed for hard hauling and short
lives—about five years. They were a key line of defense against Hitler's
strategy to strangle the life out of England, bringing food to the island,
and they also brought supplies to the United States. Manned by the U.S.
Merchant Marines, generally civilians and union men, Liberty ships carried not only food but also raw materials like timber and rubber and rare
metals needed to make war such as tungsten and magnesium. And they
carried troops, the essential human cargo. A merchant ship was as fundamental to the war effort as a bomber, the most important vessel on the
U-boats' target list. Nazi war planners estimated that the destruction of

150 merchant ships a month would defeat England. In the previous year, 1942, the Axis had sunk 1,661 ships, mostly merchants, 1,151 of them destroyed by submarines.

That is why U.S. shipyards were turning out Liberty ships at speeds never before seen, just forty-one days per ship sometimes, although the record was four days, fifteen and a half hours for a single craft out of Richmond, California. Unlike German crewmen who were present during the construction of their subs, from the laying down of the keel to installing the final light switches, the U.S. merchant crews received their ships at launching from laborers new to the marine construction workforce, blacks, and especially women. Rosie the Riveter and Wanda the Welder labored around the clock by the thousands in Mobile, Portland, New Orleans, Savannah, Sausalito, and a dozen other places. The steel magnate Henry Kaiser oversaw half a dozen companies managing Liberty ship production using the assembly-line methods of Henry Ford.

The Wilmington docks were gone from the *Richard Caswell*'s view. "First officer, dismiss your men," Suggs said.

They broke rank, among them men who had never left their hometowns until the war. The slowest to move were the Black Gang, the handful of men who knew that the vast and noisy engine room below would be even hotter than topside. They had been baptized with their name when ships were powered by burning coal, and they spent their days covered in carbon dust. They were engineers but also oilers, firemen, and wipers who tended pistons and valves, main engines and auxiliaries, day and night. Black Gangers Tommy Pike and Benjamin Groutner headed down for their shift.

Fourteen U.S. Navy personnel were aboard under separate command to defend crew and cargo from attack, and they scattered too. Some went to man the two forward guns, others the single aft gun.

Only then, when the first waves of the open sea were breaking upon the bow, would Captain Suggs pivot and climb narrow metal stairs to the wheelhouse. Before the *Richard Caswell* had weighed anchor, a U.S. Navy officer had come aboard to present Suggs with an envelope containing the ship's orders. For security reasons, Suggs had delayed opening the envelope until they were under sail. But it was also protocol for Suggs to wait—he had learned this at his alma mater, the U.S. Merchant Marine Academy in Great Neck, New York.

Suggs pulled out a piece of cream-colored paper, light as tissue, read carefully, and closed his eyes. Not yet forty, with an open face lightly tanned, Suggs felt the corners of his lips turn up in a faint smile. His ship would not join one of the England-bound transoceanic convoys, now sometimes numbering a hundred vessels yet still prey to the U-boat wolf packs that skillfully picked off individual craft. Then his brow furrowed. At least the North Atlantic convoys were protected by a loose circle of escort ships. The *Richard Caswell* would sail to the South Atlantic, alone.

Looking out the wheelhouse windows, Solomon Suggs saw blue-gray clouds rolling up from the south. It was winter in the Southern Hemisphere, not the steamy summer of his hometown of Bradford, Florida, along the green banks of the Suwanee River. The helmsman kept his eyes straight ahead, but he might have heard an exhalation that signaled the weight of responsibility falling on the captain's shoulders.

"We sail," Suggs announced, "south for the Argentine."

Two thousand miles from the *Richard Caswell*'s position, *U-513* was thirteen days out of flotilla headquarters on the coast of Nazi-occupied France, cruising the surface of the mid-Atlantic. The U-boat was the length of three freight cars, though only as wide as one, with diesel engines that could reach eighteen knots surface speed, almost twenty-one miles an hour. Her low profile served as protection from enemy ships, and she ran past the Azores without incident, bound under clear skies for the coast of Brazil.

It was nearly a miracle that *U-513* sailed at all. Returning from her previous patrol, she had met another U-boat at the harbor entrance at Lorient, on the Bay of Biscay. *U-513*'s captain on that voyage graciously allowed the other captain to dock first. An honor guard and a military band waited on the pier to greet the U-boats as minesweepers finished their duty. They missed one, though; the forward sub hit the mine, blowing a huge hole aft of the control room, and sank fast. The horrified crew of *U-513* launched a rescue, but only eleven men out of fifty-three on the other sub were saved.

In port, *U-513*'s engineer officer suffered a case of nervous shock that paralyzed his legs, so he was replaced. The captain, a veteran who already had led three patrols on *U-513*, left the ship too; he was replaced by a much younger man, Kapitänleutnant (Lieutenant Commander) Friedrich Guggenberger. Six weeks later, *U-513* was once more at sea.

Topside, standing tall and slim, the twenty-nine-year-old Guggenberger lifted his Zeiss binoculars and scanned the seascape. He saw only a blue-green expanse animated by foaming waves. His former hunting ground in the Mediterranean had been more richly blue, more dangerous, more exciting. *U-513* was well beyond the uninhabited Ascension islands in the mid-Atlantic and, except for a two-funnel steamer it chased and lost south of the Canary Islands, had found no prey. In the Mediterranean, not only did more enemy ships crawl about a smaller expanse of water, but Guggenberger could attack targets ashore, as he boldly had done at Jaffa, destroying fuel-storage tanks.

Guggenberger swung himself into the hatch, closed it, and descended the metal ladder. Stepping from the bottom rung into the control room, he stood in place for a moment, allowing his pale blue eyes to adjust to the unnaturally ivory light. In port, fresh fruit and vegetables had been packed into every corner of the sub and were now ripening. The food emitted a mix of sickly sweet smells that collided with the ship's odors of diesel fuel, a single toilet that served the entire crew, and unwashed men—water was a luxury. Guggenberger removed his wet rubber poncho and handed it to an aide, perhaps wishing he had spent another few minutes in the open air.

Men turned from their stations and saluted. Faces looked rough because shaving, too, was a luxury. Some, of course, showed barely a beard. At this point Germans were being pulled into the war as young as fifteen or sixteen.

Even before they had set eyes on him, everyone aboard had heard of Guggenberger. The submarine ace had destroyed more than sixty thousand tons of enemy shipping since the war began. Most famously, as chief of the submarine *U-81*, he once made a daring run past Gibraltar and into the Mediterranean to sink the British aircraft carrier *Ark Royal*.

That enemy ship was the prize above all others that Germans had yearned to destroy. The *Ark Royal* was one of the ships that joined the

British blockade at the Plate River in 1939, when the *Graf Spee* went down. Two years later, in May 1941, she was one of dozens of vessels hunting the powerful German battleship *Bismarck*, whose very name struck British sailors with terror. When the *Bismarck* destroyed the mighty HMS *Hood*, an imperial legend known for showing the flag at ports around the world as a symbol of British power, Winston Churchill said, "I don't care how you do it, you must sink the *Bismarck*."

The *Ark Royal* found the *Bismarck* in the Denmark Strait, crippled it with torpedo bombs, and chased it until, pummeled by the *Ark* and its sisters, the ship went down. Six months later off Gibraltar, Guggenberger sank the *Ark Royal* with a single, well-placed torpedo to its starboard side. The act wrought vengeance for two thousand men lost on the *Bismarck* and, as a British chronicler wrote, "destroyed the very core of the Royal Navy's striking power in the Mediterranean." Hitler himself presented Guggenberger with the Knight's Cross of the Iron Cross, the highest military award of the Third Reich.

National hero or not, the new captain imposed a regime that spurred grousing on *U-513*. Repeated routine submersions, emergency exercises, and crash dives ran the crew ragged, testing men and machine. When Guggenberger considered diving time too slow, crewmen had to cut holes into the space above the forward torpedo tubes to increase air circulation and shave seconds from descent. These extra moments could mean the difference between life and death.

More than once, Radioman Second Class Hans Zophel leaned out of the cubbyhole where he monitored radio transmissions and sound outside the sub to call for quiet, and the order passed along the length of the sub like a stone skipping on a lake. But they were false alarms, just rattling the men and making them sweat.

When Guggenberger finally hit his bunk, lying without a pillow, a cloth under his boots to keep the bedcover clean, he probably exhaled with the frustration of a man of action hitched to a drag sail. Perhaps he pulled out a photo of his wife of only three months. Or of his father, wearing the black dress uniform of an officer in the Kaiser's navy. His father was lost in the Battle of Heligoland in the North Sea during World War I at British hands, a few months before Guggenberger was born.

•   •   •

On June 21, the first day of winter in the Southern Hemisphere, Guggenberger finally encountered the enemy he so wanted to engage, off Brazil.

The Swedish cargo steamer *Venezia* had just loaded tobacco, coffee, cocoa, cocoa butter, and drums of vegetable oil in Bahia's port, Santiago. Bound for Buenos Aires, she sailed past colonial-era Portuguese fortifications. Stockholm sold iron ore to Nazi Germany, allowed passage of German soldiers across its territory, and otherwise cooperated with Berlin. At the same time, Sweden shared intelligence with Great Britain and sheltered Jews. It played both sides, its way of remaining "neutral."

Guggenberger gave the order to launch the torpedoes. Any cargo floating in the Atlantic that did not belong to Italy or Germany might end in Allied hands and had to be destroyed. Should the U-boat's action result in a political flap for targeting a vessel of a neutral country, the deed could always be blamed on the Italians. The *Venezia* went down so quickly its radio operator had no time to send an SOS. Its demise only became known a week later when surviving members of the crew reached land.

Four days later, lookouts on *U-513* spied a ship about which there could be no doubt of neutrality, the U.S. oil tanker *Eagle*. In the darkness, the low, unlit profile of the U-boat was all but invisible. The *Eagle*'s crew didn't know what hit them. Recovering quickly, however, the *Eagle* returned fire, forcing Guggenberger to dive.

"Alarm, alarm," repeated voices. For the next twelve hours *U-513* pursued the *Eagle*. The American tanker was old, built in San Francisco in 1917, but managed evasion until a point called Cabo Frio, just north of Rio de Janeiro. There Guggenberger was able to position the U-boat to fire two torpedoes that damaged the *Eagle*. He ordered a third, anticipating the deathblow, but the *Eagle* turned sharply to port and the torpedo missed its bow by fifteen feet.

U-513 fell away, but the sub had found her pace, vanquishing the *Venezia* and wounding the American tanker.

Late on June 30, *U-513* was chasing a large steamer south of São Paulo when a rain squall fell like a curtain between the vessels. Midnight came and went. When the air cleared, the prey was gone, but a smaller steamer, the Brazilian merchant *Tutoya*, appeared in range, and

Guggenberger hit it midship with a single torpedo. The *Tutoya* sank bow first, with the loss of the ship's master and six crew. Two days later, Guggenberger sank the U.S. Liberty ship SS *Elihu B. Washburne*, bound for New York full of coffee, a provision for troops almost as critical as ammunition. Within seventy-two hours the U-boat destroyed two more ships, the English merchant *Incomati* and an American freighter bound for New York with a cargo of hides and leather, the *African Star*. On *U-513*'s voyage, she was served by *Milchkühe*, the Nazi "milk cow" supply subs whose only purpose was to refuel fighting U-boats. Now Guggenberger had to call for another kind of supply: more torpedoes.

One night the U-boat decided to take stock of Rio's harbor defenses. So close did it stand to shore that the men took turns coming onto the deck to gaze at the city's lights. Guggenberger discovered that a single old destroyer patrolled the harbor's entrance. He ordered attack positions and maneuvered several times, but the position was never right. *U-513* slipped below, staying in place. Hours later the sub broke surface and, to the crew's shock, found itself only fifteen hundred yards ahead of the destroyer.

"Flood! Quick dive tank. Flood!" Guggenberger commanded. Loose objects flew, men fell hard against iron walls. When no depth charge or torpedo came, *U-513* headed for open sea. Apart from skill and valor, Kapitänleutnant Friedrich Guggenberger was blessed with luck.

He was also blessed with hard information about enemy movements. Operation Bolívar might have been under pressure from J. Edgar Hoover's men, but Axis vessels continued to be on the receiving end of the *Abwehr* intelligence. And there was likely an Enigma Machine aboard *U-513*— submarines had them, too.

Wrapped in a greatcoat against the Southern Hemisphere winter, Solomon Suggs stood on the bridge of the *Richard Caswell*. A cargo of tungsten, the miraculous metal mined in Argentina's northern highlands, awaited the Liberty ship in the harbor at Buenos Aires. Four times as hard as titanium and twice as hard as steel, tungsten, when mixed with ordinary carbon, became a key component in manufacturing armor-piercing weapons strong enough to stop the tanks of the Nazi *Wehrmacht*.

In Buenos Aires, Suggs staggered shore leaves, limiting them to four hours, and did not leave the ship himself, supervising deliveries that came by hand and crane and their placement in the holds. The *Richard Caswell* turned around in forty-eight hours.

Steaming out of the harbor and bound for New York, the Liberty ship carried nine hundred tons of the tungsten, cargos of canned meat, animal hides for army boots, manganese ore, and fertilizer. The Plate River roiled around it, carrying the dirt of Paraguay, Uruguay, and Argentina and giving waters the cast of coffee made with the dregs. Suggs steered fast and clear in the middle of the river, which was so broad that neither shore was visible. Pale, blue-white fingers of salt water entered the stream, embracing the *Richard Caswell*, pulling it toward the open sea.

A cadet appeared. "Message from the first officer, sir," he said. "Approaching mouth of the River Plate." The war had required young cadets like this boy to forgo the usual four years of marine education and full training.

"North," Suggs ordered. "North, for Florianopolis."

Close to the bustling cities of coastal Brazil, Florianopolis possessed such an independent sense of itself as a tropical island that its road signs pointing northeast said simply, "The Continent." Rumor ran that points on its sandy rim served as U-boat refueling stations operated by Brazilian collaborators. But Suggs felt confident about the isle and its nearby seas. Its port hosted a base for U.S. Navy ships, including seaplane tenders that accompanied the hunt for U-boats.

Some future day, these months would be remembered as the most deadly in the Battle of the Atlantic, when U-boats destroyed more Allied vessels than in any other period of the war. England nearly starved. Winston Churchill, otherwise stalwart in his memoirs, wrote that the Battle of the Atlantic "was the only thing that ever really frightened me."

On *U-513*, Captain Friedrich Guggenberger took a message from the radioman. A U.S. merchant ship would pass the waters off Florianopolis during the night. The spies of Operation Bolívar were doing their job. And the ship was carrying tungsten! The metal had become one of the most valuable on earth. Could it be recovered? Would its crates bob in salt water, even for a while? The Americans had once saved blocks of rubber from a sunken ship near the mouth of the Amazon, paying local fishermen for each boatful they recovered, so the idea wasn't far-fetched. And the intelligence gave the sub an advantage: time to prepare.

The *Richard Caswell* and *U-513* sailed toward each another throughout the day. The sea was enormous, but the encounter was as inevitable as the coming night. Merchant ships often lost to U-boats. But the merchants were armed with U.S. Navy gunners, and the contest could go the other way.

On the night of July 16, 1943, dead winter in the Southern Hemisphere, the moon rose full, blue light falling on icy waves. The wind seemed to blow up from Antarctica, only a few hundred miles south. On the *Richard Caswell*, perhaps only the Black Gangers like Pike and Groutman felt warm in their hissing, clanging, three-tiered engine rooms amid the fiery boilers.

About 9:00 p.m. from a position on deck, Guggenberger spied the tower of a ship breaching the horizon, a tiny but unmistakable reflection of moonlight coming his way. In fuller profile, the vessel revealed itself to be a U.S. merchant ship. His submarine black against black even in moonlight, Guggenberger decided not to submerge. He called orders to battle stations.

"Fire!"

At 9:15, 150 miles southeast of Florianopolis, a torpedo struck the *Richard Caswell* on the starboard side at the aft end of the engine room, killing three men on watch and destroying the ship's engines. The navy guards began to fire all ten guns in the direction from which the missile came. Officers and crew scrambled, and Suggs assessed damage and chances for survival. He made a call: "Abandon ship!"

In less than ten minutes, seven officers, thirty-four crewmen, twenty-four armed guards, and two passengers boarded three lifeboats and one raft and pushed away. Master Suggs, the last to leave, boarded a second raft with two officers and three crewmen, including the Black Gangers Pike and Groutman.

On *U-513*, Guggenberger watched through his binoculars as the last raft pushed off from the U.S. ship. Then an extraordinary thing happened. The raft began returning to the damaged *Richard Caswell*.

Seeing that the ship did not sink at once, Suggs returned with the men in the raft to collect the ship's papers and smash every piece of equipment they could.

When Guggenberger saw what the Americans were doing, he ordered a second torpedo fired. It struck at the forward end of the engine room. The explosion blew the captain and crewmen, including Pike and Groutman, over the side, ripping apart the midship deck and superstructure. In minutes the *Richard Caswell* broke in two and sank. Of those who had reboarded, there were no survivors.

Three days later, on July 19, 1943, a U.S. Navy plane from the seaplane tender USS *Barnegat* spotted *U-513* and sunk it with depth charges. The British Admiralty paid tribute to crews of the German U-boat corps like the men of *U-513* after the war: "Their morale was unimpaired to the bitter end." Besides *U-513*, 782 submarines went down in the war. The loss of life was staggering. Twenty-eight thousand men of the submarine fleet died out of a total seagoing strength of thirty-nine thousand.

The *Barnegat*'s airplane pilot dropped life belts and rafts to men struggling in the waters, and within four hours the *Barnegat* arrived to pick up the survivors of *U-513*, including Guggenberger. Three days later, the *Barnegat*'s other plane reported seeing survivors in another raft, and the ship hurried to the indicated position. There the *Barnegat* found two rafts lashed together and boarded seventeen survivors from the SS *Richard Caswell*. In Rio the *Barnegat* transferred its German prisoners to authorities and disembarked the men of the *Richard Caswell*—at separate berths.

Friedrich Guggenberger was imprisoned in U.S. camps, making two escapes. On his second escape he was recaptured just ten miles from the Mexican border. After the war and repatriation, Guggenberger attended the Naval War College in Newport, Rhode Island. He was promoted to admiral in the German Navy and served as deputy chief of staff of NATO's Allied Forces in Northern Europe.

In October 1943, three months after Solomon Suggs was lost at sea to a torpedo fired by Guggenberger's U-boat, his son Solomon Jr. signed on as an able seaman on the Liberty ship *Edward D. White* out of Brunswick, Georgia.

12.

SMOKING COBRAS

High in the Apennine Mountains stands a medieval tower among ruined walls, a reminder of ferocious fighting between Nazis and Allies that upended life in one small town during the campaign Germans called "Winter Storm." Today gardens with chestnut trees and trim houses dot the slopes of Sommocolonia—the name echoes its Roman origins. The town is whisper quiet, giving little hint of the fire and shelling that tore through this and every other city and hamlet along the Gothic Line where war raged through the 1944–45 winter, one of the worst in European history.

On the seventieth anniversary of the end of World War II in Italy, members of the *Alpini* mountain fighting unit, each wearing the distinctive traditional *capello* with its black raven's feather, placed a wreath of laurel leaves at Sommocolonia's marble memorial to the fallen. Then young and old sat down to an outdoor banquet that finished with dishes made with chestnuts, an homage to how the townspeople survived when the food ran out. They recounted stories of fear and loss and valor. From a tower on a promontory overlooking the Serchio River Valley, three banners flew: the Italian *Tricolore*; the U.S. Stars and Stripes; and the blue orb of the nighttime sky set in a field of gold and green, the flag of Brazil.

Twenty-five thousand Brazilians fought on the side of the Allies during the invasion of Italy, the only Latin American force to fight in Europe during World War II. Its veterans are fewer every year, and the Brazilian Expeditionary Force (BEF) is on the verge of being forgotten in Brazil. But their story is worth remembering.

From July to December 1944, convoys of troopships sailed from Rio de Janeiro to Italy. U-boats threatened, and U.S. ships escorted the convoys for stretches on the ocean. Ninety-two-year-old Nery Prado recalled that a U.S. vessel pulled up alongside his ship in the mid-Atlantic to salute the Brazilians.

"It was at the equator, before the American ship veered off," Prado told me at his home in Curitiba, in southern Brazil. "All their men were on deck, dressed in white, and we were all on deck, too. We sang 'God Bless America' together, Americans and Brazilians." Sitting on his living room sofa Prado sang it again, in Portuguese. *"Deus salve America . . ."*

"It was something you never forget," he said.

The first five thousand Brazilians arrived in Italy in July 1944, weak from seasickness and dysentery, having zigzagged across the Atlantic avoiding submarines. They came ashore without weapons—an ignominious landing—because Allied planners had decided they would receive arms after arrival, not before. Worse, their green uniforms resembled the enemy's. Neapolitans mistook them for German war prisoners and greeted them with jeers and foul language. The Brazilians might have expected to salve their hurt pride that night in decent barracks, but they were trucked to a "base camp" that turned out to be nothing but a grove of fruit trees at the foot of Mt. Vesuvius. They slept in the open air.

Thus rose the first of the misunderstandings, differences in perception and operational behavior that would riddle the relationship between the Brazilians and the Americans. On the day the BEF arrived, a U.S. Army major reported, "The weather was very hot and calm." The Brazilian commander, General João Baptista Mascarenhas de Moraes, referred to those first days as "terribly cold." The diminutive Mascarenhas, who wore round, metal-rimmed glasses, was an old-school Brazilian officer whose expectations of a certain kind of welcome were clearly violated.

Without familiar food, some Brazilians nearly starved in the first weeks until they could stomach GI rations, mysterious meats in dull gold cans, not the rice, beans, and manioc flour to which they were accustomed. When they received new uniforms, they found the American-size boots too big, and stuffed them with paper or cloth. Three months later, when they reached the district of the Barga commune called Fornaci di Barga, some enterprising soldiers took advantage of a break in the firing to have their footwear refitted by a cobbler in exchange for a ration of food.

In his memoirs, General Mark Clark, commander of the Fifth Army to which the BEF was attached, wrote, "We did, however, get combat jackets and winter underwear for them quickly, and then they were properly prepared to go into the line."

To say the Brazilians were "properly prepared" with clothing, as Clark wrote, was not to say they were prepared, despite the general's opinion, "to go into the line" against troops of German field marshal Albert Kesselring. One of Hitler's most accomplished strategists, Kesselring commanded the Axis front in Italy with highly trained and experienced soldiers. Brazil's most recent—and only other—overseas deployment had been three centuries in the past, in 1648, when soldiers from Portuguese-held Brazil were part of an expedition to drive the Dutch from Angola and take control of the slave trade that powered the sugar industry.

As they prepared in Brazil to fight in Europe, troops had used weapons from the 1920s and 1930s such as single-shot Mauser rifles, World War I–era Hotchkiss machine guns, and Schneider artillery of the kind transported on the backs of mules. At an old royal hunting ground near Pisa, the men got a crash course in their new U.S. arms.

Mascarenhas and his troops faced a dangerous military situation in Italy. The Allies had secured Sicily, Monte Cassino, Rome, and most of the south, but German forces and thousands of Italians who had agreed to serve in the German army after Italy surrendered in 1943 held strong in much of the center of the country, and almost all of the wealthy north. Tens of thousands of Allied troops had just been taken away from Italy to prepare for the invasion of France, leaving the Allies short of men. Yet all of Italy north of Rome remained contested.

The rest of Europe was in flames. On the day the first Brazilians arrived in Naples, a conspiracy to assassinate Hitler had just failed, and the Fuehrer ordered the mobilization of all Germans for the war. U.S. general George Patton's tanks were advancing on German lines; the Russians were advancing on Warsaw.

Incongruously, amid intensive instruction and exhausting exercises, the newly arrived troops reveled in extracurricular events, as if they could not leave behind a particularly Brazilian spirit of celebration. On August 19, when Winston Churchill arrived dressed in a lightweight suit and pith helmet, his ever-present cigar in his mouth, for a battlefield visit at a marshy, forested stretch of coast called Tiro de Bolo, the Brazilians stood in formation, resplendent in their new uniforms. A few days later they commemorated the Brazilian Day of the Soldier with songs and a dress parade. This proclivity for conviviality almost killed some troops who liked to gather informally around campfires at night despite blackout orders. More than once, the fires' glow drew attacks from planes of the Fascist Italian Air Force.

After three weeks of training at Pisa and the inevitable graduation parade, the Brazilians were thrown up against thousands of the most seasoned troops of Adolf Hitler's *Wehrmacht*. "The German position in Italy was as strong as any previous time in the Italian campaign," wrote the Fifth Army's historian, Lieutenant Colonel Chester G. Starr. Mascarenhas feared his men would serve as cannon fodder.

The Brazilians met the enemy at the Gothic Line. Built by fifteen thousand Italian slave laborers working under the Todt Organization, the engineering company at the service of the Reich, the Line was a snaking path of steel shelters and protective bunkers running 180 miles long and ten miles deep from just south of La Spezia on Italy's west coast across the Apennines to a point between Pesaro and Ravenna on the east coast, on the Adriatic Sea. To halt the Allies' advance north from Rome, Kesselring had the bulwark designed to be impregnable, with two thousand concrete emplacements for anchoring eighty-eight-millimeter antiaircraft and antitank guns, minefields, and defense positions carved into mountains. Of Kesselring's twenty-seven German divisions and parts of six Italian divisions—half a million men—eighteen divisions were stationed on the Line.

It was the landmines that took some of the first Brazilian lives. German soldiers fought skillfully and without quarter. By this time *Wehrmacht* veterans had fought dozens, if not hundreds, of battles, skirmishes, and firefights in Europe and Africa.

Even off the battlefield, however, away from the enemy, Brazilians were thrown out of commission or worse because of inadequate preparation. Men who had never been inside a car suddenly found themselves behind the wheel of ten-ton trucks, driving mountain roads gone slick and muddy with rain; thirty-six drivers and passengers died in accidents in the first month. Seventy-one years later, a veteran named Eronides João da Cruz still wanted to insist on the valor of his fellow soldiers while lamenting their lack of training. "In all the action, Brazilians showed we were not weak, but at first, inexperienced," da Cruz told me.

And many were ill. Nery Prado remembers that of six teenagers who left their coffee-growing farms together to volunteer for the BEF, only he and one other passed a physical. "You have to be healthy to die," he said ruefully. Yet medical screening in Brazil was inconsistent. To the consternation of Brazilian and U.S. medics, men who never should have been in Italy in the first place had to be treated for complications of conditions such as tuberculosis or hepatitis, or transported home.

And language was a problem unforeseen—or ignored—by Brazilians and Americans. General Clark assigned his aide, Captain Vernon Walters of Connecticut, as liaison to General Mascarenhas. Walters had been raised in Europe and spoke several languages, including Portuguese. But the energetic young officer, who later would serve as an advisor to presidents from Harry Truman to Ronald Reagan, was only one man, often in demand by several officers at once. And he didn't get much help in translating from the Brazilian soldiers, although thousands of them spoke not only their native Portuguese but also Italian or German or Japanese, the languages of their immigrant heritages, and many spoke French. Bilingual Brazilians became on-the-spot interrogators when German or Italian troops were captured. Only a handful spoke English, however, and most of them were quickly trained as radio operators. There were virtually no other Portuguese speakers among the Americans. The South Americans regarded their monolingual U.S. trainers as regrettably undereducated.

• • •

The Brazilians' first skirmishes on the front north of the Arno River were true trials by fire. Nobody ran, but the Brazilians were clobbered. On September 18, the harried troops finally scored a victory—and at a critical point on the Gothic Line. Near Camaiore, a town located in a district of green plains in western Tuscany, Lieutenant General Euclides Zenóbio da Costa led the assault.

Zenóbio, a fit-looking fifty-one with the commanding posture of a graduate of Brazil's top military schools, had a reputation for bravery and the ability to get things done. He also commanded abiding loyalty from men who had served with him in Brazil—many followed him to Italy. On September 17, orders came to Zenóbio: take Camaiore.

"He did not waste time," wrote the Brazilian general chief of staff, Floriano de Lima Brayner. "[Zenóbio] commanded, with bits of recklessness, launching and directing the departure of the vehicles, not worrying about the dangers surrounding him."

The Brazilians routed the Germans. Liberating Camaiore "in Zenóbio's pure and impulsive style" was a small victory in a major, ill-fated Allied offensive called Operation Olive. The plan was to storm the Gothic Line and break through to Italy's important cities of the north before winter set in. By the end of September, however, Operation Olive was sputtering. The Allies were losing too many men, too much equipment. Every time the Germans seemed to disappear, they attacked with rearguard actions. Churchill had miscalculated: he did not believe the Germans would defend Italy.

The Brazilians matured as a fighting force in the valley of the meandering Serchio River, which flows through northern Tuscany for seventy-eight miles between the Apuan Alps and the Apennines. On one side of the vale rises the coastal range glinting with the white peaks from which Michelangelo took his marble. On the other, ancient settlements like Sommocolonia crown heights along the Apennine range called the backbone of Italy. The Northern Apennines, running from the Ligurian Sea south of Genoa southeast across the Italian peninsula nearly to the Adriatic below Rimini, were "the most formidable mountain barrier [the Fifth Army] was ever to face in combat operations in Italy," wrote Starr, the Fifth Army historian.

Unfortunately, the Brazilians arrived in the Serchio Valley just when torrential rains began, sweeping trucks from roads, threatening troops on foot with flash floods and the kind of mud that could swallow a man. With Zenóbio in the lead, men slogged their way up the river, town by town and bridge by bridge.

On October 6, however, they took the district of Fornaci di Barga so fast that they captured its munitions and aircraft-parts factory before the Germans could blow it up. A German squad returned under cover of darkness to sabotage the place. A long firefight ensued, and four Brazilians died. But in the morning the factory was intact, in Brazilian hands.

By this time the Brazilians were working in concert with the only Italian partisan unit that would remain undefeated during the war, organized by the legendary "Pippo," Manrico Ducceschi. A student who had once attended the elite *Alpini* Cadet Officer Course, Pippo had the honor of being the Germans' "most wanted" guerrilla resistance fighter. The Brazilians seemed taken aback at their first sight of the guerrillas, "armed to the teeth," a partisan wrote, "but without uniforms of any kind." The *partigiani* made reconnaissance patrols and reported their intelligence to the Brazilians. On at least two occasions they searched for Brazilian troops who had lost contact with commanders, escorting them back to base. Reports from the time say that of all the Allied units, the Brazilians, Latin in temperament, respectful of the Italian fighters' local knowledge, worked best with the *partigiani*.

From Fornaci di Barga a Brazilian patrol set out to reconnoiter the most valuable prize in the southern sector of the Serchio, just three miles away: Barga itself, a walled city with a distinctive cathedral that dominated the landscape, the finest example of Romanesque architecture in the valley.

The people of Barga had been suffering death and occupation. The parish priest, Lino Lombardi, noted in his journal the day and time of every cannonade that burst in the hills, every shell that hit a house, every soul he buried in those terrible months in late 1944. Nearly sixty, with hair almost entirely gray and black-rimmed glasses that gave his round face an owlish look, the *prete* wore a wide-brimmed hat and flowing black cassock that flapped in the wind as he hurried among Barga's steep narrow streets. His flock, he wrote, looked inconsolably grim, "like anyone with a loved one dying."

Farmers and townsmen hid at the sight of uniforms, afraid of being swept into the Todt Organization's ranks of slave labor. Families mourned their dead young men who had been among tens of thousands of Italians sent by Mussolini to fight alongside Hitler's divisions on the Russian Front.

Not far away, German massacres of women, children, and the elderly, from twenty to seventy persons at a time, were taking place as warnings, or punishments. In a scorched-earth operation in August, in a hill town less than twenty-five miles from Barga named Sant'Anna di Stazzema, SS troops took reprisals for a partisan operation by going door-to-door, rounding up more than 700 residents, including 130 children, and murdering them and burning their bodies. In the town of Marzabotto, a Waffen-SS unit slew some 770 unarmed residents in an operation that took five days. Burying their bodies was forbidden. One day Lombardi and some parishioners went to an old estate amid olive groves and vineyards to give food to a "herd" of people who had been rounded up in German raids as slave workers. They were "a pitiful spectacle of men in clothes worn out and torn," he wrote, "shoes almost gone, shabby and suffering . . . reduced to a semi-bestial state."

Beginning in July, the Black Brigade, drawn from Mussolini's loyal Fascist troops, had occupied Barga. By autumn, they turned the town over to the Germans, who blew up the local aqueduct as they left town at the Allies' approach and took positions in the surrounding heights. For towns like Barga, liberation could not come soon enough.

At 12:15 p.m. on October 7, 1944, Lombardi, returning from saying Mass in an outlying parish, encountered the Brazilian reconnaissance patrol that had set out from Fornaci. The unit, Lombardi noted with surprise, was "composed of soldiers of the most various colors, from white to black, commanded by a dark non-commissioned officer." Unless a man had fought in Mussolini's conquest of Ethiopia or served elsewhere in Africa, an Italian may never have seen a black person before setting eyes on the Brazilians.

Mussolini's Racial Laws, in effect from 1938 to 1943, discriminated against Jews but maligned blacks too, considering them less than fully human. Publications like the slick government magazine *La Difesa della Razza* (The Defense of the Race) promoted Fascist myths of Italian "racial" and cultural dominance over Jewish and African people. For Father Lombardi, the first sight of his deliverers, Brazilian soldiers "of the most various colors," was a symbol of what had gone terribly wrong in Italy itself.

"I thought sadly about all the racial pride which in recent years had been one of the flagships of the Regime, and also about the fact that we, the people of an ancient civilization, were under [the Brazilians'] control, even though friendly, in the middle of a war," he wrote.

On October 11 at precisely 10:30 a.m., Lombardi noted "for the record" that the Brazilian forces entered Barga in jeeps, many of which, he wrote with delight, "were marked with the names of the Virgin and the saints and with sacred images." Crowds lined the streets, visibly thankful at the promise of an end to their suffering. Partisans, some of whom had been in the town for two days, took a drier view of the grand arrival.

Pippo's lieutenant had already taken control of the city hall and overseen mild reprisals, setting Fascist sympathizers to work clearing rubble from the streets, shearing the heads of a few women deemed too friendly to the enemy. Now the *partigiani* looked appalled at the South Americans' relaxed, triumphal demeanor, "exposed, in the open, without prudence, smiling and merry, almost as if they were in a parade."

Someone warned people to get out of the streets. German cannons rained fire. When shooting broke out again at midnight, Lombardi "jumped" from his bed and ran down to shelter with the thirty *brasiliani* who had bivouacked for the night inside the thick walls of the lower cathedral complex.

It may be about this time that the Brazilians, noting the distinctive unit insignias worn on shoulder patches by Americans, Indians, South Africans, and others who fought with the Fifth Army, wanted one for themselves. The choice of an image was easy. A saying attributed to Hitler used to make the rounds in Brazil: "The Brazilians will fight when the snake smokes." Thus the Smoking Cobras were born, their symbol a snake in pouncing position with a pipe in its mouth, smoke rising from the bowl.

By all accounts the people of Barga were glad to be "occupied" by the Brazilians. An Italian historian who gathered postwar descriptions of the time concluded that the South Americans "created with their joyous presence in the city, a climate of euphoria absent for long months." Women cooked pasta with tomato sauce and gave it to the soldiers, men handed out bottles of wine; the Brazilians, in turn, gave away so much of their own food and personal items that a provisioning crisis ensued. Part of the problem was their prodigal sharing with the partisans too, upon whom they counted for patrolling. "Our food improved," wrote one partisan, because Brazilians "split [with us] the little food they had with them." They also loaned partisans their Bren machine gun, a Tommy gun, ammunition, and hand grenades. Even today among Barga inhabitants too young to have experienced the war, faces glow and stories spill out at mention of *i brasiliani*. In a remark that signified how they had been incorporated into local folklore, the town mayor declared to me that months after the Brazilians left, children were born who grew up to have a remarkable capacity for soccer.

THE LONGEST WINTER

On three nights in early November 1944, the Brazilian soldiers crowded into trucks and made a seventy-five-mile drive east and north of the Serchio Valley, at times without headlights, on curves skirting precipitous cliffs. At dawn they arrived at new frontline positions.

All around rose mountains white with the season's first dusting of snow. The soldiers stared in wonder; the powder gave the heights an air of enchantment. It was the first snow most had seen. Eventually sleet, frozen mud, and icy boot-grabbing drifts that slowed every move would become menaces as hostile as any enemy, rotting feet, and burning skin. But the first snows were lovely to behold, if amazingly cold.

The South Americans were charged with taking the 3,240-foot-high Monte Castello, perhaps the highest mountain many had seen. The mount had to be wrested from the Germans so the Allies could move on to the Po

Valley and, finally, down to Bologna, the largest city of the north. "Bologna by Christmas!" was the Allied watchword. In his memoirs, Marshall Kesselring said Monte Castello was "of maximum importance for the possession of Bologna and the routes of communication toward the south, north and northwest." Monte Castello was key to maintaining positions in the east all the way to the Adriatic. The Germans had defended it to the hilt with the concrete pillboxes and troops of the 232nd Panzer division.

In November and December the Brazilians brutally—there is no other way to say it—hurled themselves against the mountain's icy slopes. Monte Castello became their obsession, their white whale. "Frankly, you Brazilians are either crazy or very brave," a German captain told a captured Brazilian lieutenant. "I never saw anyone advance against machine guns and well-defended positions with such disregard for life."

The Smoking Cobras had launched their first assault in a debilitated physical state, operating on their sixty-eighth straight day without rest. They lost twelve men, and another forty-five were so badly injured that they had to be evacuated. They charged the mountain again the next day, a frontal assault without reinforcements. The Germans picked off the Brazilians as if they were performing target practice.

After acrimonious exchanges with U.S. commanders whom the Brazilians blamed—justifiably or not—for the failures, General Mascarenhas demanded control of the Allied attempt to take the mountain. His troops, after all, were in the lead. General Clark agreed. The risk was great, but the wiry, determined Mascarenhas was resolved to redeem the honor of the Smoking Cobras. He had to justify Brazilian presence in the European theater not just politically, but as a fighting force. But the next assault on November 29, the first under Brazilian command, went terribly.

In the confusion of preparation, some units hadn't received food and fought hungry all day. One new battalion was rushed into position without time to perform reconnaissance, so at daybreak they stood in full view of the Germans lined up on elevations. At one point a single enemy fragmentation grenade killed nine Brazilians. Far from redeeming themselves in American eyes or their own, the Smoking Cobras simply looked bad. Allied officers acknowledged their tenacity but began to doubt the viability of the Brazilian Expeditionary Force.

Unbelievably, the Brazilians immediately set a date for what they characterized as their decisive assault on the mountain. They sent the attack plan to the U.S. high command, which gave its approval. At Zero Hour—6:00 a.m.—on the morning of December 12, incessant rain was turning the slopes into icy marshes. Thick fog hampered air cover and visibility for artillery fire. By late afternoon General Zenóbio ordered a retreat. Forty-nine men died, with another six missing in action. Recriminations flew. Washington had approved the attack plan, the Brazilians said. Brazilian commanders were incompetent, some Americans said.

Worst for the soldiers, the bodies of fallen comrades lay scattered in the snow, unreachable because the territory was under enemy control. The Germans buried some of the dead; later a Smoking Cobras patrol came across a marker that read, in German, "Here Lie Three Brave Brazilian Soldiers."

There would be no "Bologna by Christmas." It was the lowest point in the life of the Brazilian Expeditionary Force.

The Smoking Cobras settled in for the kind of weather they had never known at home: freezing nights barely tempered by canvas tents. Trench foot was rampant—it caused peeling, bloody skin, and the foul odor of incipient necrosis. Enemy gliders dropped flyers. "Why have you abandoned your country, radiant and full of sun, and fight now here in the fog, the mud and the filth, awaiting a horrible winter, with its snowstorms and interminable avalanches? Is this worth the $95 you receive every month? A bullet-riddled body or a burial in Italy should be better paid."

The messages in Portuguese addressed the Brazilians as "comrades" and were signed "German soldiers." At night, music meant to induce yearnings for home poured forth from the "Green and Gold Hour," a Portuguese-language German radio show named for the colors of the Brazilian flag. Sometimes the announcer advised listeners that Americans "who are not esteemed by anyone in this world" had hoodwinked the Brazilian soldiers into crossing the sea while the Allies were poised to invade Brazil and capture its minerals and other natural resources. The transmission was required listening because it carried the soccer scores from home.

In December, the Brazilians received their winter camouflage outfits—all white. One day they reported the puzzling arrival of a cargo of "long boards and some pointed sticks with rings on them." Vernon Walters inspected the delivery and discovered a quantity of skis and poles for soldiers going out on patrol—in many places drifts were already too deep for walking. Eventually a designated ski instructor, Lieutenant Francis Sargent, later a governor of Massachusetts, would arrive to give regular lessons, but meanwhile the polyglot Walters, also an expert skier, was ordered to begin. He invented "a whole new Portuguese vocabulary to describe the various maneuvers and movements on skis," he wrote. But after a few classes, the soldiers protested they could not descend the hills or stop. Their complaints were tested when a disabled B-25 with U.S. markings approached from the north, spit forth men on parachutes, went into a screaming dive, and crashed in flames. Walters told the Brazilians he was pushing off for division headquarters to report the downed paratroopers. "Follow me," he ordered. All successfully made it down the hill.

The Brazilians learned to ski halfway between Florence and Bologna, above BEF headquarters at Porretta Terme, a town on the Reno River known since Etruscan times for its thermal baths. Shelling boomed nightly, and by day the Germans pounded surrounding roads so intensely that Mascarenhas brought in smoke machines so the enemy couldn't see Allied traffic; nearly everyone suffered from burning eyes and mouths and a feeling of seared lungs. Most divisions had headquarters situated well behind the fighting, but the BEF headquarters was on the front.

Nevertheless, when Lieutenant General Willis Crittenberger, commander of the Fifth Army's IV Corps, visited Mascarenhas and suggested relocation, the Brazilian general would have none of it.

"General Crittenberger, you are an American," Mascarenhas said. "You have many headquarters in Italy. You can move them forward, sideways or backwards and no one is going to pay any attention. This is the only Brazilian headquarters in Italy and when I move it, it is going to be forward and not backward."

General João Baptista Mascarenhas was a superb strategist with a supremely doughty personality, at home among the other Allied officers.

But lower-ranking officers also embodied persistence and daring in that winter campaign.

Lieutenant Max Wolf, a tall, blue-eyed lieutenant from the German south of Brazil, joined the BEF in the footsteps of his admired superior officer in the National Police Force, Lieutenant General Zenóbio, arriving late in 1944. Wolf was the son of an Austrian immigrant who owned a coffee-roasting plant. He had proven himself under fire in Brazil, having been severely wounded while fighting would-be government usurpers alongside Zenóbio in São Paulo in 1932. A thirty-three-year-old widower with a ten-year-old daughter at home, Wolf was one of eight hundred *teuto-brasileiros*, "German" Brazilians, in BEF ranks.

During the ill-fated December 12 attack on Monte Castello, Max Wolf had held his position when most other new arrivals, terrified at facing the enemy within hours of reaching the field, had fired wildly, revealing their places and drawing fire. After the battle he volunteered to lead a four-man resupply unit carrying ammunition to advanced positions, collecting the wounded and dead on return. The next day Wolf accompanied a superior officer on a probing mission, insisting on walking ahead.

"Captain, your life is more useful to the country than mine," Wolf said.

For the next weeks Max Wolf, charismatic and apparently tireless, led volunteer units to assess enemy lines, perform special missions, and engage enemy patrols. One day Zenóbio called for volunteers to reclaim the body of a fallen captain that was being used as bait by Germans— they fired on soldiers trying to rescue his remains. Leading a small unit under cover of darkness, Wolf brought back the dead captain. He gathered intelligence, took German prisoners, and once ferreted out an Italian civilian who had been orienting German artillery against the Brazilians with lights from his house.

By late January, troops were calling Max Wolf the "King of the Patrollers," a sobriquet he bore good-naturedly. On March 7, a Brazilian company crossing a field at night was surprised by explosions of consecutive mines, sending bodies flying, killing or wounding thirteen, and, not inconsequentially, felling telephonic lines that troops used to communicate with command posts. Leading three other volunteers, Wolf negotiated the minefield

and repaired the lines. He had already received medals for valor from Zenóbio for previous actions. In the wake of the minefield action, the gravel-
voiced U.S. general Lucien Truscott, who had taken over as Fifth Army
commander from Clark, presented Wolf with the Silver Star.

When Max Wolf took command of a new unit called the "Special
Platoon" in April, other soldiers quietly assumed the squad was destined
for "suicide missions." However, photos show the company's men looking relaxed, hearty and smiling. Brazilian news correspondents arrived
at the front and wanted to interview one man: Max Wolf. He complied,
but seemed unexpectedly shy in the spotlight.

An iconic photo from the files of a Rio de Janeiro newspaper, shot
on April 12, 1945, shows Wolf wearing a steel helmet and battle fatigues,
arms akimbo, standing about a yard forward of his men, who appear at
ease, some of them grinning, one carrying a bazooka, the others Thomp-
son submachine guns. He is looking to the side, as if distracted, or preoccupied. The patrol was charged that day with gathering intelligence vital
to Allied forces planning the giant Spring Offensive. Was the foe dug into
place, or in retreat? They must find out.

Two hours after the picture was taken, the Special Platoon cautiously
approached a stretch of open fields dotted with farmhouses on the rolling
outskirts of the town of Montese. Made of rocks and gypsum, fortresslike
in appearance, the houses were sometimes used as defenses by Germans
who hid behind or inside them; an approaching soldier could be met by
machine-gun or rifle fire. On the other hand, the houses might be sheltering
frightened, unarmed civilians. Or they might be holding Germans ready to
surrender, which happened occasionally in these last months of the war.

In an eerie midafternoon silence, Wolf dispersed his men on opposite flanks and walked ahead of them some 150 feet. He crossed a clean
field with no cover. A long burst of machine-gun fire exploded from a
farmhouse. Max Wolf fell face forward into the dirt, where snow had recently melted away.

The Brazilian command reported his death without mentioning the
fact that, as platoon leader, Wolf should never have been the one to take
the risky position of *esclarecedor*, the one who walked ahead. Nor did
the report suggest the episode was suicidal. Instead, it commended Max

Wolf for "unexcelled bravery" in circumstances that "did not defeat his spirit, in which he neither flinched nor faltered."

For many who survived the winter of 1944–45, bravery consisted in confronting obstacles less spectacular than those for which Max Wolf is remembered. "The war was about being cold," said Pedro Rossi, who was a twenty-five-year-old artilleryman at the time. "So many lost their legs from the cold."

I met the former Captain Rossi by chance in 2015, standing before an eternal flame at a commemorative pool in a rolling, ten-acre monument to the Brazilians in Pistoia, twenty miles south of their old headquarters at Porretta Terme. Rossi, ninety-five, wore a straw hat against the sun but still held himself with military bearing. He was making his third return visit to the battlefields, he said, accompanied by his son and daughter-in-law. Together we crossed a field of headstones, each marked with the name of one of the 455 Brazilians who died in Italy, including Max Wolf. Rossi spoke of the vicissitudes of the weather that year, and still sounded amazed that he and his friends had pulled through. As we walked among the tombstones, however, his voice fell to nearly a whisper. "Those who died were the real heroes," he said.

On the edge of the field we stepped into a small museum and paused before a display of shells and arms. Rossi picked up a war-era machine gun and handled it gingerly, familiarly. He recalled the minutes before midnight on December 31, 1944. "We were young. It was New Year's Eve," he said, pointing the vintage weapon high. "So I fired into the air. A celebration, you see. And somebody from the others—a German—fired too." He lowered the gun. "We were young."

As it happened, a few older officers had been entertaining the same idea that night, at almost the same moment, according to Vernon Walters's account. Colonel Ademar de Queirós, operations officer of the Brazilian divisional artillery, ordered guns and mortars fired to welcome in 1945, the Year of Victory. Not to be outdone, the Germans launched a salvo so fierce it caused plaster to fall inside the Brazilian headquarters, demolishing a celebratory buffet. Officers dived for cover. Walters jumped under a table where he had just placed his contribution to the party, a large round of hard-to-obtain cheese. The shelling stopped. The phone rang. Chief operations officer Colonel Humberto de Alencar Castello Branco answered to hear de Queirós's cheerful voice. "How did you like that fireworks display we put on?"

"Ademar, never do that again," huffed Castello Branco. "The whole German answer just landed on us. We're lucky to be here to answer the phone."

The doggedness of Mascarenhas, Max Wolf's audacity, and the perseverance of artilleryman Pedro Rossi, multiplied a hundred ways among Brazilian soldiers over that European winter, might stand for how the Smoking Cobras transformed themselves from an ill-prepared division operating with a sense of defeat into a force that would emerge from the war with justifiable pride. Combat itself was their training. The turnaround manifested itself, of all places, at their old nemesis, Monte Castello.

Fifty Italian partisans joined the Smoking Cobras, increasing their effectiveness. The 92nd division, called the Buffalo Soldiers, black troops with white officers in a still-segregated U.S. Army—a fact that shocked the Brazilians—fought alongside them. And from the United States another unit arrived, trained to fight under the most difficult mountain conditions: the 10th Mountain Division of Colorado.

The Colorado unit's white-clad sports skiers, forest rangers, and outdoorsmen turned soldiers had already captivated the American public. They were featured on the cover of the *Saturday Evening Post* and the popular radio programs of adventurer Lowell Thomas, himself an avid skier. On February 18, the 10th surprised the Germans with a silent, fifteen-hundred-foot nighttime ascent of the Riva Ridge, considered unassailable day or night. Once in command of the ridge, they were able to take the heavily fortified Mount Belvedere, the highest peak in the Apennines at forty-nine hundred feet. With the heights taken, the way was cleared for yet another Brazilian assault on nearby Monte Castello.

The men of the 10th, with their insignia of red crossed swords on a blue field under the bold word "MOUNTAIN," shared their knowledge of survival skills with the Brazilians, such as how to use snowshoes and how to build a snow cave. Culturally, however, there was distance between them. One night a Colorado soldier listened amazed to the goings-on across the ridge.

Walt Disney was a "Goodwill Ambassador" in Rockefeller's Latin America propoganda campaign for the Allies.

The "Brazilian Bombshell" Carmen Miranda embodied an attractive, good-natured image of Latin America. By war's end she was the highest-paid woman in the United States.   Billboard *magazine ad, 1943. Wikimedia Commons*

Nazi groups in Blumenau, Brazil, invited locals to sports events, dancing, speeches, games and films like the German language movie *Germany Awakes.*

Fundaçao Cultural de Blumenau

The German-built *Graf Zeppelin,* here flying over Buenos Aires in 1934, made the world's first regularly scheduled transatlantic passenger flights, from Berlin to Rio.

Archivo General de la Nación Argentina, Wikimedia Commons

A Nazi flag flies in a park in Santa Catarina, in southern Brazil.

Fundaçao Cultural de Blumenau

As civil war and repression wracked Spain, Spanish-language culture flourished in Argentina, one of the ten wealthiest countries in the world. Cosmopolitan Buenos Aires was home to Jorge Luís Borges, Federico García Lorca and some of the region's best filmmakers.
Horacio Coppola, Wikimedia Commons

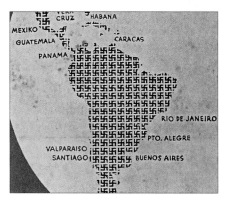

Cover detail from *The Overseas German Observer,* a Nazi monthly published in Germany that reached Joinville, Brazil.
Arquivo Histórico de Joinville

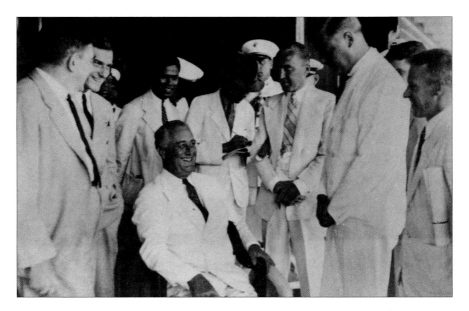

Franklin D. Roosevelt's greatest fear in the lead-up to war was Axis penetration of Latin America. The president made a cruise to Latin capitals to promote his Good Neighbor policy. *Franklin D. Roosevelt Presidential Library*

Germans in Colombia established the first airline in the Americas in 1921, three years before Delta, the oldest operating U.S. airline. *Utopia Airport*

Nazis sponsored loyalty groups for all ages in southern Brazil.

Fundaçao Cultural de Blumenau

A boy from a Nazi youth group in Brazil salutes.

Arquivo Histórico de Joinville

Italians, and skilled German crews who immigrated to Latin America after World War I, ran airlines that crisscrossed southern skies.

SCADTA: Utopia Airport

A class in Guatemala City's German School, 1938. Most "German" parents in Guatemala raised children to be Guatemalan without forgetting German roots. Brazil had 1500 German schools.

Los alemanes en Guatemala, 1828–1944, *Regina Wagner*

Only in May 1942, when U-boats sank two of its oil tankers, did Mexico give up the neutrality it had tried to preserve.

Secretariat of Public Education, Mexico

Manuel Ávila Camacho of Mexico saw himself as a wartime president. Mexican airmen fought against the Japanese in the Philippines.

Secretariat of the Interior, Mexico

Lazaro Cardenas (in suit), Mexico's greatest president, nationalized the country's railroads and nationalized oil, upsetting the monopolies of international companies.

Doralicia Carmona Dávila, Wikimedia Commons

"We recognize a mutual interdependence of our joint resources," Roosevelt declared in Mexico in 1943.
Leon Helguera, United States Office of War Information

A controversial "secret map" divided post-war South America into four Nazi territories. Its background is black due to the mimeograph technology used to create this copy that arrived at the White House.
Franklin D. Roosevelt Presidential Library

The Brazilians "must have been really happy because they were making all kinds of noise . . . as if they were going from one party to another," he wrote. "The Germans would surely hear this outfit sooner or later."

Early on the morning of February 21, the Brazilians launched their fifth assault on Monte Castello, not a disastrous frontal assault as they had attempted before, but on its flanks. By late afternoon, as the battle raged, testy U.S. generals visited Mascarenhas's command to ask why the BEF's reserve did not go into action to complete the conquest of the mountain. Mascarenhas said the time wasn't opportune. The generals conceded that the Brazilian was, after all, in charge, but as soon as they left Mascarenhas sent a message to Zenóbio. The crest must be reached while it was still daylight to afford artillery support. "We will not lose the confidence of the American commanders," Mascarenhas said.

Zenóbio's field commander said he was maintaining a slow pace to avoid undue casualties. "But my dear fellow," answered Zenóbio, "do you want to conquer Monte Castello with men or with flowers?" At 4:20 p.m. Brazilian artillery commenced pounding the mountain in a merciless barrage. An hour and a half later Zenóbio picked up the phone and called Mascarenhas. "The mountain is ours," he said.

At home in Brazil the press went wild. The nation now surely would be invited to join the other five world powers in the Supreme Allied Council, said the Rio daily *A Manhã*, reflecting the hopes of a nation. Brazil would help shape the postwar world.

The Smoking Cobras became unstoppable, taking the city of Castelnuovo on March 5 and helping to take the town of Montese overlooking the lush Pantaro Valley in April, after a wrenching four-day battle that cost 426 dead and wounded. A few days later, Mascarenhas received news that a well-supplied German division, its officers veterans of the African and Italian campaigns, was attempting to break through to the Po Valley from the south toward Parma, among Italy's most prosperous cities. The Brazilians blocked the roads and met the Germans at Collechio, a town eight miles southwest where they set up mortar positions in front of a church. When a field commander wanted to stop fighting and camp for the night, Mascarenhas objected. "The old general acted with the enthusiasm of a lieutenant," the soldier said. Zenóbio, too, fought hard.

"That Zenóbio was crazy," recalled a Brazilian soldier who was firing mortars during the battle. Writing after the war, the soldier recalled that, faced with incoming fire, "like everyone else, I was lying down, with that machine gun firing close." But Zenóbio "didn't move, didn't lie down, did nothing of the sort."

At nearby Fornovo, the Brazilians made their last stand of the war. Outnumbered by *Wehrmacht* infantry and Panzers, soldiers of the Fascist Italian National Republican Army's *Bersaglieri*, and *Alpini* mountain soldiers, the Brazilians led Allied troops to a standstill with the enemy. Mascarenhas demanded unconditional surrender; the Germans refused. A local priest was enlisted to carry notes back and forth across the lines. The Brazilians guaranteed safety. Unable to escape or counterattack, the Germans saw they were trapped.

In their last act of World War II, the Smoking Cobras captured fourteen thousand enemy soldiers and three generals—members of the German 90th *Panzergrenadier* and the iconic Italian Bersaglieri Corps, and the entire 148th division of the German army.

IT ONLY REMAINS TO GO HOME

And now—now it only remains for me to light a cigarette and go home. Dear God, only now am I remembering that people die. Does that include me? Don't forget, in the meantime, that this is the season for strawberries. Yes.

—CLARICE LISPECTOR, WHO NURSED BEF SOLDIERS IN NAPLES

By June 1945, almost all the Brazilians in Italy had shipped for home—a few who married Italian women stayed or later brought their wives to Brazil. In July in Rio de Janeiro, General Clark, Vernon Walters, and other U.S. officers sat in a reviewing stand in sight of Sugar Loaf Mountain. General Zenóbio led parading troops down the boulevard on the sparkling bay. The city's old cannons fired rounds of salutes, hundreds of boats gathered in the harbor, church bells rang, and crowds cheered.

Within a few weeks, however, the veterans of the Brazilian Expeditionary Force were being purposely ignored by a dictatorship that feared soldiers who had fought for democracy. "They turned their backs on us," Eronides João da Cruz told me. "We were intelligent and trained, but here we were treated as dogs." Da Cruz could not find a job when he returned. The force was disbanded, its soldiers scattered around the country. The government did not allow them to unite as a veterans' group until the 1970s.

General Mascarenhas, the old-school officer who led the Brazilian division through glory and low times, wrote a series of memoirs after his return.

Minister of war General Eurico Gaspar Dutra, who had visited troops in the Serchio Valley, helped to depose President Vargas in 1945. Dutra was elected president in 1946, and Brazil returned to democracy under a new constitution. But Dutra turned back the clock on Vargas's populist development programs. He broke unions, lowered wages, and cooperated enthusiastically with postwar U.S. free-market economic policy.

Vargas remained so popular, however, that when the next elections were held, he won the presidency again in free and fair voting. General Zenóbio became minister of war. But Vargas's enemies among top generals eventually demanded the president's resignation. It was Zenóbio who delivered the news on the night of April 26, 1954. Two hours later, Vargas shot himself in the chest with a Colt police revolver.

The fiercely anticommunist Brazilian military established a dictatorship supported by the United States from 1964 to 1985 that included officers of the Smoking Cobras. When Dutra was president, he had established with U.S. assistance the national Superior School of War that taught anticommunism and the U.S. view of the Cold War; several plotters of the 1964 military coup graduated from the school.

Castello Branco, Mascarenhas's operations officer in Italy, became chief of state in the coup. Vernon Walters, by now a close friend of Castello Branco, was serving as U.S. defense attaché in Rio. Castello Branco abolished political parties and ordered jurists to draw up a new, authoritarian constitution.

In 1960, the remains of the men who had been interred at the monument in Pistoia were transferred to Brazil, where they rest at a monument in the Flamengo neighborhood of Rio. In the state of Minas Gerais, home of many soldiers on the front line at Monte Castello, a small museum with BEF artifacts invites visitors, while elderly veterans in the state of Parana sometimes gather at the Expeditionary Museum in Curitiba. In the coastal city of Fortaleza on the Brazilian hump, a neighborhood christened Montese commemorates the battle for that Italian city.

Apart from these, there are few traces of the Smoking Cobras in Brazil today. When I asked at the main tourist information center in São Paulo, Brazil's largest city, where I might find a monument to the Brazilian Expeditionary Force, young staff members said it was news to them that Brazilians had participated in the war.

In Italy, however, numerous reminders remain. At Pistoia, Mario Pereira, the son of late BEF veteran Miguel Pereira, tends the monument visited by increasing numbers of Brazilian diplomats, veterans, and travelers. "They find it on the internet," said Pereira. There is a museum for the history of the Smoking Cobras and the Colorado division in the town of Iola de Montese; a spectacular monument to the Brazilians in the shape of a towering silver arc in sight of Monte Castello; and plaques of remembrance in small towns liberated by the Smoking Cobras in the provinces of Pisa, Modena, and Bologna.

And there is the annual ceremony with the picnic and laying of the laurel wreath at Sommocolonia, overlooking the Serchio Valley. A room attached to the parish church holds gas masks from both sides, flags torn by bullet holes, uniforms marked with bloodstains gone black, and flyers from the Germans to their Brazilian "comrades."

Against a stone wall is a plaque showing the bright green cobra with a smoking pipe in its mouth. A salute is rendered in Italian and Portuguese in bold black letters:

IN MEMORY OF THE SOLDIERS OF THE BRAZILIAN EXPEDITIONARY
FORCE WHO, TO DEFEND LIBERTY AND DEMOCRACY,
CROSSED THE OCEAN TO FIGHT IN THE SECOND WORLD WAR.

PART V

The End Without an End

13.

RATLINES

In 1949, Walter Rauff, who developed the mobile gas vans in which thousands died during Hitler's Reich, was sailing on a ship out of Genoa headed for South America on an escape route run by the Vatican. Rauff had spent his time since the end of the war working for U.S. and Israeli intelligence agencies and starting a Syrian intelligence service in Damascus based on the Gestapo. Now he looked forward to a comfortable life in the Southern Hemisphere.

Rauff was part of the greatest mass flight of criminals of the century—fascists with blood on their hands who came to the Americas after the war by way of the system known as the Ratlines (*Rattenlinien*).

The Roman Catholic Church had a powerful reason to help Nazis like Rauff, who were viscerally against Bolshevism. After the Russian Revolution in 1917, Communists waged a war against religion, turning Russian Orthodox churches into museums or wedding halls, killing hundreds of priests, and torturing believers who clung to their faith. They plundered and liquidated monasteries and convents, ridiculed and eliminated objects of popular reverence. Atheism became the law of the land.

As World War II ended, certain understandings were clear from the Vatican's point of view: Communists were bent on spreading their system to the world, and conflict between communism and the Church was a zero-sum game—only one could survive. Fascists could be depended upon never to accommodate themselves to communists of any kind. They had experience in the fight and must be saved. This was the same thinking that drove Western intelligence agencies looking ahead to the Cold War to hire Nazi war criminals like Walter Rauff.

In a remarkable feat of casuistry, those who greased the Ratlines purported that the good in National Socialism—its hate for Bolshevism—could be separated from the bad. The Vatican imagined that because of its sacred origins, history, possessions, and ways of thinking, the Church was the repository of the values of Western Civilization, which was under threat. If fascists were allies in the new war, so be it.

In the popular imagination, the escape routes to Latin America were a project of Nazis intent on establishing a Fourth Reich, as described in 1972 by one of the most successful thrillers ever, *The Odessa File* by Frederick Forsyth. The book was fiction. SS officers like Rauff helped comrades escape, and once in Latin America, they often openly associated with each other. But the Ratlines involved a tangle of participants far wider and more insidious than what *The Odessa File* described.

To move those on the lam, the Church used its vast infrastructure, from Vatican City to bishoprics to village parishes. Routes in Italy, to which escapees from the Reich began to flee as early as 1944, went through safe houses including convents and along the self-explanatory "monastery route" taken by Adolf Eichmann. Funds often came from projects for legitimate refugees and persons left stateless after the war, but in one spectacular case, a Nazi slush fund created by an SS counterfeiting operation produced gold and cash that supported escapes.

Operation Bernhard, as the scheme was called, was based in one of the charming mountain districts of the South Tyrol, where the old Habsburg town of Merano lies in a balmy green valley circled by snowy alpine peaks. Since the 1850s, Merano has been a destination for the ill or merely idle. Famous writers including Franz Kafka and Ezra Pound came for the climate and waters reputed to bring health and well-being. From a promenade dotted with palm plants along the Passer River, a visitor can hire a taxi to drive through an elegant spa district into hills covered with apple orchards and centuries-old castles now used as private houses or hotels.

In 1943, a businessman working with the SS, Friedrich Schwend, bought one of the rambling old castles, Schloss Labers. Perfect for his assignment, Schloss Labers looked out across the Passeier Valley to a ring of peaks, snowcapped even in summer. Guards could see anyone approaching. Schwend took on the identity of an SS major by the name of Wendig, who had been killed in an Italian partisan attack. Sometimes as Schwend, sometimes as Wendig, he oversaw Operation Bernhard over the next two years, a complex plot to undermine the economy of Great Britain and, eventually, of the United States. Schwend answered directly to Heinrich Himmler, an architect of the Holocaust and chief of the SS. By flooding the market with false sterling notes, they aimed to do what the Luftwaffe and food blockade had failed to do: bring England to its knees.

Operation Bernhard also manufactured counterfeit documentation for the Reich's worldwide espionage web. The project hid gold and valuable artifacts in old mining tunnels in southern Austria should it be required for future Nazi needs, for a guerrilla war in case of Berlin's defeat, or for the security of SS personnel after the war. Eventually, profits from Operation Bernhard helped to fund the Ratlines.

Today Schloss Labers is listed on travel sites as a hotel, but one April day when I visited it was closed for the season. Through the windows of a vast enclosed porch I could glimpse a grand salon with high ceilings. The place included several outbuildings, perhaps once used to store valuables or loads of currency. Mountain hikers passed on a Sunday afternoon, but in photos from the World War II era I had seen in the Merano civic archives, Schloss Labers looked isolated on its promontory, unrelievedly bleak. Schwend lived comfortably with a full household staff, his children enjoying a Christmas tree that rose almost to the high ceiling and decorating eggs at Easter. On the roof, hidden from below, stood an antiaircraft gun.

Merano was virtually an outpost of the Reich, occupied by Nazis, and Schwend did not seem to fear for himself, taking out his white horse regularly in the mornings for a ride through the hills. But a contingent of

Waffen-SS soldiers from the *Sonderstab-Generalkommando III Germanisches Panzerkorps*, the special staff of the headquarters of the Third German Armored Corps, kept guard atop the house and behind bushes. Schwend seemed to travel quite a bit, but he otherwise cut a quiet figure in the hills.

An agent of the U.S. Army's Intelligence Division later called Schwend's Operation Bernhard "the most elaborate and far reaching scheme that an invading army ever devised for the wholesale counterfeiting of the money and credentials of other countries."

At the Sachsenhausen concentration camp, just north of Berlin, SS *Sturmbannführer* Bernhard Kruger oversaw 140 Jewish engravers, jewelers, and other skilled craftsmen who created plates for the bogus British pounds sterling, and to a lesser extent for U.S. dollars. They used a special rag commissioned from a paper factory in northern Germany and special inks. The Jewish artisans stayed alive as long as they produced quality work, while prisoners around them were annihilated or starved to death. The currency was shipped from Sachsenhausen to Merano by train, brought up to Schloss Labers and stored in hidden passages, then distributed along Schwend's global networks.

Agents of the operation purchased art and gold with false notes in the galleries of Paris and Berlin, the souks of the Middle East. They paid the Reich's spies. They laundered bills by buying real estate. Sometimes Himmler, Schwend's boss, squabbled with other branches of the Nazi bureaucracy over Operation Bernhard: the German foreign ministry and the central bank did not want to destabilize global monetary systems, even those of enemies. Occasionally the frustrated *Reichsbank* found itself stuck with the worthless currency.

Schwend's phony money, including fake U.S. military payment certificates—scrip—did disrupt economies slightly, especially in Italy. But Operation Bernhard's beautifully crafted notes did not destabilize the world's currencies, as planners hoped. Schwend did not have enough time. "Had this counterfeiting operation [been] fully organized in 1939 and early 1940, results of World War II may have been quite different," said the Holocaust scholar Rabbi Marvin Hier. But the scheme did support the escape of fascists from Europe to South America.

Trucks laden with money and gold left Schloss Labers heading south to Rome. Among the spires and cupolas of the Eternal City, Operation Bernhard's riches and infrastructure of transport and safe houses contributed to the Ratlines that were already under protection of the Church.

Communist Stalin might exterminate people by the thousands and watch millions starve, and fascist Hitler might kill millions for being the people they were born—Jews, homosexuals, Roma, the disabled. But members of the Church saw a difference between the two, and believed they could live with one worldview but not the other. The anticommunist ardor of certain princes of the Church made the Ratlines work.

An Austrian bishop in the Vatican, Alois Hudal, protected many of the most infamous Nazi war criminals, including Rauff, Eichmann, and Franz Stangl, commander of the Treblinka death camp. As a seminarian Hudal, the son of a shoemaker from Graz, delved into the history of the Eastern Orthodox Catholic Church, separated from Rome for a millennium over doctrinal issues. He became obsessed with a guiding principle— a desire, really—that would remain with him for his entire life: someday the Eastern Church in the Balkans would reunite with Rome. This could only happen, he believed, if Communist Russia were rendered decisively weak, unable to impose itself upon Eastern Europe. For Hudal, a strong Germany was Christianity's sacred bulwark, the West's only hope of keeping atheistic Bolshevism from sweeping across the continent.

While volunteering as an army chaplain in World War I, Hudal wrote a book of sermons for soldiers that previewed his beliefs later in life. The sermons conflated national loyalty with "loyalty to God." Later, Hudal also wrote about Jews, who were linked, he warned, to the "nefarious" tendency toward democracy. Jews were the portal to liberalism and Bolshevism, and Christianity must stand up to them. Nazism was a tool for the purpose.

In time, Hudal fancied himself as a mediator between Germany and Rome, saying that the Vatican's line with Hitler was too severe. He maintained that the Fuehrer was not an extremist, although some of his followers were. A Christianized National Socialism might save the world.

By the 1940s, Hudal was a bishop responsible for a complex of church and seminary classrooms called Santa Maria dell'Anima that covered an entire city block in Rome. Set among narrow, winding streets near the Piazza Navona, the strong, pale ocher walls of the Anima loomed in contrast to graceful, white Italianate churches nearby. A visitor can still see seminarians riding bicycles, their long cassocks flying, arriving at the Anima. Above the door are the words *speciosa facta est* ("fair she is"), from an antiphon in the Marian vespers, an allusion to the Blessed Mother, her arms open to the stranger. One of the most notorious war criminals who sought help at the door was a perpetrator of the infamous 1944 Ardeatine massacre, which still stands as a symbol in Italy for the egregious Nazi killings of civilians between September 1943 and the end of the war in May 1945. The SS officer's trajectory from occupied Rome, where the slaughter occurred, to receiving a safe passage to Argentina shows how the Ratlines worked.

"HE WAS VERY CONTROLLED, VERY COLD . . ."

On March 23, 1944, an armed division of 160 SS police made up of ethnic Germans from South Tyrol marched along the narrow Via Rasella in the center of occupied Rome, not far from the Trevi Fountain. A bomb exploded and several troops fell. Italian partisans spilled from hiding places, firing submachine guns and pistols, then disappeared among the streets and around corners. Thirty-three SS police died.

News of the attack reached Hitler in his Wolf's Lair bunker in the East Prussian forest. The response was furious. "He is roaring," reported one officer to the others. "He wants to blow up an entire quarter of the city, including everyone who lives there."

An order went out to kill ten Romans for every SS trooper who died on the Via Rasella.

SS captain Erich Priebke was on the job. At age thirty-one, the light-haired German presented a slim, attractive figure. Priebke had worked in swank hotels in London and Capri before volunteering for the elite "political soldiers" corps in 1936; he interpreted between Mussolini and Hitler when the Fuehrer came to Rome. Part of his job was to serve as liaison between the SS and bishops close to the pope. At night, Priebke took advantage of the after-hours social life for the privileged that percolated through the occupied city. An undercover OSS agent met Priebke at a party and found him "charming, cold and personable, good looking, impeccably uniformed."

At Gestapo headquarters on Via Tasso, however, Priebke could be vicious. "He was very controlled, very cold," said a woman whose husband was one of the prisoners Priebke tortured. "He hit him often with brass knuckles."

Priebke's Gestapo office received the orders to round up 330 Italians and execute them within twenty-four hours in reprisal for the fallen SS police. "The whole of that night we searched the records and could not find a sufficient number of persons to make up the number required for execution," he later said. Military police nabbed pedestrians on the streets and brought in others because they were Jews. A dozen men who had been released from a prison across town and were picking up their things at the door to leave were grabbed to fill the quota.

The ultimate register of victims in Priebke's hands represented a cross-section of Romans, among them sixty-eight military men, including forty-two officers of the Italian army loyal to King Victor Emanuel, who had ceded to the Allies in September 1943. Others were farmers, craftsmen, artists, merchants, a diplomat, a priest, six students, doctors, a lawyer, and civil servants.

Late on the morning of March 24, Priebke and another officer ordered the men into commandeered meat trucks and drove the Appian Way to an area of tunnels where early Christians, forbidden to bury their dead inside the city walls, had constructed underground tombs. They stopped at a former stone quarry known as the Ardeatine Caves, between the catacombs of San Callisto, which holds the crypt of sixteen popes, and of Santa Domitilla, where first-century Christian martyrs are interred.

Troops marched five men at a time to a cavern about a hundred feet away as Priebke crossed their names from his list. A farmer secretly watching from a nearby copse noted the moment of the first shot: 3:30 p.m. Soldiers were instructed to eliminate each person with a single shot at the closest possible range, aiming at a certain angle so the bullet entered the brain from the cerebellum, killing instantly. They were not to place the gun barrel in contact with the neck, lest the captive twitch or move in reaction, slowing the process. A medic climbed among the corpses with a flashlight and confirmed that each man was dead. When a few soldiers appeared to balk, Priebke himself shot two of the Italians, to move the process along.

Massacres take time. Hours passed. When troops began to react with revulsion or appeared shaken by the work, officers distributed cognac; aim became less precise, so that three or four shots, not just one, might be needed to kill. Some who died were in their seventies. Outside, those waiting, like nineteen-year-old Gino Cibei and his younger brother Duilo, fourteen, could hear the shots and only wait their turn.

When the job was done the Germans set an explosion that collapsed the vault of the cave, entombing any wounded who might still be alive. Three months later, after the Allies took Rome, soldiers removed the fallen rocks and exhumed remains, but forensic scientists could not identify all the bodies.

At the end of the war, tens of thousands of Germans, including officers like Erich Priebke, were held in crowded Italian prisoner-of-war camps while the Allies sorted out who they were. Priebke kept his head down. On New Year's Eve 1946, he escaped with some fellow captives, cutting through perimeter wire while British guards were drinking, and the Polish guards were already drunk.

He made his way to South Tyrol, where his wife and two small boys had moved. The Priebke family—he never changed his name—blended seamlessly into the local Germanic culture. Other refugees from the Reich were all around—you didn't have to worry about being denounced. The wife and ten children of Martin Bormann, Hitler's private secretary and one of the Reich's most powerful men, settled in Merano to await (ultimately in vain) her husband's arrival.

By 1944, many of Merano's big hotels and clinics had been converted into Nazi military hospitals. Meran—the town's name in German—became an officially designated *Lazerettstadt*, a "hospital city." Red crosses on white flags flying from rooftops sheltered neighborhoods from Allied bombs. They protected Nazi officials and collaborators already on the run.

In 1948, Priebke saw not only that Hitler's closest collaborators had been tried at Nuremberg but also that former Nazis at various levels were continuing to be charged elsewhere with war crimes. SS *Obersturmbann-führer* Herbert Kappler, head of the Gestapo in German-occupied Rome and Priebke's superior, was already in jail, and Italians wanted Priebke for the Ardeatine massacre. He decided it would be prudent to leave Europe.

Many looking to escape went to Madrid or Lisbon, where certain neighborhoods were well known as refuges for those seeking a way out of Europe. Small Merano, then with a population of about eighteen thousand, offered as many opportunities to get on a Ratline as either of those bigger cities. Priebke started by seeking out a local Roman Catholic cleric.

Parish priests, especially in northern Italy, commonly confirmed the Catholic faith and good standing of Nazi fugitives and collaborators. Whether a priest was still sympathetic to Mussolini's Fascism, which had given concessions to the Church in exchange for support, or was an admirer of the Reich because it fought communists or was anti-Semitic, the cleric would attest in writing that a person seeking documents was a practicing Catholic of good character, allowing him entrance to the Church escape system. To protect himself, Priebke underwent a "rebaptism." Mayors, too, and other city officials like those in Merano provided written recommendations asserting that a person on the run had presented proof that he was stateless, another victim of the shifted borders that affected millions at the war's end.

With the references, refugees both real and bogus could obtain documents from the International Committee of the Red Cross (ICRC), certifying their status as persons unable to return to their homelands. Migration officials accepted the ICRC papers as identification for international travel, as good as a passport. The ICRC failed to vet those who received the certificates, or officials knew who they were and issued papers anyway.

At Santa Maria dell'Anima, Bishop Hudal greeted Erich Priebke warmly. The former SS officer later described the bishop as "a gentle man." Before Priebke left the seminary, Hudal handed him a blank Red Cross passport stamped with an Argentine visa on which his family could travel.

Not far away, another cleric was sheltering entire groups of Croatian fascists. The church of San Girolamo degli Illirici, whose pleasing travertine facade faces a small plaza on the Tiber, is a half hour's walk along the river from Hudal's Santa Maria dell'Anima. Until the 1890s, a sweep of stone steps descended from the door of San Girolamo down to the Port of Ripetta. Today the riverine port is gone, but San Girolamo and the stolid building complex to which it belongs remain in place, as they have for more than five hundred years.

In the mid-1940s, brusque young men in civilian clothes, visibly armed, kept guard all around. Sometimes they exchanged a Nazi-like salute and cried out in the Croatian language, *"Za dom spremni!"* ("For the homeland, ready!") The true protector of the fugitives inside, however, was San Girolamo's director, the Reverend Krunoslav Draganović.

Tall, with thinning hair and piercing brown eyes, Draganović was a native of Bosnia-Herzegovina who had thrown in his lot early with the Ustashi, the revolutionary Croatian independence movement. Its founder, Ante Pavelić, bombed civilian trains and collaborated in political assassinations, including the 1934 murder of King Alexander of Yugoslavia. Ustashi thinking was a dark brew of nationalism, fanatic Roman Catholicism, and fascism, its mission to defend Europe's Christian civilization from threats by "Eastern" Serbs. When Hitler and Mussolini handed the "Independent State of Croatia" to Ante Pavelić on a platter, Ustashi forces murdered more than two hundred thousand Orthodox Christian Serbs, thousands of Freemasons, Moslems, and Communists, and almost all of the land's Roma and Jews. Draganović held a minor post in the government before coming to Rome. He considered Pavelić a "torchbearer of freedom."

Sometimes Krunoslav Draganović was called the "Golden Priest" for using bars of ore from the Croatian treasury to guarantee new lives for thousands of ordinary Croatians who fled a new communist regime at the war's end. At San Girolamo, he sheltered the former Ustashi government's finance minister, propaganda minister, deputy foreign minister, commander of the gendarmerie, and commander of the air force. When Ante Pavelić arrived in Rome disguised as a humble Peruvian priest, Draganović helped him get a travel passport from the International Red Cross and passage on a ship out of Genoa to Buenos Aires. San Girolamo was a destination for some of Friedrich Schwend's gold and money that left Schloss Labers.

THE "WORLD-DANGER OF BOLSHEVISM"

Hudal, Draganović, and other clerics who aided travelers on the Ratlines reflected Church thinking at the highest levels. Pope Pius XI, who reigned from 1922 to his death in 1939, set the tone. A librarian by profession, Pius XI did not sympathize with Nazi territorial goals or methods, but he saw Hitler as the only world figure besides himself who was truly standing up to the "world-danger of Bolshevism." His 1937 encyclical, *Divini Redemptoris*, cast the fight against universal communism in the light of the age-old "struggle between good and evil." The world was in convulsion, the pope said, with people "in danger of falling back into a barbarism."

The danger was "Bolshevistic and atheistic Communism, which aims at upsetting the social order and at undermining the very foundations of Christian civilization." Historically, the Catholic Church shared political and social rule with kings and governments. But in communist countries, the Church would not have a dominant role and might not be tolerated at all.

Men like Hudal and Draganović lived within a clerical culture that had coexisted for years with Italian Fascism, an ideology that the pope viewed as keeping socialism and communism at bay in the heartland of the Church. The Vatican itself created the atmosphere for development of the Ratlines with public ambivalence about condemning Nazism, but the position had its roots in the Holy See's collaboration with Mussolini.

In the 1929 Lateran Treaty, Mussolini recognized Vatican City as a sovereign, independent state ruled by the pope. Il Duce mandated Catholic education in schools and promised the Church money. In return, the Vatican pledged to stifle political opposition by Catholic democratic groups and to support Mussolini's Fascist state. Bishops were required to take a loyalty oath to the government. The pope was overjoyed at the restoration of Vatican property and churchly privileges that had been suspended since the unification of Italy in the nineteenth century.

"Newspapers throughout the country, including the Vatican daily, hammered on the theme that the historic event could never have happened if Italy had still been under democratic rule," wrote Vatican scholar David Kertzer. "Only Mussolini, and fascism, had made it possible."

Pius XI envisaged an Italian confessional state where Catholicism would be the official religion, figuring he could Christianize Fascism. Instead, Mussolini created his own political religion, sometimes riding piggyback on Catholic tradition. When Il Duce promulgated the racial laws in 1938, he quoted from medieval anti-Semitic Catholic tracts.

When Vatican secretary of state Eugenio Pacelli, scion of one of Rome's finest families, succeeded to the papal throne in 1939 as Pius XII, an important difference between the two prelates emerged. By the end of his life the old pope, Pius XI, had come to regard militaristic Nazism, with its suppression of individual liberties, to be just as threatening as atheistic and materialistic communism. In *Mit brennender Sorge* (With Burning Concern), written in German to the German Church, he condemned Nazi "neo-paganism" and the "so-called myth of race and blood."

His successor, Pius XII, did not make such public condemnations of the Nazis. He was openly impressed when fascist forces crushed the leftist forces of Republican Spain with the help of Hitler's air force, and he blessed Italian troops on their return from fighting with Franco. In Spain, fascists showed they could stop communism.

As papal nuncio in Germany from 1917 to 1929, Pacelli signed the Concordat with Hitler meant to protect twenty million members of the German Catholic Church. There were trade-offs in the deal—bishops had to swear allegiance to the Reich. But an understanding prevailed that the pope's first obligation was to protect the Church so its priests could administer the sacraments that give the faithful the graces necessary for salvation.

Whether Pius XII did not want to unleash Hitler's wrath on Catholics under Reich control or whether his will was weak, the fact remains that as pope he acted with an excess of caution. He did not roundly condemn the mass killing of Jews. He failed to excommunicate the Fuehrer, a baptized Catholic. He did not support the Italian resistance—partisans were suspect because most were communist.

In his role as the bishop of Rome, Pius XII also tread lightly in 1944 lest occupying Nazis destroy the Eternal City and the independent Papal State. The day after the massacre at the Ardeatine Caves, the official Vatican mouthpiece *L'Osservatore Romano* lamented equally the Nazi troopers' deaths and the dead of the cave who were "sacrificed for the guilty parties who escaped arrest." In this way the papacy cast guilt for the Gestapo murders not on the Germans but on the partisans who fled the Via Rasella.

The Vatican did not by itself run the Ratlines. But the popes gave a green light for clerics to implement escape routes amid the confusion and pain caused by movements of people torn by the war.

William Gowen of the U.S. Army Counter Intelligence Corps (CIC), who was looking for Ante Pavelić in 1946, got word that up to ten truckloads of purloined gold had been unloaded at Draganović's San Girolamo from a convoy bearing Vatican license plates. He couldn't find it. Later, when Draganović had been recruited into the U.S. intelligence network, he confirmed to Gowen that the convoy arrived, commanded by an Ustashi lieutenant colonel. According to one report, a Croatian stash of US$530 million—a staggering amount for the time—flowed "through the Vatican's pipeline" to Spain, then to Argentina. The Vatican denied it.

What is clear from the Holy See's own records, however, is that no other state had a network with such capacity for knowing where people were and moving them as the Vatican had. For the most part, the Vatican systems were used to assist legitimate wartime refugees at a time of terrible displacement. Through the Vatican Refugee Organization, which aided twelve million legitimate refugees in Europe between 1945 and 1953, some of those running from justice also obtained the coveted *cartas di reconicimento*, the friendly letters that got them travel documents from the ICRC.

The papal Office of Information tracked missing persons through its networks of parishes and monasteries and facilitated correspondence between families and loved ones in POW camps or at the front. The office maintained a wartime central index of persons on four million cards.

Working closely with the inventor Guglielmo Marconi, Pope Pius XI established Vatican Radio in 1931; the station broadcast a million wartime messages, often to reconnect families.

From 1940 to 1946, agencies operating out of the Vatican helped about 860,000 persons, mostly civilians, to repatriate or move to safe havens. Probably some 30,000 were war criminals and collaborators who took the Ratlines. After the war the Vatican directly interceded with Washington and London for certain war criminals and Nazi collaborators sheltering in Italy, including some protected by Hudal and Draganović, lest they be extradited to countries where they would face a death sentence.

Almost all the escape routes ran through the Church infrastructure, but members of the Roman Catholic Church were not the only ones to use the Ratlines to abet fugitives. The Allies also used them to move their former foes to freedom.

The desire for advance information is no doubt rooted in the instinct for survival.

—ALLEN DULLES, *The Craft of Intelligence*, 1963

Allen Dulles, who became the first civilian director of the CIA and America's longest-serving spymaster, spent World War II as the OSS chief in Berne in an enchanting fourteenth-century home with a commanding view of the Alps and the sinuous Aare River. Along with Stockholm, Madrid, Lisbon, and Istanbul, the Swiss capital was considered an "intelligence metropolis" for the amount of espionage and counterespionage that went on there. Disaffected Nazis found their way to Dulles's mansion, sometimes entering by a partially hidden back door. The American spy spoke fluent German and squeezed out pertinent information. Sometimes the intelligence he received also helped his clients at Sullivan and Cromwell, the New York law firm where Allen and his brother Foster, later secretary of state, were partners.

The OSS cultivated certain Nazis, bringing them onto the payroll to fight postwar communism. In the spring of 1945, Walter Rauff, then the

Nazi chief of intelligence in northern Italy, participated in Operation Sunrise, Dulles's secret scheme to negotiate a separate surrender of German soldiers and Mussolini's troops in that part of the country, just days before the official end of the war. Friedrich Schwend of Operation Bernhard also took part. Later Rauff worked for the CIC, and Schwend collaborated with the OSS.

When U.S. intelligence agencies discovered the Ratline routes, they began to use them to move agents and valuable contacts, fascist or not, to safety. Just as anyone with money for a ticket could take a train, so too it seemed that anyone with the right contacts could travel a Ratline. Among Friedrich Schwend's lieutenants in his shady business were several Jews who, after the war, used the old routes of Operation Bernhard to shepherd Holocaust survivors illegally to Palestine. At one time, Schloss Labers housed Jews on one floor and fugitive Nazis on another.

From the perspective of Dulles and the likes of Draganović, Hudal, and Rauff, in the wake of the Axis defeat, the next war was looming between the civilized West and the forces of the East represented by the Soviet Union. SS captain Klaus Barbie, known as the Butcher of Lyon for the torture he inflicted personally on Gestapo prisoners, once asked Draganović why he was going to such efforts to help him escape to Bolivia. Draganović replied, "We have to maintain a sort of moral reserve on which we can draw in the future."

More fascists and collaborators took the Ratlines to Argentina than to any other country in Latin America. In general, President Juan Perón agreed with their politics. At the same time, he wanted the immigrants to help modernize the country and to support his nuclear and aviation programs. He valued military and industrial experience and admired the political systems of Hitler and Mussolini. He knew Fascist Italy especially well.

In 1939, forty-four-year-old army lieutenant Juan Domingo Perón lived in Merano, learning mountain warfare while attached to a crack *Alpini* combat unit and becoming familiar with Mussolini's armed forces. He skied on the slopes that encircled the city. He rode fine horses in the hippodrome near the barracks. Tall and athletic and with a dazzling smile, the vigorous Argentine cut a dashing figure in uniform.

From Merano, Perón went to Rome to serve as adjutant to the defense attaché at the Argentine embassy. He saw the efficiency of Mussolini's police state and the effectiveness of his cult of personality, and he recognized the power of Il Duce's grand public displays. In Mussolini's Italy, Perón said later, ordinary people—workers—had a part in national life that they never had before, and the same happened in Hitler's Germany, "an organized state for a perfectly ordered community, and a perfectly ordered population, where the state was the instrument of the people. I thought that this ought to be the political form of the future, the true people's democracy, the true social democracy."

Perón was not a notably devout Catholic, but in Rome he cultivated Argentina's representatives to the Holy See. Unusually for a man of his relatively low rank, he was received by the pope in a private audience. The visit was almost certainly approved by the Vatican's sharp intelligence agents, who knew a rising star when they saw one.

After two years in Europe, Juan Perón returned to Buenos Aires "at a moment when the [political] battles, as usual, were being rigged," he said in a 1960s interview. "I asked myself, 'What would happen if someone began to fight for real and announced "I'm going to play to win"'?"

Perón became one of a circle of officers who ousted the Argentine president in a popular coup in 1943. Now a colonel, he exuded a magnetism born of physical prowess and self-confidence. J. Edgar Hoover sent the State Department a description of Perón's manner provided by the FBI's spy network.

"He improvises," said Hoover's report. "He does not boast about his physical power, but he shows it. He takes off his jacket and walks up and down with his regulation Kahki [sic] shirt, exhibiting the pistol in his belt. He bangs the table and does not hesitate when referring to other chiefs and officers, or in stating that he will fix that situation 'by blows.' But he does all this laughing. If he becomes flustered over a discussion, it only lasts a second."

Perón made no secret of his admiration for Il Duce, Franco, and the Fuehrer. When he left Rome in 1941, Germany was at its high point of wartime strength. He wanted to ensure that Argentina would play a part in the new world order to come.

• • •

In 1943, Perón was a central player in a secret plan that proposed Argentina as a broker, in collaboration with the Vatican, to end the war. In the audacious scheme, a victorious Germany would get a formal bridge to the Western Hemisphere through Argentina. The pope would be assured of protection for the Eternal City and the Vatican would govern Jerusalem, keeping the Holy Places safe from Zionists and Moslems. Argentina would reclaim the Falkland Islands and acquire a powerful ally—the Reich— against "Bolshevist penetration" of Latin America.

Perón covertly sent a personal envoy to the Vatican and the Reich to propose a postwar "triangle of peace," tethered at its points by Germany, the Vatican, and Argentina. Part of the inspiration was General Francisco Franco's interpretation of *hispanidad*, the idea that Spanish and Portuguese speakers the world over were united in their Catholic faith and support of the Reich, especially in the face of British and U.S. imperialism. Mostly, however, Perón's idea centered on the concept of Argentina as a natural leader of the region. He believed that alongside the Vatican, Latin America with Spain and Portugal could create a new global sphere of political influence.

As the Argentine journalist and historian Uki Goñi has written, "The country's powerful nationalist military officers and Church dignitaries dreamt of converting Argentina from a secular republic into a Hispanic 'Catholic Nation' that could act as a counterweight to its 'materialistic' northern cousin, the 'Anglo-Saxon' United States."

Perón's envoy, a well-connected Catholic nationalist named Juan Carlos Goyeneche, traveled to the Reich to pledge Argentina's support. There are conflicting versions about whether he met with Hitler, but it has been confirmed that he met with SS chief Himmler and with Hitler's foreign minister Joachim von Ribbentrop at the minister's Westphalia estate, where he sat through an extended rant against "international Jewry." But Goyeneche received assurances that Argentina would be rewarded commercially for its loyalty when the Reich won the war. "We could take everything that Argentina produced no matter how much it might be," Ribbentrop said.

Then Goyeneche raised the issue more important than any other to

Argentine national pride—the Falkland Islands, claimed by the British. Seldom has such an apparently insignificant bit of land weighed so heavily in the history of a country.

The Falklands—*Las Malvinas* in Spanish—are three hundred miles from the Argentine coast off Patagonia and scarcely populated even today. For much of their history, the islands were notable principally for scrubby hills, penguins, and albatross, a convenient repair stop for ships rounding the Horn or engaged in the "wrecking trade," recovering cargo and timbers from disabled ships.

For Britain, however, the Falklands are an imperial outpost in reach of Antarctica. During World War I, the British successfully defended the Falklands from an attack by German admiral Graf Maximilian von Spee, who died along with his two sons and more than two thousand other men. The bitter memory of the defeat of their national hero gave Germans, too, a stake in liberating *Las Malvinas* from the British.

Would the victorious Reich support the Argentine claim to the Falklands? The answer pleased Perón's envoy.

The clear-eyed, stern-looking Ribbentrop, formerly the ambassador to the Court of St. James, compared the Falklands to that "grotesque example" of British Gibraltar, which lies "without question . . . on the Iberian peninsula," thus rightfully belonging to Spain. He warned that "unless Argentina takes care," the United States might take over the Falklands. Ribbentrop said the islands were "nearer Argentina than to England," and expressed "great sympathy" for the Argentine claim.

It must have been music to Goyeneche's ears then, to hear Mussolini also express support for Argentina's claim at a meeting in Rome. At another location in the city, in an office of polished mahogany walls, Vatican secretary of state Luigi Cardinal Maglione made a discreet but pointed inquiry of another Argentine diplomat, its ambassador to the Holy See. Was Argentina willing "to apply its immigration law generously in order to encourage at the opportune moment European immigrants to seek the necessary land and capital in your country?" Yes.

In February 1946, the same month that Juan Perón was elected president, Argentine bishop Antonio Caggiano traveled to Rome carrying another diplomatic message: Argentina was "willing to receive French persons, whose political attitude during the recent war would expose them, should they return to France, to harsh measures and private revenge"— that is, onetime Nazi collaborators.

Caggiano was accompanied by an Argentine bishop with strong ties to Action Française, an ultranationalist movement that disdained the French Revolution and modern democracy. They met with the Vatican's Russia expert, Eugène Cardinal Tisserant, who believed the Russians were on the verge of taking control over Europe. Soon visas stamped on ICRC passports were forthcoming for French and Belgian Nazi collaborators hiding in Italy and Spain.

The three clerics who met in the Vatican may have been presuming that the men they helped to escape would form an anticommunist political brain trust upon which Argentina might draw. Nevertheless, the ship that carried the Argentine bishops home also carried the first officially documented wanted Nazi collaborator to disembark in Buenos Aires, and he was not an intelligence agent, secret police veteran, or professional intellectual. He was an aviation industry genius.

The Frenchman Émile Dewoitine, one of Europe's most important jet plane designers, had worked for the Reich, Japan, and Spain. Within a year in Argentina, collaborating with Perón's aviation team, he built the IA-27 Pulqui, the first combat jet fighter in Latin America, making the country only the fifth in the world to develop a jet fighter on its own. In 1947, aviation expert Kurt Tank, the aeronautical engineer and test pilot who flew the prototype of the first landplane to cross the Atlantic and created warplanes for the Luftwaffe, arrived and proceeded to devise an Argentine jet fighter along the lines of the Soviet MiG-15. The resulting Pulqui II, however, was a casualty of an Argentine economic crisis in the early 1950s, with just five prototypes built. The only one that saw combat flew in support of rebels that brought down Perón's government in 1955.

Perón wanted to import as many German and other refugee technicians as he could to further industrialization. The Americans and the Russians had already claimed thousands, but Perón wanted his share, too, even though he had less money and international standing with which to work. It was not a bad idea, a British Foreign Office memorandum noted, for Argentina to profit from trained specialists so that industrialization would not be dominated by North Americans. For the first time in the country's history, industrial production became greater than agricultural production, with arms production greater than any other branch.

For all the emphasis on bringing in trained experts to promote development, Perón's Ratline system was in the hands of some of the most unsavory men in Argentina: Rodolfo Freude, Perón's spy chief and head of his propaganda apparatus; Pierre Daye, who wrote for an anti-Semitic, ultra-collaborationist review in France; René Lagrou, once leader of the Flemish SS in Belgium; and Carlos Fuldner, an Argentine who grew up in Germany, joined the SS, and translated for the Blue Division, a unit of Spanish and Latin American volunteers who fought for Germany on the Soviet front. The Ratline agents had their own covert headquarters in the presidential Information Bureau and Central State Intelligence office located in the Casa Rosada, the pink-colored White House in Buenos Aires.

Pierre Daye later exulted about a two-day meeting that Perón held with this team, remarking on the president's "courage" in receiving the men in the "national official palace." There should have been no surprise. In the 1960s, Perón gave his opinion of the Nuremberg trials, calling them "an infamy, unworthy of the conquerors." Perón was a military man who seemed to consider that demanding justice for certain acts in wartime was a weakness. "Now we realize that [the Allies] deserved to lose the war," he said.

It is difficult to say for certain how many refugees came on the Ratline escape routes to Latin America. Argentina, for instance, has a European face, with a small indigenous population and strong historical immigration from Italy, England, Germany, and Spain. Newcomers blended into the ordinary flow of immigrants; arrival records of the period that might have told us more were destroyed. What is clear is that the arrivals came from many countries, not only Germany. Thirty thousand Croatians went to Argentina. Some newcomers were fortunate to get jobs in branches of the Reich's businesses—IG Farben, Volkswagen, Hoechst, Bayer, Krupp. Others scraped out a modest living.

Friedrich Schwend of Operation Bernhard made his way to Peru, probably in 1946, some reports say with a good deal of Operation Bernhard treasure. Schwend became a successful businessman, an experience he shared with many other new arrivals. "Life here is much easier," he wrote to a brother-in-law in Genoa in 1959. "A shame you didn't make tracks over here immediately after the end of the war."

Others who traveled the Ratlines to Latin America were among the era's most wanted war criminals.

- **Ante Pavelić**, the Ustashi founder helped by Krunoslav Draganović, became a security advisor to Juan Perón. In Buenos Aires, he declared a Croatian state in exile, tried to breathe new life into Nazism among followers, and railed against the Yugoslav Communist regime of Josip Broz Tito. After Perón's fall in 1955, Pavelić took refuge in Paraguay, where he worked as a security advisor to the ruthless dictator Alfredo Stroessner. He died in Spain in 1959 from wounds suffered in a 1957 assassination attempt by a Serbian patriot in Buenos Aires.
- **Joseph Mengele,** the gap-toothed "Angel of Death," was a physician at Auschwitz who condemned those he judged unfit for work to immediate extermination in the gas chambers. He performed cruel experiments on the living. Mengele had an obsession with developing a method of producing twins, believing German women might offset war losses with multiple births. With Bishop Hudal's help, Mengele escaped to Bolivia. He lived for a time in Paraguay and then migrated to Brazil, where he drowned in 1979 at age sixty-seven after suffering a stroke while swimming off the coast near São Paulo.
- **Adolf Eichmann,** who managed the transportation logistics for moving hundreds of thousands of Jews for elimination in deaths camps, went to Argentina with Hudal's help. There he lived quietly for fifteen years until 1960, when an Israeli team of security and intelligence agents kidnapped him and brought him to Jerusalem, where he was tried and hanged in 1962. (Hudal also helped Eichmann's deputy, Alois Brunner,

go to Syria, where he worked as a consultant on Nazi torture and interrogation methods.)

- **Klaus Barbie,** the Gestapo chief with the penchant for personally involving himself in the torture of his victims, signed a 1944 order sending forty-four Jewish children and their seven caregivers from a home near Nice to the death camps. Barbie noted dutifully that the home had been "cleaned out" but that "neither cash nor other valuables could be secured." After the war, the U.S. CIC hired Barbie as an informer. When the French demanded him for trial, U.S. agents and Draganović arranged for his escape to Bolivia. There he worked for West German intelligence and may have continued to work for U.S. intelligence, as he boasted of aiding in the capture of Che Guevara, a CIA-advised operation, although the boast has never been proven. Extradited to France, Barbie died in prison in 1991 at age seventy-seven.

- **Eduard Roschmann,** the "Butcher of Riga," oversaw the murders of twenty-four thousand Jews in a Latvian forest and presided over the murders of German, Austrian, and Czech Jews who had been delivered to a Latvian ghetto. Arrested in Graz, Roschmann escaped from Dachau, which had been turned into a prison camp, got in touch with Hudal, and traveled safely to Argentina, where he became a citizen. An unclaimed body found in Asunción, Paraguay, in 1977 may have been that of Roschmann, but its identity was never confirmed.

- **Franz Stangl** oversaw the death camps at Sobibór and Treblinka and a facility of the "euthanasia" network that killed disabled children and the gravely ill. Stangl went to Brazil. In 1969, at age fifty-seven, he was extradited to Germany and died three years later in jail.

- **Gustav Wagner,** known as "The Beast" for his personal brutality, was Stangl's deputy commander at the Sobibór camp in German-occupied Poland where more than two hundred thousand died. In 1948, Hudal gave Wagner a Red Cross passport. He sailed for Brazil, where he lived for thirty years. In

October 1980, he was found at home in São Paulo with a knife in his chest, an apparent suicide.

After the war Erich Priebke, the SS officer who presided over the massacre at the Ardeatine Caves, lived a full life for fifty years in a city in the foothills of the Andes, about a thousand miles southwest of Buenos Aires. Priebke arrived with his wife and two sons at a ski and vacation destination, Bariloche, in 1948. Long settled by Germans and Austrians, Bariloche looks as if it belongs in Bavaria, with woody alpine architecture and vistas of tall mountains. Priebke ran a German deli and served as director of the German school and chairman of the cultural association.

This cozy state of affairs came to an abrupt end in 1994 when an ABC-TV team, following a tip from the Nazi-hunting Simon Wiesenthal Center, pinned down Priebke's whereabouts. The network flew journalist Sam Donaldson in with his crew, posing as ski enthusiasts. On a Bariloche city street, Donaldson identified himself to Priebke and staged a classic ambush interview. "Oh my," said Priebke, confronted about the Italian massacre. "At that time an order was an order."

Priebke was extradited to Italy, convicted in 1996 for the Ardeatine massacre, and placed under house arrest. He lived for seventeen years in an apartment that belonged to his lawyer, dying in 2013 at age one hundred. Neither Argentina nor Priebke's German hometown wanted his remains. The papal vicar for the Holy City forbade any priest in Rome to celebrate a funeral Mass; the mayor and the police chief ruled out a public ceremony.

An ultra-traditionalist Catholic order offered to hold a funeral Mass outside Rome at its headquarters south of the city limits. Protesters gathered, mobbing the hearse. A crowd of neo-Nazis fought back. Police managed to carry Priebke's coffin inside, but the street riot lasted well into the night, and the service was canceled. Authorities buried Priebke in a secret location. It was the only way, they said, to prevent his resting place from becoming a pilgrimage site for modern fascists.

Walter Rauff's 1949 voyage from Milan landed in Ecuador, from which he moved to Argentina and finally to Chile. There he worked for

the West German Federal Intelligence Service and as an advisor to dictator General Augusto Pinochet's secret police. He died of a heart attack at
age seventy-eight in 1984.

A wreath with a swastika lay at the church door the night of Rauff's
wake. The next morning, his coffin was brought to the general cemetery
in Santiago. Two hundred mourners attended the funeral. When Rauff's
family left, five men stayed behind at the grave to raise their arms in the
Nazi salute.

14.

CONNECTIONS, THE COLD WAR

War once begun has few limits in time or space, as these chapters show. During the years in which I examined the era of World War II in Latin America, I often thought of later wars I covered as a journalist in Mexico and Central America, and of the South American Cold War dictatorships. Some four hundred thousand persons died or disappeared in political violence in Latin American countries in the 1970s and 1980s, most of them civilians, almost all at the hands of militarized governments supported by the United States.

The fascists of Europe possessed characteristics in common with the authoritarians of Latin America. They defined groups as internal enemies, "the enemy within." They tortured individuals to get information, for punishment, or for the pleasure of the torturers, and they tried to hide crimes of mass killings. They stole babies. They "concentrated" undesirables in camps, and counted on collaboration from professionals—medics, psychiatrists. Hitler's secret "Night and Fog" decree (*Nacht-und-Nebel-Erlass*) of 1941, which ordered resisters of the Reich to be taken clandestinely and eliminated without a trace—as if swallowed by "night and fog"—prefigured the process that created thousands of Latin Americans disappeared by the 1980s, the *desaparecidos*.

I wondered whether the horrors of World War II were connected to the spasms of terror that shook Latin states thirty years later. Or do tyrannies simply have similarities that mirror each other? Perhaps there is such a thing as a cycle of violence that inevitably repeats itself, with shared characteristics, erupting here then erupting there, never to be completely extinguished?

I arrived at no definitive answers to these questions. But I met individuals who considered them in thoughtful ways, including a torture survivor, a forensic anthropologist, a pedagogical psychiatry educator, and a physician whose lifetime spanned Hitler's Reich and New World fascism. Simply to listen to Gunter Seelmann, eighty-five, the physician, was to feel a connection between the tyrannies.

On the night of November 9, 1938, in Aachen, Germany, seven-year-old Gunter was sleeping in his grandmother's bed. Above was the attic from which he had watched the sleek silver *Graf Zeppelin* glide through the sky. Below was the small factory where his father made bedding and the storefront where the products were sold.

At some moment he awoke to shouting, the sound of glass shattering. His father's shop windows were being smashed. Later, those hours would have a name: *Kristallnacht*, the Night of the Broken Glass. Gunter's father and uncle were taken to a work camp, Buchenwald.

In midmorning, his grandmother walked Gunter through streets to the place where their synagogue had stood the day before. "I saw the smoke, still rising from the ruins," he said. "I will never forget it."

Gunter's father was released but never spoke to him of Buchenwald. Only twice did his son see him show deep emotion: once on the train platform as the family left for exile, and again later in Chile when he received a package from his longtime friend from Aachen, Otto Frank. Inside was a copy of a diary written by Frank's daughter Anne, one of three thousand that he had printed in 1947 in hope that others might read her story.

Relatives of the Seelmann family stayed behind in Germany and perished. In Concepción, Chile, about 250 miles south of Santiago, Gunter learned Spanish, studied medicine, and married a dynamic nursing educator, Hanni Grunpeter, whose Czech Jewish family had fled Europe, too.

In 1970, when physician and former minister of health Salvador

Allende became the first Marxist in history to be elected president of a democratic country, Gunter was the head of a pediatric hospital. At the time, Chile had one of the highest infant mortality rates in the world. "It is not possible to bring health and education to a population with poor nutrition, dressed in rags and who work in a landscape of merciless exploitation," Allende had written. Gunter and Hanni agreed, and took posts in the new administration.

Allende angered the international business community by nationalizing production of Chile's major resource, copper, as well as the telephone system, both American owned. He upset the land-based oligarchy by introducing land reform in an attempt to feed the country—much of the best land had lain fallow or was held for speculation.

Washington funded the opposition. In 1970, a CIA coup plot failed. Nixon's secretary of state Henry Kissinger called the voters who elected Allende "irresponsible," explaining that "the issues are much too important for the Chilean voters to be left to decide for themselves."

On the morning of September 11, 1973, forces commanded by General Augusto Pinochet surrounded the presidential palace, La Moneda, symbol of South America's longest-running democracy. Allende refused to surrender, citing his constitutional duty. He addressed the nation by radio in farewell.

Go forward knowing that, sooner rather than later, the great avenues will open again where free men will walk . . .

Helicopter gunships assaulted La Moneda and Chilean Air Force jets bombed the palace until Pinochet's troops swooped inside around 2:30 in the afternoon. Allende had committed suicide.

Soldiers rolled up in a van before Gunter's house and drove him to a transport that took him to a concentration camp on an island in Concepción Bay. He became one of more than 30,000 persons imprisoned and abused by the Pinochet regime in the next seventeen years, at least 2,279 of them executed by the state. (Twenty-one of those killed, noted Gunter, were doctors.)

For eight months, Gunter went through interrogations, being "treated not very well," he said blandly, disinviting further questions about his time on the island. Helmut Frenz, a Lutheran clergyman, intervened for him with a German diplomat, saying, "If the German fascists didn't kill him, the Chilean fascists will kill him." Gunter and his family accepted exile in Germany, "the last place I wanted to go," he said, where he remained until 1985.

At his house in Santiago in 2017, sitting tall in a chair, Gunter inscribed a book and handed it to me, his *Political Memories*. "I was much younger," he said, pointing to the cover, where he stands looking handsome and serious to the left of a seated Allende during a municipal electoral campaign.

On the back cover are printed his words, "History does not repeat itself and no one wants it to." Nevertheless, Gunter compared the Nazi and Chilean intelligence systems to each other, both "very good, with unions, parties, and organizations successfully infiltrated." The Chilean National Intelligence Directorate, called the DINA for its initials in Spanish, became Pinochet's feared secret police. Sometimes the DINA is called Chile's Gestapo.

In Europe, Jews in the millions were eliminated because they had been born Jews, not because of their actions or associations as people were in Chile. "The killing of the Shoah was industrialized," Gunter said. He sat back and seemed to ponder. Nevertheless, he said, "the ideologies were the same; they tried to establish fascism here, taking all the decisions over the lives of persons."

Night had fallen, and with his long view of history, Gunter Seelmann worried about the present. "We are in a very critical moment now, authoritarian regimes again are looking for enemies.

"It seems like a cycle," he said. "A cycle of dictatorships and the desire for power by war. Sometimes men have to demonstrate the bestial side of themselves."

In Argentina Ana Maria Careaga, a torture survivor, told me she believes that the "beast in human nature" wreaks havoc if ordinary people deny the signs of its emergence, or if they deny its existence once it has seized power over society. Ana Maria was sixteen years old and four months pregnant on June 13, 1977, when soldiers pulled a black hood over her head and delivered her to the Athletic Club in Buenos Aires, one of three hundred torture sites under the dictatorship. She was blindfolded around the clock, hung from her arms and legs, shocked in her private parts with an electric cattle prod.

Even now, Ana Maria said, some deny the extent and depravity of the violence of those years. Reports and human rights advocates put the number killed during the dictatorship at thirty thousand, but in 2017 President Mauricio Macri said that he "didn't know" how many died, that the number may be as low as nine thousand. Another government official said, "There was no systematic plan for the disappearance of people."

Today Ana Maria Careaga is a psychotherapist in Buenos Aires, with long, dark hair and dark eyes, who keeps a thick volume about Nazi concentration camps on her office shelf. One evening after her last patient had left, she filled our discussion about torturers and the tortured with references to Freud and Hitler and Primo Levi and the phenomenon of surviving. Of fifteen hundred persons to pass through the chambers of the Athletic Club, only about three hundred left the place alive.

When Ana Maria was captured, her mother Esther Ballestrino de Careaga was a leader of the Mothers of the Disappeared of the Plaza de Mayo, known by the Spanish word for mothers, *Madres*. Esther Careaga cofounded the *Madres* in 1976 when security forces kidnapped two of her sons and she met other mothers searching for their children.

To denounce Ana Maria's kidnapping, a delegation of the women went to the office of the English-language *Buenos Aires Herald*, not to government-controlled papers where they assumed a notice would not see print. The Argentine journalist Uki Goñi told me that "the Mothers of the Disappeared used to come into the office in a group. Sometimes Esther would then come back alone and talk, and sometimes I would just hold her hand."

Esther Careaga held a PhD in chemistry and worked in a laboratory where she supervised a young assistant, Jorge Mario Bergoglio, who later became a Jesuit priest. In 2013, Bergoglio became Pope Francis. "I remember her as a great woman," Francis told two journalists who published a book of "conversations" with him. "She taught me the seriousness of the work." They stayed friends. Careaga showed him that Marxists could be "good people." During the dictatorship, however, Argentines could be condemned for the books they read. When Ana Maria disappeared, Esther called Father Bergoglio to administer last rites to a relative at her house, but it was a ruse. When he arrived, she begged him to take away the family's books about Marxism and communism. He did.

After four months in captivity, Ana Maria Careaga was freed, and the family flew to Sweden. Soon, however, Esther Careaga, then fifty-nine, bought a ticket to return.

"Why have you come back?" Uki Goñi asked the first time he saw her again. She replied, "There are other children who remain disappeared, other mothers still looking."

Shortly before Christmas, Ana Maria called to tell her mother the happy news that her baby boy had been born healthy. But Esther wasn't there.

Security forces had captured her with five other *Madres* and two French nuns and brought them to the Naval Mechanics Training School, an elite center on green acres in the center of Buenos Aires. As cadets and officers went about classes, guards pushed the women through a door attached to the base commander's private residence and into a basement where data about their personal characteristics was neatly recorded on official forms. They climbed flights of stairs to take places on the floor among other prisoners in a stinking, darkened room. Any pregnant women captives around them who had reached their seventh month were moved to a smaller room with pale walls where they received a glass of milk and a piece of fruit every day, besides the prisoners' gruel. When they gave birth, attended by doctors and nurses, the new mothers were killed and the babies trafficked through officers and their friends.

Ana Maria said she lived in a state of "permanent uncertainty" after her mother disappeared. To deprive loved ones of knowledge about the missing or their fate is a way of inflicting mental punishment on survivors. In Central America, relatives told me a disappearance in the family felt like experiencing a death over and over, a never-healing wound. They longed at least to bury the remains of their dead.

·   ·   ·

During the Cold War, Latin governments tried to hide murders while pursuing deniability, "the way the Nazis did," Patricia Bernardi of the Argentine Forensic Anthropology Team told me. Patricia has been a member since 1984, when the team was founded, and since then has worked all over the world. I had come to know her at a place called Dos Erres, the site of a Guatemalan massacre, where she labored for several days in 1992, much of that time deep in a well where bodies of unarmed peasants killed by the army had been tossed. In Latin America, she said, police and courts denied arrests, denied the existence of the torture centers. The military and secret police also learned from French methods in Algeria and counterinsurgency methods taught at the U.S. School of the Americas.

In Argentina, prisoners were injected with a soporific and taken to an armed forces aircraft, often a helicopter, in which they were flown over the Atlantic or the River Plate and dropped to their deaths. In 2005, Bernardi's team exhumed bones buried in a grave marked "unknown" that had initially been found on a beach in late 1977.

"We saw they were bones of older women," she said, which was unusual, because *desaparecidos* were typically under age thirty-five. The cause of death, the scientists determined, was "multiple fractures consistent with a fall from a great height." With a thumbprint, they made a match: Esther Careaga. Ana Maria accompanied her older sister to confirm the identification of their mother with a DNA test.

Patricia Bernardi said she was taken aback by the identification of the remains. "Every person is important," she said. "But here was the president of the *Madres*."

"The torturers were defeated, both the Nazis and the Argentines," Ana Maria Careaga had told me. They could not hide what they had done, and "they both failed in the final solution."

The next day I visited the former naval school where Ana Maria's mother had been held, commonly called ESMA for its initials in Spanish. I could not help but think of a visit I once made to Auschwitz. Just as in the Reich, in Argentina clerks obeyed a compulsion for order by maintaining detailed records of the doomed. Doctors and nurses kept the detained well enough for torture and interrogation. An ESMA room used to store goods confiscated from captives, from clothing to furniture to

electric fans, reminded me of a mountain of shoes I had seen at Auschwitz, taken from Jews before they were executed. Auschwitz captives
were forced to labor, notably at the IG Farben factory to produce artificial
rubber; ESMA captives were forced to repair and shine up the confiscated goods for sale to profit the navy and support the torture site.

"When they took out the Jews for interrogations, they beat them on
the way even harder than the rest of us," Ana Maria said of the Athletic
Club. "I could hear the guards playing Hitler's speeches, loud, while they
were torturing them." Prisoners held elsewhere tell of seeing Nazi swastikas drawn by guards on the walls of torture chambers and along halls,
and in one case the Spanish word for "nationalism," spelled tellingly with
a "z," *nazionalismo*. Jews were 1 percent of the Argentine population;
they accounted for 12 percent of the victims of the self-styled "Western
and Christian" regime.

Many Cold War Latin strongmen admired Italian Fascists and Nazis. However, everyone I spoke to in the region told me that the major outside influence on the Cold War regimes was not European fascism but the United
States National Security Doctrine, Washington's strategy to prevent the
spread of communism and maintain a "stable" climate for U.S. business.

In the early 1960s, when the Cuban revolution had succeeded and
movements in other countries were challenging sclerotic, oligarchic regimes, President John F. Kennedy called Latin America "the most dangerous area in the world." At a meeting of journalists and Florida officeholders
in 1963, he said, "We . . . must use every very resource at our command
to prevent the establishment of another Cuba in this hemisphere."

The immediate result of the National Security Doctrine was ten military coups in Latin America between 1961 and 1964 against governments
bent upon reform. The CIA abetted three more against elected civilian
governments: Guatemala (1954), Brazil (1964), and Chile (1973). Latin
armies supported the status quo, opposition was subversion, and "irreg-
ular warfare" was the strategy against *subversivos*, the internal enemy
considered communist. U.S. trainers and advisors directed the transformation of the continent's regular armies into counterinsurgency forces.

"Communist," however, was a profoundly elastic term. It included anyone agitating for change. U.S. military manuals show that popular movements—students, labor—and public political demonstrations were considered communist-inspired. U.S. Army and CIA instructors taught how to use pain in interrogations and to weaken prisoners' resistance by threatening their families. The manuals taught methods of assassination. As happened during the Reich, organizations that might have protested the brutality were dismantled one by one, first communists, then political parties from liberal to conservative, labor and student federations, courts and legislatures, and the independent press.

Hundreds of faith-inspired individuals died for denouncing the Latin American violence. Others, including churchmen, supported armed forces claiming that they were doing God's work against communism. By the 1970s, armies presented themselves as crusaders in a holy war, the only instrument capable of securing national survival in the face of the Soviet Communist threat. Where the institutional Church lined up with the strongmen, the dream of Christianized fascism held by some during World War II finally came to pass—in Latin America.

Some key civilians and former military personnel participated in "anti-insurgency" through the World Anti-Communist League (WACL), a militant global organization led after 1980 by Major General John Singlaub. His career had begun with the OSS and continued in South Korea, where he was chief of staff of both U.S. Army and UN forces. WACL members from Mexico to Argentina included former Nazi collaborators, neo-Nazis, and Central American death squad leaders. The men (they were exclusively men) who attended regular meetings in Latin America learned from each other by sharing experiences and techniques against the common enemy, *subversivos*. In the 1980s, President Reagan named WACL members as ambassadors to Guatemala, the Bahamas, and Costa Rica and sent congratulations to a San Diego conference with "best wishes for future success."

What fright the face of fascism causes!
They carry out their plans with such precision.

—VÍCTOR JARA, *"Estadio Chile"*

In Argentina and Chile, people often speak of the Cold War dictatorships in language that calls up World War II: *Nazi, Holocaust, genocide.*

In a Buenos Aires café, a history professor who belonged to a Perónist teachers' group in the 1970s spoke about having to cull her books. "Sometimes I wonder why I survived and others disappeared," she said. "My father-in-law survived Auschwitz. When I asked him how, he said, *'Puro azar.'*" Pure chance. "I think that's why I'm here, *puro azar.*"

An employee at the La Chacarita cemetery in Buenos Aires showed me tombs of the famous—the aviator Jorge Newbery, the tango icon Carlos Gardel, Juan Perón (his remains were transferred after political vandals raided the grave and cut off Perón's hands). "Of course there are no remains here of those who died in our Holocaust," she said, referring to the disappeared.

Even the word "genocide" takes on a particular life in Latin America. Perpetrators of a range of human rights crimes are called *genocidios.*

Such words have precise legal meanings that some experts say do not perfectly fit the Latin violence. But coming from the lips of the persons I was meeting, they stood for the worst experiences a people could have.

Echoes of World War II sounded especially sharp when I heard the term "concentration camp." We associate it with Nazi death camps, but it also described other kinds of incarceration, such as at Crystal City in Texas, U.S. camps in Panama, or Camp Algiers where Latin American Jews were held in Louisiana. Those in Chile and Argentina, however, were death camps.

In Chile, thousands captured in sweeps immediately after the coup were dragged to soccer stadiums in Santiago where they went through physical and psychological torture, like false firing squads. Victor Jara, the internationally renowned folk singer and activist, sang to keep up the spirits of fellow prisoners in the Estadio Chile until guards recognized him. For three days they beat him in a locker room, breaking more than fifty bones, before riddling his body with gunfire and dumping him with other corpses outside a cemetery.

"Anyone who sees us will know what fascism really means for our family," Jara's British-born widow Joan told an interviewer. "Our daughters will never be the same people."

High-ranking officials such as Orlando Letelier, Allende's ambassador to the United States and foreign minister, were taken to Dawson Island, a frigid speck in the Straits of Magellan. Letelier was among thousands who died in Operation Condor, the secret 1970s network of intelligence services of South American countries that shared information and eliminated each other's enemies as they killed their own people, even reaching into Europe and the United States. Released from prison on condition he leave Chile, Letelier, an economist, went to Washington. A Condor agent placed a bomb on Letelier's car that exploded as he rounded Sheridan Circle on September 21, 1976, killing him and an American colleague, Ronni Moffitt.

The United States was complicit in Condor's operation. For instance, to communicate secretly with each other, the Condor chapters used an encrypted system through a U.S. communications installation in the Panama Canal Zone that covered all of Latin America.

The camp at Dawson Island was reputedly designed by the Nazi war criminal Walter Rauff. Another Nazi veteran, former corporal and army nurse Paul Schaefer, linked the repressive methods of the Reich with the New World in a bizarre and ghoulish forced-labor camp he founded in 1961 called Colonia Dignidad (Dignity Colony).

"They thought they would build a place where they would do good works and live like good Christians," Horst Schaffrick told a London newspaper about his parents Helmut and Emi, who sold their house in Germany and gave the money to Schaefer on the promise of a new life in Chile. "They found nothing but slavery and suffering."

Acting as an evangelical preacher, Schaefer controlled the colony with terror, public "confessions," sedatives, and sexual abuse of children who were separated from their parents. His huge, isolated farm, where all but his favorites were obliged to work, was surrounded by barbed wire and sensors hidden among bushes to prevent escape. German colonies, with German-style architecture and use of the German language, are not uncommon in the area, so Colonia Dignidad raised less suspicion than it might elsewhere. Schaefer befriended local landowners from the oligarch class that supported Pinochet. Authorities permitted him to run a state within the state.

During the dictatorship, Schaefer gave the DINA free rein to import captives and torture them at Colonia Dignidad. Of about 350 prisoners brought to the Colonia, half died there. At times, Schaefer participated. Samuel Fuenzalida, a nineteen-year-old guard based at DINA's Villa Grimaldi site in the winter of 1974, testified that he accompanied "a German" to the Colonia with a prisoner. After several hours, Schaefer suddenly appeared from "a kind of secret door" with a black German shepherd. "'*Fertig*,' he said. It was a word that I've never forgotten. *Fertig*. It means it's over, it's done. And I [understood] that . . . the prisoner was dead."

In 2005, Paul Schaefer was found guilty of sexually abusing children, and he died in jail at age eighty-eight. Today Colonia Dignidad has become Villa Baviera, a tourist destination where residents—including some who lived with Schaefer—are staff. German meals are served, Bavarian music piped from speakers. It is available for rent as a wedding venue.

Many places in Latin America where Cold War massacres occurred or men and women disappeared are memorialized respectfully, just as the killing places of World War II are marked by stones or engraved tablets or made venues for tours. I have always left such sites feeling angry with the perpetrators who caused the pain and deaths, and sad. There has been one exception: Villa Grimaldi outside Santiago.

Villa Grimaldi's grassy grounds and a restaurant called "Paradise" were a gathering place for the best and brightest of Allende's Popular Front government, a place to relax, to hammer out plans. In 1974, when Pinochet's intelligence apparatus launched the selective repression phase of state terror, homing in on opponents one group at a time, Villa Grimaldi became one of the DINA's foremost torture centers.

Alberto Rodriguez, a professor of pedagogical psychology, is also the vice president of an association that developed Villa Grimaldi as a garden-like destination where the public might come and see where the worst of human behavior once displayed itself. With local members of base Christian communities, they wrestled the land in the 1990s from the intelligence service, which had been trying to cover up what happened there by breaking the site into lots for a housing development. They restored buildings and installed explanatory plaques, working to preserve history, educate the public, and honor the forty-five hundred persons who entered Villa Grimaldi's walls through a heavy wooden door to be tortured and often killed. "Everyone who survived remembers the sound of that door closing," said Rodriguez, who asked me to call him by his nickname, Beto.

Noisy green parrots flew from one lush araucaria tree to another, the scent from a garden of roses wafted through the air. I remarked on the beauty of a place that had seen such horror. "We live with this contradiction," he said.

Some survivors, said Beto, remember the scent of the roses in the midst of their torture. Others perfectly recall the design and color of the tiles on which we walked—they could be seen under the lower part of a blindfold. Beto opened the slim door of a replica of a windowless cell. With my arms extended I could not turn around. Thirty-nine square inches of floor space for three to five prisoners. When a captive returned from being tortured, the others would stand to give him or her room to lie upon the floor, diagonally corner to corner. "They stroked him, called him by his name," Beto said. (On entry to such camps, guards called persons by numbers.) "Imagine the compassion."

Beto Rodriguez was telling me that a place that brought out the worst in man also brought out the best. On Good Fridays, hundreds, including many young people, come in procession to remember the dead and survivors and to demand justice in legal cases. They pass a monument inscribed with captives' names, called the Wall of Life.

Beto is easygoing and serious at once. To him, it seemed, Villa Grimaldi was not only a torture site but also a monument to resistance. His concept of Villa Grimaldi, indeed the spirit behind its transformation into a memorial, was one of admiration for those who paid the ultimate price for their beliefs. He had spent a lifetime thinking about it, and his view of things made it possible for me, eventually, to walk away feeling at peace, not depressed. He could not have greater authority on the subject.

"My mother died here," he said.

He saw the look on my face and added quickly, "But coming does not upset me."

"Look, I was detained too—I was only six months old," he said, and smiled, moving the conversation to the plane of dispensing information.

Beto's mother and father, Catalina and Rolando, were political activists and adherents to liberation theology that embraced the Church's "preferential option for the poor." At the intelligence agency headquarters, Catalina, age twenty-nine, was able to give the baby Beto to his grandmother before Catalina was brought to Villa Grimaldi, where she was tortured along with her father—Beto's grandfather—and other relatives. Witnesses said on the night of November 18, 1975, they heard agents call for boiling oil to pour down the captives' throats. Later they were found dead.

Beto's father and mother had pledged to each other that if one fell, the other would continue in the struggle. Beto's father Rolando refused to leave the country. "His friends said they tried to convince him, saying, 'Think of Beto, think of your son,'" Beto told me. But his father said, "I'm thinking of all the Betos of the world." DINA agents found Rolando Rodriguez and another activist on October 20, 1976, and killed them.

In a small, climate-controlled building, we looked at iron lengths pulled up from the sea—pieces of train rails. DINA agents tied bodies to the rails and army pilots dropped them into the Pacific where currents carried them away. On September 12, 1976, however, the tortured body of Marta Ugarte, the Communist Party education delegate in Allende's government, washed up on a Chilean beach, having become separated from the rail used to weight it, a discovery that served to corroborate the regime's system of disposal.

We passed an empty swimming pool. When DINA occupied the Villa, officers brought their families to party and splash, as prisoners were being abused nearby. I thought back to my visit at the ESMA in Buenos Aires, attached to the home of the base commander, where during the time it was used as a torture center an officer threw a *quinceañera*, a fifteenth birthday party, for his daughter and guests.

Beto said it did not faze him to make the rounds at Villa Grimaldi. "Why?" I had to ask. "Why do you do this?"

He repeated the pact his parents made to each other. "If one falls, the other carries on."

Could totalitarian systems return to the Americas? "I cannot guarantee it would never happen again," he said. All people have to do is "do nothing." He repeated something I have heard over and again in these latitudes.

People say they didn't see what was happening, but the truth is they looked away. To say they didn't know is a lie.

Overhead, parrots squawked and flew into the piney araucaria trees; a couple of bats and the first night birds flew out to catch insects above the branches. In the changing light, the brilliant pink bougainvillea alongside the dread door of death caught the sun's rays and seemed to hold them for a moment. I noticed the door was chained shut, which turned out to be a symbol of determined hope. Beto said the key was in safekeeping, so no one could walk through again.

ACKNOWLEDGMENTS

My deep appreciation goes to very special women who gave me support and *posada* during the years it took to report and write this book: June Erlick; Rasa Gustaitis; Nancy McGirr; Elissa Miller; Jean Molesky-Poz; Lucia Newman. Thank you to my agent Andy Ross who remained faithful and pushy throughout, and to my wonderful editor Elisabeth Dyssegaard and the skillful staff at St. Martin's Press. Besides those I interviewed for these chapters, individuals in many countries contributed to the book, and I was nurtured by their enthusiasm for the idea of exploring a largely hidden chapter in the history of Latin America. Thank you, Maria Dolores Albiac; Marion Archibald and Russ Archibald; Adelfo Cecchelli and Margarete Bunje Cecchelli; Berlin Juarez; Susana Kaiser; Christine Kim; Rosalin Kleman de Mata; Ronnie Lovler; Andrea Gandolfi; Bernardo Mendez Lugo; Maxine Lowy; James McCarville and Haydee McCarville; Jorge Mario Martinez; Charles Munnell; Marco Palacios; H. Glenn Penny; Mario Pereira; Craig Pyes; Frank Viviano; Regina Wagner; Bill Yenne.

I could not have written *The Tango War* without one of the greatest American institutions, the public library, especially the San Francisco Public Library system. Other groups and institutions whose staffs I thank in particular are Arquivo Histórico José Ferreira da Silva, Blumenau;

Asociación Mutual Israelita Argentina; Bletchley Park; Brazilian Military Cemetery of Pistoia; "Carlos Chiyoteru Hiraoka" Museum of Japanese Immigration to Peru; Centro de Investigaciones Regionales de Mesoamerica; Curitiba Museu do Expedicionário; Espacio Memoria y Derechos Humanos ex-Esma; Franklin D. Roosevelt Presidential Library & Museum; Fundação Cultural de Blumenau; German American Internee Coalition; Gruppo di Studi "Gente di Gaggio"; Hemeroteca Nacional de Guatemala; Historical Archive of Joinville; Londres 38, Espacio de Memorias; Hoover Institution on War, Revolution and Peace; Japanese Peruvian Oral History Project; Marc Chagall Jewish Cultural Institute; Mechanics' Institute Library San Francisco; Merano Jewish Museum; Museo Iola di Montese; Museu Histórico da Imigração Japonesa do Brasil; Museu Pomerano-Centro Cultural de Pomerode; Museum of Memory, Santiago; National Archives, College Park; National Japanese American Historical Society, San Francisco; the Rockefeller Archive Center; SS Jeremiah O'Brien Liberty Ship Memorial; St. Frediano Historical Collection, Sommocolonia; Centro de Documentación e Investigación Judío de México, A.C.; Royal Geographic Society, London.

Robert DeGaetano and our daughter Maria Angelica DeGaetano have my deepest gratitude, not only for their own intellectual contributions to these pages but also for the many ways large and small they sustained me in these years. I cannot thank them enough.

SOURCES

1. THE FIGHT FOR SOUTHERN SKIES

BOOKS

Conn, Stetson, and Byron Fairchild. *The Western Hemisphere.* Vol. 1, *The Framework of Hemisphere Defense.* United States Army in World War II. Washington, DC: Center of Military History, United States Army, 1960.

Corn, Joseph J. *The Winged Gospel.* London: Oxford University Press, 1984.

Daley, Robert. *An American Saga: Juan Trippe and His Pan Am Empire.* New York: Random House, 1980.

Dobson, Alan P. *FDR and Civil Aviation: Flying Strong, Flying Free.* Basingstoke: Palgrave Macmillan, 2011.

Espiniella, Fernando. *El tango y la aviación argentina.* Buenos Aires: Editorial Dunken, 2012.

Hilton, Stanley E. *Hitler's Secret War in South America, 1939–1945: German Military Espionage and Allied Counterespionage in Brazil.* New York: Ballantine Books, 1982.

Hoffman, Paul. *Wings of Madness: Alberto Santos-Dumont and the Invention of Flight.* New York: Hyperion, 2003.

Hyde, H. Montgomery. *Room 3603: The Story of the British Intelligence Center in New York during World War II.* New York: Farrar, Straus and Giroux, 1962.

Lear, John. *Forgotten Front*. New York: E. P. Dutton & Co., 1943.

Reiss, Curt. *Total Espionage*. New York: G. P. Putnam's Sons, 1941.

Stevenson, William. *A Man Called Intrepid: The Secret War*. New York: Harcourt Brace Jovanovich, 1976.

Vidal, Gore. "On Flying." In *United States: Essays 1952–1992*. New York: Random House, 1993.

Winters, Nancy. *Man Flies: The Story of Alberto Santos-Dumont, Master of the Balloon, Conqueror of the Air*. Hopewell, NJ: Ecco Press, 1997.

JOURNALS

Hall, Melvin, and Walter Peck. "Wings for the Trojan Horse." *Foreign Affairs* 19, no. 2 (January 1941): 347–69.

Schwab, Stephen I. "The Role of the Mexican Expeditionary Air Force in World War II: Late, Limited, but Symbolically Significant." *Journal of Military History* 66, no. 4 (October 2002): 1115–40.

DOCUMENTS

"Otto Lilienthal's letter to Moritz von Egidy in Berlin." January 1894. Berlin, Archives, Otto Lilienthal Museum, http://ikareon.de/olma/el1852.htm.

NEWSPAPERS

"Aviation Pioneer Scored a First in Watch-Wearing." *New York Times*, October 25, 1975.

Calvo, Dana. "The Saga of the Aztec Eagles." *Los Angeles Times*, July 25, 2004.

Wyllie, John Philip. "Escuadron 201 Pilot Recalls Mexico's Role in WWII." *La Prensa San Diego*, May 9, 2003.

ONLINE RESOURCES

"Condecoran al xalapeño Héctor Porfirio Tello." YouTube video, 10:30. Posted by Al Calor Politico TV. November 20, 2015. https://www.youtube.com /watch?v=ipg99rlUhJo.

2. BLACK GOLD, OIL TO FUEL THE WAR

INTERVIEWS

Galindo, Sergio Hernández; Kerber, Victor; Matsumoto, Ernesto

BOOKS

Brown, Jonathan C. *Oil and Revolution in Mexico.* Berkeley: University of California Press, 1993.

Chew, Selfa A. *Uprooting Community: Japanese Mexicans, World War II, and the U.S.-Mexico Borderlands.* Tucson: University of Arizona Press, 2015.

Galindo, Sergio Hernández. *La Guerra contra los japoneses en México durante la segunda guerra mundial, Kiso Tsuru y Masao Imuro, migrantes vigilados.* Mexico City: Itaca, 2011.

Gardner, Lloyd C. *Economic Aspects of New Deal Diplomacy.* Madison: University of Wisconsin Press, 1964.

Gellman, Irwin F. *Good Neighbor Diplomacy: United States Policies in Latin America 1933–1945.* Baltimore: Johns Hopkins University Press, 1980.

Grayson, George W. *The Politics of Mexican Oil.* Pittsburgh, PA: University of Pittsburgh Press, 1980.

Harrington, Dale. *Mystery Man: William Rhodes Davis, Nazi Agent of Influence.* Dulles, VA: Brassey's, 1999.

Higham, Charles. *Trading with the Enemy: An Exposé of the Nazi-American Money Plot, 1933–1949.* Toronto: Delacorte Press, 1983.

Jones, Halbert. *The War Has Brought Peace to Mexico: World War II and the Consolidation of the Post-Revolutionary State.* Albuquerque: University of New Mexico Press, 2014.

Katz, Friedrich. "International Wars, Mexico, and U.S. Hegemony." In *Cycles of Conflict, Centuries of Change: Crisis, Reform, and Revolution in Mexico,* edited by Elisa Servín, Leticia Reina, and John Tutino. Durham, NC: Duke University Press, 2007.

Mancke, Richard B. *Mexican Oil and Natural Gas: Political, Strategic and Economic Implications.* New York: Praeger, 1979.

Mayer, Jane. *Dark Money: The Hidden History of the Billionaires behind the Rise of the Radical Right.* New York: Doubleday, 2016.

Meyer, Lorenzo. *Mexico and the United States in the Oil Controversy, 1917–1942.* Translated by Muriel Vasconcellos. Austin: University of Texas Press, 1977.

Niblo, Stephen R. *Mexico in the 1940s, Modernity, Politics, and Corruption.* Wilmington, DE: Scholarly Resources Inc., 1999.

Schuler, Friedrich E. *Mexico between Hitler and Roosevelt: Mexican Foreign Relations in the Age of Lázaro Cárdenas, 1934–1940.* Albuquerque: University of New Mexico Press, 1999.

Smith, Peter Seaborn. *Oil and Politics in Modern Brazil.* Toronto: Macmillan of Canada/Maclean Hunter Press, 1976.

Stevenson, William. *A Man Called Intrepid: The Secret War*. New York: Harcourt Brace Jovanovich, 1976.

Townsend, William Cameron. *Lázaro Cárdenas: Mexican Democrat*. Ann Arbor, MI: George Wahr Publishing Company, 1952.

Ueno, Hisashi. *Los Samuráis de México: La verdadera historia de los primeros inmigrantes japoneses en latinoamérica*. Kyoto: Kyoto International Manga Museum, 2008.

3. WHITE GOLD, THE STORY OF THE RUBBER SOLDIERS

BOOKS

Bunker, Stephen G., and Paul S. Ciccantell. *Globalization and the Race for Resources*. Baltimore: Johns Hopkins University Press, 2005.

Dean, Warren. *Brazil and the Struggle for Rubber*. Cambridge: Cambridge University Press, 2002.

Garfield, Seth. *In Search of the Amazon: Brazil, the United Nature of a Region*. Durham, NC: Duke University Press, 2013.

Goodman, Jordan. *The Devil and Mr. Casement: One Man's Battle for Human Rights in South America's Heart of Darkness*. New York: Farrar, Straus and Giroux, 2010.

Grandin, Greg. *Fordlandia: The Rise and Fall of Henry Ford's Forgotten Jungle City*. New York: Henry Holt, 2009.

Hall, Anthony. "Did Chico Mendes Die in Vain?" In *Green Guerrillas, Environmental Conflicts and Initiatives*, edited by Helen Collinson. London: Latin America Bureau, 1996.

Lacey, Robert. *Ford: The Men and the Machine*. New York: Ballantine Books, 1987.

Loadman, John. *Tears of the Tree: The Story of Rubber, a Modern Marvel*. Oxford: Oxford University Press, 2005.

McCann Jr., Frank D. *The Brazilian-American Alliance, 1937–1945*. Princeton, NJ: Princeton University Press, 1973.

Revkin, Andrew. *The Burning Season: The Murder of Chico Mendes and the Fight for the Amazon Rain Forest*. Boston: Houghton Mifflin Company, 1990.

Sguiglia, Eduardo. *Fordlandia: A Novel*. Translated by Patricia J. Duncan. New York: Thomas Dunne Books, 2000.

Shoumatoff, Alex. *The World Is Burning*. New York: Little, Brown and Company, 1990.

Vargas Llosa, Mario. *The Dream of the Celt*. Translated by Edith Grossman. New York: Farrar, Straus and Giroux, 2010.

Wolfe, Joel. *Autos and Progress: The Brazilian Search for Modernity*. Oxford: Oxford University Press, 2010.

JOURNALS

De Guzman, Doris. "History of the Synthetic Rubber Industry." *Independent Chemical Information Service (ICIS)* (May 12, 2008). http://www.icis.com /resources/news/2008/05/12/9122056/history-of-the-synthetic-rubber -industry/.

Logsdon, Jonathan R. "Power, Ignorance, and Anti-Semitism: Henry Ford and His War on Jews." *Hanover Historical Review* (1999).

Wendt, Paul. "The Control of Rubber in World War II." *Southern Economic Journal* (January 1947).

DOCUMENTS

"Picture story of the visit of President Getulio Vargas of Brazil to Belterra site of the Ford Rubber Plantation, October 8, 1940." 1940. The Henry Ford–Benson Ford Research Center. https://beta.worldcat.org/archivegrid/collection/data /69930928.

Wagner, Regina. "Guatemala Rubber Industry." Unpublished manuscript, 2016.

Wilkinson, Xenia Vunovic. "Tapping the Amazon for Victory: Brazil's 'Battle for Rubber.'" Doctoral dissertation, Georgetown University, 2009.

"World War II on the Home Front," wartime posters. U.S. War Production Board. http://www.learnnc.org/lp/editions/ww2-rationing/5911U.S.

NEWSPAPERS, MAGAZINES

"Detour on Rubber." *Pittsburgh Post-Gazette*, February 4, 1943.

McConahay, Mary Jo. "Amazonian Futures." *Choices: The Human Development Magazine* 6, no. 2 (April 1997): 19–25.

Rohter, Larry. "Brazil 'Rubber Soldiers' Fight for Recognition." *International Herald Tribune*, October 13, 2006.

ONLINE RESOURCES

Branford, Sue. "The Life and Legacy of Chico Mendes." *BBC News*, December 22, 1988. http://news.bbc.co.uk/2/hi/7795175.stm.

"Brazil at War 1943 US Office of the Coordinator of Inter-American Affairs

World War II." YouTube video, 9:41. Posted by Jeff Quitney. November 7, 2012. https://www.youtube.com/watch?v=3VcsM8RRS9o.

Darby, Kenyatta, and Matthew. "World War II and Rubber." The History of Rubber. http://historyofrubber.weebly.com.

"Fordlandia: The Rise and Fall of Henry Ford's Forgotten Jungle City." Transcript of Democracy Now! video, 46:00. July 2, 2009. https://www.democracy now.org/2009/7/2/fordlandia_the_rise_and_fall_of.

Oliveira, Wolney. "Borracha Para A Vitória." YouTube video, 54:38. Posted by Jozafá Batista. November 26, 2012. https://www.youtube.com/watch ?v=Lw4uK5bienI.

"The Charles Goodyear Story." Goodyear Tire and Rubber Company. Reprinted from the January 1958 issue of *Reader's Digest*. https://corporate.goodyear .com/en-US/about/history/charles-goodyear-story.html.

4. "WHERE THEY COULD NOT ENTER": JEWISH LIVES

INTERVIEWS

Guggenheim, Hans; Lowy, Maxine; Scliar, Judith; Skolnick, Paul; Unger, David; Unger, Manuel

BOOKS

Agosin, Marjorie. *Among the Angels of Memory*. San Antonio, TX: Wings Press, 2006.

———. *Dear Ann Frank*. Lebanon, NH: Brandeis University Press/University Press of New England, 1998.

Columbus, Christopher. *The Journal of Christopher Columbus (during His First Voyage, 1492–93) and Documents Relating to the Voyages of John Cabot and Gaspar Corte Real*. Translated by Clements R. Markham. Boston: Adamant Media Corporation, 2001.

Correa, Armando Lucas. *The German Girl*. New York: Atria Books, 2016.

Elkin, Judith Laikin. *Jews of Latin America*. New York: Holmes and Meier, 1998.

Gertz, René. *O Fascismo no Sul do Brasil*. Porto Alegre: Mercado Aberto, 1987.

Gleizer, Daniela. *El exilio incómodo, México y los refugiados judíos*. Mexico City: Colegio de Mexico, 2011.

Gutfreind, Ieda. *A imigração judaica no Rio Grande do Sul, Da memoria para a história*. São Leopoldo: Editora Unisinos, 2004.

Lesser, Jeffrey. *Welcoming the Undesirables: Brazil and the Jewish Question*. Berkeley: University of California Press, 1995.

Levine, Robert M. *Tropical Diaspora: The Jewish Experience in Cuba*. Princeton, NJ: Markus Weiner Publishers, 2010.

de Magalhães, Marionilde Dias Brepohl. *Pangermanismo e nazismo, A trajetória alemã rumo ao Brasil*. Campinas São Paulo: Editoria da UNICAMP/FAPESP, 1998.

Morais, Fernando. *Olga*. São Paulo: Editora Schwarcz, 2008.

Morimoto, Amelia. *Los japoneses y sus descendientes en el Perú*. Lima: Congreso de la República del Perú, 1999.

Perera, Victor. *The Cross and the Pear Tree, a Sephardic Journey*. New York: Alfred A. Knopf, 1995.

Scliar, Moacyr. *The War in Bom Fim*. Lubbock: Texas Tech University Press, 2010.

Sepan, Nancy Leys. *The Hour of Eugenics, Race, Gender and Nation in Latin America*. Ithaca, NY: Cornell University Press, 1996.

Wiazovski, Taciana. *Bolchevismo & judaísmo, A comunidade judaica sob o olhar do DEOPS (Inventário DEOPS)*. São Paulo: Arquívo do Estado/Imprensa Oficial, 2001.

JOURNALS

Birnbaum, Ervin. "Evian: The Most Fateful Conference of All Times in Jewish History: Part II." *NATIV* (February 2009). http://www.acpr.org.il/nativ/0902-birnbaum-E2.pdf.

DOCUMENTS

Histórias de Vida: Imigração Judaica No Rio Grande Do Sul. Porto Alegre: Instituto Cultural Judaico Marc Chagall, nd.

NEWSPAPERS

Bloomekatz, Ari B. "Mexican Schindler Honored." *Los Angeles Times*, December 1, 2008.

ARCHIVES

Photos and oral histories, Marc Chagall Jewish Cultural Institute, Porto Alegre, Brazil.

ONLINE RESOURCES

Peralta, Pablo. "The History of the Bolivian Schindler." Translated by *Bolivian Thoughts in an Emerging World*, September 4, 2015. https://bolivianthoughts .com/2015/09/04/the-history-of-the-bolivian-schindler/.

Tauber, José Kaminer. "La primera presencia." *Enlace judío*, August 21, 2012. http://www.enlacejudio.com/2012/08/21/la-primera-presencia/.

"The Evian Conference." United States Holocaust Memorial Museum. https:// www.ushmm.org/outreach/en/article.php?ModuleId=10007698.

"The Righteous among the Nations." The World Holocaust Remembrance Center. http://db.yadvashem.org/righteous/family.html?language=en&itemId=5604975.

5. NAZIS AND NOT NAZIS, IN THE LAND OF THE WHITE BUTTERFLY

INTERVIEWS

Reiche, Olga; Sapper, Arne; Sapper, Maya; Wagner, Regina

BOOKS

Friedman, Max Paul. *Nazis and Good Neighbors: The United States Campaign against the Germans of Latin America in World War II*. Cambridge: Cambridge University Press, 2005.

de Magalhães, Marionilde Brepohl. *Pangermanismo e Nazismo: A trajetória alemã rumo ao Brasil*. Campinas São Paulo: Editora da UNICAMP/FAPESP, 1998.

Newton, Ronald C. *The "Nazi Menace" in Argentina, 1931–1947*. Palo Alto: Stanford University Press, 1992.

Terga Cintrón, Ricardo. *Almas Gemelas: un estudio de la inserción alemana en las verapaces y la consecuente relación entre los alemanes y los k'ekchies*. Coban: Imprenta y Tipografía "El Norte," 1991.

Wagner, Regina. *Los alemanes en Guatemala 1828–1944*. Guatemala City: Universidad Francisco Marroquin, 1991.

JOURNALS

"O Dirigivel 'Graf Zeppelin' Sobrevoando Blumenau." *Blumenau em Cadernos* (October 1998).

Seyferth, Giralda. "A liga pangermânica e o perigo alemão no Brasil: Análise sobre dois discursos étnicos irredutíveis." *História: Questões & Debates* 10 (June–December 1989).

ARCHIVES

Photos and ephemera, Arquivo Histórico de Joinville, Joinville, Brazil.

Photos and oral histories, Arquivo Histórico José Ferreira da Silva, Blumenau, Brazil.

Newspapers collection, Hemeroteca Nacional de Guatemala, Guatemala City.

Photos and family histories, Center for Meso-American Research, Antigua, Guatemala.

ONLINE RESOURCES

Personal accounts, Latin American Germans, The German American Internee Coalition, http://gaic.info.

6. IN INCA COUNTRY, CAPTURING "JAPANESE"

INTERVIEWS

Diogo, Adriano; Galindo, Sergio Hernández; Panfichi Huamán, Aldo; Igei, Ginyu; Kerber, Victor; Maoki, Libia; Naganuma, Kazuharu; Naganuma, Kazumu; Naganuma, Kazushige; Okujara, Mario Jun; Shimizu, Grace; Shimomura, Carlos; Shimomura, Flor de Maria; Tsuneshige, Cesar; Yaga, Rolando Tamashiro

BOOKS

Corbett, P. Scott. *Quiet Passages: The Exchange of Civilians between the United States and Japan during the Second World War.* Kent, OH: Kent State University Press, 1987.

Gardiner, C. Harvey. *Pawns in a Triangle of Hate: The Peruvian Japanese and the United States.* Seattle: University of Washington Press, 1981.

Higashide, Seiichi. *Adios to Tears: The Memoirs of a Japanese-Peruvian Internee in U.S. Concentration Camps.* Seattle: University of Washington Press, 2000.

Hirabayashi, Lane Ryo, Akemi Kikumura-Yano, and James A. Hirabayashi, eds. *New Worlds, New Lives: Globalization and People of Japanese Descent in the Americas and from Latin America in Japan.* Stanford: Stanford University Press, 2002.

Masterson, Daniel M., with Sayaka Funada-Classen. *The Japanese in Latin America*. Chicago: University of Illinois Press, 2004.

Robinson, Greg. *A Tragedy of Democracy: Japanese Confinement in North America*. New York: Columbia University Press, 2010.

Rocca Torres, Luis. *Los japoneses bajo el sol de Lambayeque*. Lambayeque: Universidad Nacional "Pedro Ruiz Gallo," 1997.

Russell, Jan Jarboe. *The Train to Crystal City: FDR's Secret Prisoner Exchange Program*. New York: Simon and Schuster, 2016.

Shinto, Victor Aritomi. *Encuentro y Relaciones Diplomáticas entre Perú y Japón: A cien años de la Inmigración Japonesa al Perú*. Lima: Editorial Perú Shimpo, 1999.

Taneshiro, Takeo, ed. *Internees: War Relocation Center Memoirs and Diaries*. New York: Vantage Press, 1976.

Yamashita, Karen Tai. *Brazil-Maru*. Minneapolis: Coffee House Press, 1993.

JOURNALS

Watanabe, José. "Wall," translated by Michelle Har Kim. *Asian American Literary Review* 2, no. 1 (Winter/Spring 2011).

DOCUMENTS

Galindo, Sergio Hernández. "Orígenes del autoritarismo: la concentración de japoneses en México durante la segunda guerra mundial." *El XX mexicano. Lecturas de un siglo*, coordinated by Carlos San Juan Victoria. México: Itaca, 2012.

Letters, photos, and ephemera, Shimomura family.

ARCHIVES

National Japanese American Historical Society, San Francisco.

Oral histories, Japanese Peruvian Oral History Project.

7. INMATES, A FAMILY AFFAIR

Interviews, books, and archives cited in previous chapter, with the addition of:

INTERVIEWS

Donald, Heidi Gurcke

BOOKS

Donald, Heidi Gurcke. *We Were Not the Enemy: Remembering the United States Latin-American Civilian Internment Program of World War II*. Lincoln, NE: iUniverse, 2006.

DOCUMENTS

Letters, photos, and ephemera of Starr Gurcke, Werner Gurcke.

ONLINE RESOURCES

Kaplan-Levenson, Laine. "'Camp Algiers,' New Orleans' Forgotten WWII Internment Camp." *New Orleans Public Radio*, January 19, 2017. http://wwno.org/post/camp-algiers-new-orleans-forgotten-wwii-internment-camp-part-ii.

———. "The WWII Internment Camp, 'Camp Algiers,' Part I." *New Orleans Public Radio*, January 12, 2017. http://wwno.org/post/wwii-internment-camp-camp-algiers-part-i?nopop=1.

8. SEDUCTION

BOOKS

Baxter, John. *Disney during World War II: How the Walt Disney Studio Contributed to Victory in the War*. New York: Disney Editions, 2014.

Benamou, Catherine. *It's All True: Orson Welles's Pan-American Odyssey*. Berkeley: University of California Press, 2007.

Canemaker, John. *The Art and Flair of Mary Blair: An Appreciation*. Glendale, CA: Disney Editions, 2014.

Evans, Richard J. *The Third Reich in Power: 1933–1939*. New York: Penguin Press, 2005.

Gehring, Wes D. *Robert Wise: Shadowlands*. Indianapolis: Indiana Historical Society Press, 2012.

Giesen, Rolf, and J. P. Storm. *Animation under the Swastika: A History of Trickfilm in Nazi Germany, 1933–1945*. Jefferson, NC: MacFarland & Company, 2012.

Kramer, Michael S., and Sam Roberts. *"I Never Wanted to be Vice-President of Anything!": An Investigative Biography of Nelson Rockefeller*. New York: Basic Books, 1976.

Leaming, Barbara. *Orson Welles: A Biography*. New York: Viking, 1985.

Reich, Cary. *The Life of Nelson A. Rockefeller: Worlds to Conquer, 1908–1958*. New York: Doubleday, 1996.

Schickel, Richard. *The Disney Version: The Life, Times, Art and Commerce of Walt Disney*. New York: Simon and Schuster, 1968.

Shale, Richard. *Donald Duck Joins Up: The Walt Disney Studio During World War II*. Ann Arbor, MI: AMI Research Press, 1982.

Smith, Richard Norton. *On His Own Terms: A Life of Nelson Rockefeller*. New York: Random House, 2014.

Tota, Antonio Pedro. *The Seduction of Brazil: The Americanization of Brazil during World War II*. Austin: University of Texas Press, 2000.

Welles, Orson, and Peter Bogdanovich. *This Is Orson Welles*. New York: Harper-Collins, 1992.

JOURNALS

Feuerlicht, Maurice. "To Your Health, Jose!" *Educational Screen* 22 (October 1943): 285–88.

Fox, Stephen. "The Deportation of Latin American Germans, 1943–47: Fresh Legs for Mr. Monroe's Doctrine." *Yearbook of German-American Studies* 32 (1997).

Stam, Robert. "Orson Welles, Brazil and the Power of Blackness." *Persistence of Vision* 7 (1989).

DOCUMENTS

Marchesi, Greta. "Nelson A. Rockefeller's Office of International Affairs and the Roots of United States Hemispheric Development Policy." Research Reports, Rockefeller Archive Center, Sleepy Hollow, New York, 2010.

NEWSPAPERS, MAGAZINES

Ross, Alex. "The Shadow: A Hundred Years of Orson Welles." *New Yorker*, December 7, 2015.

ARCHIVES

Letters and materials produced by the Office of the Coordinator of Inter-American Affairs, The Rockefeller Archive Center, Sleepy Hollow, New York.

ONLINE RESOURCES

"Disney History." The Walt Disney Company. https://d23.com/disney-history/.

"Orson Welles—Four Men in the Raft (1942) [Alta qualidade e tamanho].avi." YouTube video, 46:26. Posted by João Arjona. March 26, 2012. https://www.youtube.com/watch?v=7Hy-4cI3EVc.

"Orson Welles—It's All True (1942)—The Story of Samba." YouTube video, 5:31. Posted by MrByronOrlok. December 23, 2010. https://www.youtube .com/watch?v=IevOgR1ftSc&list=PLtGZekGgqXq68IOmOtp8zM -QFLAW9A-em.

"Orson Welles—It's All True—My Friend Bonito—The Blessing of the Young Animals." YouTube video, 3:14. Posted by upcycle. November 27, 2011. https://www.youtube.com/watch?v=BZnYhyA_zH8.

"*The Story of Jazz*, Duke Ellington and Louis Armstrong." Columbia University, The Center for Jazz Studies. http://jazz.columbia.edu/event/orson -welles-presents-louis-armstrong.

Thomas, Theodore, dir. *Walt & El Grupo.* 2008; YouTube Movies, 2012, DVD. https://www.youtube.com/watch?v=4-EOG_WqhTE.

9. SPIES, MASTERS OF SPIES

BOOKS

Becker, Marc. *The FBI in Latin America: The Ecuador Files.* Durham, NC: Duke University Press, 2017.

Bogdanovich, Peter. *John Ford.* Berkeley: University of California Press, 1978.

Brown, Anthony Cave. *Wild Bill Donovan: The Last Hero.* New York: Times Books, 1982.

Cedillo, Juan Alberto. *Los Nazis en México.* Mexico City: Random House Mondadori, 2010.

Colvin, Ian. *Master Spy: The Incredible Story of Admiral William Canaris.* New York: McGraw-Hill, 1951.

Dunlop, Richard. *Donovan: America's Master Spy.* Chicago: Rand McNally, 1982.

Eyman, Scott. *Print the Legend: The Life and Times of John Ford.* New York: Simon & Schuster, 2015.

Farago, Ladislas. *Burn after Reading: The Espionage History of World War II.* New York: Walker & Company, 1961.

———. *The Game of the Foxes: The Untold Story of German Espionage in the United States and Great Britain during World War II.* New York: Bantam Books, 1971.

Freidel, Frank. *Franklin D. Roosevelt: A Rendevous with Destiny.* New York: Little, Brown and Company, 1990.

Masterman, J. C. *The Double-Cross System in the War of 1939 to 1945.* New Haven, CT: Yale University Press, 1972.

McBride, Joseph. *Searching for John Ford*. New York: St. Martin's Press, 2001.

McBride, Joseph, and Michael Wilmington. *John Ford*. Boston: DaCapo Press, 1975.

Mueller, Michael. *Canaris: The Life and Death of Hitler's Spymaster*. Annapolis, MD: Naval Institute Press, 2007.

Paz, Maria Emilia. *Strategy, Security, and Spies: Mexico and the U.S. as Allies in World War II*. University Park, PA: Penn State University Press, 1997.

Popov, Dusko. *Spy/Counterspy: The Autobiography of Dusko Popov*. New York: Grosset & Dunlap, 1974.

Powers, Richard Gid. *Secrecy and Power: The Life of J. Edgar Hoover*. New York: Free Press, 1987.

Rout, Leslie B., and John F. Bratzel. *The Shadow War: German Espionage and United States Counterespionage in Latin America during World War II*. New York: Praeger, 1986.

Smith, Richard Harris. *OSS: The Secret History of America's First Central Intelligence Agency*. Berkeley: University of California Press, 1972.

Summers, Anthony. *Official and Confidential: The Secret Life of J. Edgar Hoover*. New York: G. P. Putnam's Sons, 1992.

Waller, Douglas. *Wild Bill Donovan: The Spymaster Who Created the OSS and Modern American Espionage*. New York: Free Press, 2011.

Weiner, Tim. *Enemies: A History of the FBI*. New York: Random House, 2012.

JOURNALS

Bratzel, John F., and Leslie B. Rout. "FDR and the 'Secret Map.'" *Wilson Quarterly* 9, no. 1 (New Year's, 1985): 167–73.

NEWSPAPERS, MAGAZINES

Ahrens, J. M. "Hilda Kruger, la espía que se acostaba por Hitler y su Reich." *El Pais*, October 22, 2016.

Santibañez, Julia. "Hilda Kruger, espía nazi en México." *Vanity Fair de México*, October 20, 2016.

ONLINE RESOURCES

Roosevelt, Franklin D. "President Franklin Delano Roosevelt Address over the radio on Navy Day concerning the attack upon the destroyer U. S. S. Kearny, October 27, 1941." October 27, 1941. *American Merchant Marine at War*. http://www.usmm.org/fdr/kearny.html.

10. OPERATION BOLÍVAR, GERMAN ESPIONAGE IN SOUTH AMERICA

Books cited in previous chapter, with the addition of:

BOOKS

Anderson, Jon Lee. *Che Guevara: A Revolutionary Life*. New York: Grove Press, 1997.

Hilton, Stanley E. *Hitler's Secret War in South America: 1939–1945*. New York: Ballantine Books, 1981.

Hinsley, F. H., and Alan Stripp, eds. *Codebreakers: The Inside Story of Bletchley Park*. Oxford: Oxford University Press, 1994.

Schoonover, Thomas D. *Hitler's Man in Havana: Heinz Luning and Nazi Espionage in Latin America*. Lexington: University Press of Kentucky, 2008.

Sebag-Montefiore, Hugh. *Enigma: The Battle for the Code*. London: Cassell, 2006.

Turing, Dermot. *Demystifying the Bombe*. Stroud: The History Press, 2014.

JOURNALS

Brinson, Susan L. "Politics and Defense: The FCC's Radio Intelligence Division 1940–1947." *Journal of Radio and Audio Media* 16, no. 1 (May 2009): 2–16.

DOCUMENTS

McGaha, Richard L. "The Politics of Espionage: Nazi Diplomats and Spies in Argentina, 1933–1945." Doctoral dissertation, Ohio University, 2009.

Mowry, David P. "German Clandestine Activities in South America in World War II." 1989. United States Cryptologic History (Series IV, Vol. 3), National Security Agency.

"ISOS-ISK Broadcast locations," courtesy Bletchley Park.

11. THE BATTLE OF THE ATLANTIC: SOUTHERN SEAS

BOOKS

Blair, Clay. *Hitler's U-Boat War: The Hunted, 1942–1945*. New York: Random House, 1998.

———. *Hitler's U-Boat War: The Hunters, 1939–1942*. New York: Modern Library, 2000.

Dimbleby, Jonathan. *The Battle of the Atlantic: How the Allies Won the War.* Oxford: Oxford University Press, 2016.

Frank, Wolfgang. *The Sea Wolves: The Complete Story of German U-Boats at War.* New York: Ballantine, 1955.

"History of the Bureau of Yards and Docks and the Civil Engineer Corps: 1940–1946." In *Building the Navy's Bases in World War II*, vol. 2. Washington, DC: United States Government Printing Office, 1947.

Landsborough, Gordon. *The Battle of the River Plate.* London: Panther Books, 1956.

Mascarello Zappia, Mario, et al. *Graf Spee, De la política al drama.* Montevideo: Ediciones Cruz del Sur, 2010.

Savas, Theodore P. *Silent Hunters: German U-boat Commanders of World War II.* Boston: Da Capo Press, 1997.

Showell, Jak P. Mallmann. *U-Boat Command and the Battle of the Atlantic.* London: Conway Maritime Press, 1989.

DOCUMENTS

Bidlingmaier, (Ret'd) Kapitän zur See Gerhard. "KM Admiral Graf Spee/Pocket Battleship 1932–1939." *Profile Warship 4.* Windsor: Profile Publications Limited, 1971.

ONLINE RESOURCES

"AVP Barnegat, the Fourth Fleet Ships." Sixtant: War II in the South Atlantic. http://www.sixtant.net/2011/artigos.php?cat=recife-the-u.s.-4th-fleet-headquarters&sub=the-fourth-fleet-ships-(169-pages—325-images)&tag=40)avp-10-barnegat.

"Barnegat report." July 1943. U-boat Archive. http://www.uboatarchive.net/U-513A/U-513BarnegatReport.htm.

"Richard Caswell American steam merchant." Uboat.net. http://uboat.net/allies/merchants/ships/3013.html.

12. SMOKING COBRAS

INTERVIEWS

Biondi, Vittorio Lino; da Cruz, Eronides João; de Oliveira, Dennison; Pereira, Miguel; Pontarolli, Reynaldo; Prado, Nery; Rossi, Pedro; da Silva Filho, Jose Basilio; Viviano, Frank

BOOKS

Atkinson, Rick. *The Day of Battle: The War in Sicily and Italy, 1943–1945*. New York: Henry Holt, 2007.

Brayner, Floriano de Lima. *A Verdade Sobre a Feb. Civilizacao Brasileira, Memórias de un chefe de Estado-Maior na campanha de Itália: 1943–1945*. Rio de Janiero: Editora Civilizaçao Brasiliera, 1968.

Clark, Mark. *Calculated Risk*. New York: Harper & Brothers, 1950.

De Oliveira, Dennison. *Os Soldados Alemães de Vargas*. Curitiba: Juruá, 2011.

———. *Aliança Brasil-EUA, Nova História do Brasil na Segunda Guerra Mundial*. Curitiba: Juruá, 2015.

Dulles, John W. F. *Castello Branco: The Making of a Brazilian President*. College Station: Texas A&M University Press, 1978.

———. *Unrest in Brazil: Political-Military Crises 1955–1964*. Austin: University of Texas Press, 1970.

Ferraz, Francisco Cesar. *A guerra que não acabo, a reintegração social dos veteranos da Força Expedionaria Brasiliera*. Londrina: Eduel, 2012.

———. *Os brasileiros e a Segunda Guerra Mundial*. Rio de Janiero: Jorge Zahar, 2005.

Giannasi, Andrea. *Il Brasile in Guerra, La Força Expedicionária Brasileira in Italia (1944–1945)*. Roma: Carocci editore, 2014.

Lombardi, Lino. *Barga sulla linea gotica*. Barga: Gasperetti, 1954.

McCann Jr., Frank D. *The Brazilian-American Alliance, 1937–1945*. Princeton, NJ: Princeton University Press, 1973.

de Moraes, João Baptista Mascarenhas. *The Brazilian Expeditionary Force by Its Commander*. Washington, DC: U.S. Government Printing Office, 1966.

Morris, Eric. *Circles of Hell: The War in Italy 1943–1945*. New York: Crown Publishers, 1993.

Neto, Ricardo, Cesar Campiani Maximiano, and Ramiro Bujeiro. *The Brazilian Expeditionary Force in World War II*. Oxford: Osprey Publishing, 2011.

Starr, Chester G. *From Salerno to the Alps: A History of the Fifth Army 1943–1945*. Washington, DC: Infantry Journal Press, 1948.

Teixeira, Carlos Gustavo Poggio. *Brazil, the United States, and the South American Subsystem: Regional Politics and the Absent Empire*. Lanham, MD: Lexington Books, 2012.

Walters, Vernon. *Silent Missions*. New York: Doubleday & Company, 1978.

DOCUMENTS

Rosenheck, Uri. "Olive Drab in Black and White: The Brazilian Expeditionary
 Force, the U.S. Army and Racial National Identity." *XXIX International Congress of the Latin American Studies Association*, October 2009.

ONLINE RESOURCES

"Brazil: Prosecute Dictatorship-Era Abuses." *Human Rights Watch*, April 14,
 2009. https://www.hrw.org/news/2009/04/14/brazil-prosecute-dictatorship
 -era-abuses.

"History of the 10th Mountain Division." *Fort Drum: Home of the Tenth
 Mountain Division*. http://www.drum.army.mil/AboutFortDrum/Pages/hist
 _10thMountainHistory_lv3.aspx.

Imbrie, John. "Chronology of the 10th Mountain Division in World War II, 6
 January 1940—30 November 1945." *National Association of the 10th Mountain Division*, June 2004. http://www.10thmtndivassoc.org/chronology.pdf.

Pankhurst, Richard. "Racism in the Service of Fascism, Empire-Building and
 War: The History of the Italian Fascist Magazine 'La Difesa della Razza.'"
 Marxists Internet Archive, 2007. https://www.marxists.org/archive/pank
 hurst-richard/2007/03/x01.htm.

Zanchi, Lindano. "Pippo e i brasiliani in mediavalle." *Manrico Ducceschi detto
 "Pippa" Comandante XI Zona*. http://xoomer.virgilio.it/lpoggian/PIPPO/brasi
 liani.htm.

13. RATLINES

BOOKS

Godman, Peter. *Hitler and the Vatican: Inside the Secret Archives That Reveal
 the Complete Story of the Nazis and the Church*. New York: Free Press, 2004.

Goñi, Uki. *The Real Odessa: How Perón Brought the Nazi War Criminals to
 Argentina*. London: Granta Books, 2003.

Katz, Robert. *Death in Rome*. New York: Macmillan, 1967.

Kertzer, David. *The Pope and Mussolini: The Secret History of Pius XI and the
 Rise of Fascism in Europe*. New York: Random House, 2014.

Kinzer, Stephen. *The Brothers: John Foster Dulles, Allen Dulles, and Their Secret World War*. New York: Times Books, 2013.

Malkin, Lawrence. *Krueger's Men: The Secret Nazi Counterfeit Plot and the
 Prisoners of Block 19*. Boston: Little, Brown and Company, 2006.

Newton, Ronald C. *The "Nazi Menace" in Argentina, 1931–1947*. Palo Alto: Stanford University Press, 1992.

Page, Joseph A. *Perón: A Biography*. New York: Random House, 1983.

Phayer, Michael. *Pius XII, the Holocaust, and the Cold War*. Bloomington: Indiana University Press, 2008.

———. *The Catholic Church and the Holocaust*. Bloomington: Indiana University Press, 2000.

Posner, Gerald. *God's Bankers: A History of Money and Power at the Vatican*. New York: Simon and Schuster, 2015.

Stangneth, Bettina. *Eichmann before Jerusalem: The Unexamined Life of a Mass Murderer*. New York: Vintage, 2015.

Stavans, Ilan, and Ivan Jaksič. *What is La Hispanidad? A Conversation*. Austin: University of Texas, 2011.

Steinacher, Gerald. *Nazis on the Run: How Hitler's Henchmen Fled Justice*. Oxford: Oxford University Press, 2011.

Talbot, David. *The Devil's Chessboard: Allen Dulles, the CIA, and the Rise of America's Secret Government*. New York: HarperCollins, 2015.

Valenti, Paulo. *Merano. Breve storia della città sul confine*. Bolzano: Raetia, 2008.

Wiesenthal, Simon. *The Murderers among Us: The Simon Wiesenthal Memoirs*. New York: McGraw-Hill, 1967.

DOCUMENTS

"The 'Fosse Ardeatine' Memorial." *Commissariato Generale per le Onoranze ai Caduti in Guerra, Ministero della Difesa*, 2011.

NEWSPAPERS, MAGAZINES

Chandler, Adam. "Eichmann's Best Man Lived and Died in Syria." *Atlantic*, December 1, 2014.

Elam, Shraga, and Dennis Whitehead. "In the Service of the Jewish State." *Haaretz*, March 29, 2007. https://www.haaretz.com/israel-news/in-the-service-of-the-jewish-state-1.216923.

Iyengar, Rishi. "A Notorious Nazi War Criminal Died in Syria Four Years Ago." *Time*, December 2, 2014.

"Nazi Salute Given at War Criminal's Grave." Associated Press, in *The Day*, New London, CT, May 16, 1984.

ONLINE RESOURCES

"Exclusive: Interview with Jorge Priebke." Vimeo video, 32:37. Posted by Davide Scalenghe. November 5, 2013. https://vimeo.com/78665357.

"Nazi Capt. Erich Priebke: 'An Order Was an Order.'" *ABC News*. Sam Donaldson, October 15, 2013. http://abcnews.go.com/International/video/nazi-captain-erich-priebke-found-abc-news-20575216.

14. CONNECTIONS, THE COLD WAR

INTERVIEWS

Bernardi, Patricia; Bruzzi, Ines; Careaga, Ana Maria; Goñi, Uki; Grunpeter, Hanni; Jaksič, Ivan; Portales, Felipe; Rodriguez, Alberto; Seelmann, Gunter; Sohr, Raul

BOOKS

Anderson, Scott, and Jon Lee Anderson. *Inside the League: The Shocking Expose of How Terrorists, Nazis, and Latin American Death Squads Have Infiltrated the World Anti-Communist League*. New York: Dodd Mead, 1986.

Dinges, John. *The Condor Years: How Pinochet and His Allies Brought Terrorism to Three Continents*. New York: The New Press, 2004.

Finchelstein, Federico. *The Ideological Origins of the Dirty War: Fascism, Populism, and Dictatorship in Twentieth Century Argentina*. Oxford: Oxford University Press, 2014.

Grandin, Greg. *Kissinger's Shadow: The Long Reach of America's Most Controversial Statesman*. New York: Metropolitan Books, 2015.

Lowy, Maxine. *Memoria latente. Una comunidad enfrentada por el desafío de los derechos humanos en Chile*. Santiago: LOM Ediciones, 2014.

Menjivar, Cecilia, and Nestor Rodriguez, eds. *When States Kill: Latin America, the U.S., and Technologies of Terror*. Austin: University of Texas Press, 2005.

Nelson-Pallmeyer, Jack. *School of Assassins, Guns, Greed, and Globalization*. Maryknoll, NY: Orbis Books, 2001.

INDEX